澳華
Encounters

Musical Meetings between
Australia and China

Edited by **Nicholas Ng**

First published in 2012
Australian Academic Press
Level 5, Toowong Tower
9 Sherwood Road
Toowong QLD 4066
Australia

www.australianacademicpress.com.au

© 2012 Copyright for each contribution in the book rests with the identified authors.

Copying for educational purposes
The Australian Copyright Act 1968 (Cwlth) allows a maximum of one chapter or 10% of this book, whichever is the greater, to be reproduced and/or communicated by any educational institution for its educational purposes provided that the educational institution (or the body that administers it)
has given a remuneration notice to Copyright Agency Limited (CAL) under the Act.

For details of the CAL licence for educational institutions contact:
Copyright Agency Limited, 19/157 Liverpool Street, Sydney, NSW 2000.
E-mail info@copyright.com.au

Production and communication for other purposes
Except as permitted under the Act, for example a fair dealing for the purposes of study, research, criticism or review, no part of this book may be reproduced, stored in a retrieval system, or transmitted in any form or by any means electronic, mechanical, photocopying, recording or otherwise without prior written permission of the copyright holder.

National Library of Australia Cataloguing-in-Publication entry:

Author:	Ng, Nicholas, 1979-
Title:	Encounters : musical meetings between China and Australia / Nicholas Ng.
ISBN:	9781922117069 (pbk.)
	9781922117076 (ebook)
Subjects:	Music--Chinese influences--Congresses.
	Music--Australia--Congresses.
	Music--Western influences--Congresses.
Dewey Number:	780.6

Typesetting and Cover design by Maria Biaggini — www.thelettertree.com.au

CONTENT

Acknowledgements — vi

Foreword — vii
Emeritus Professor Colin Mackerras, AO
Griffith Business School, Griffith University

Introduction — ix
Musical Meetings
Nicholas Ng

Part One
Historical Perspectives

Chapter 1
The Gangzhou Yueju Quyishe
("Gangzhou Society Cantonese Opera Group") in Melbourne, Australia
Wang Zhengting — 3

Chapter 2
Australian encounters with an imagined China
in early musical entertainment
Aline Scott-Maxwell — 20

Chapter 3
By the Bund and beyond: Music-making in the Shanghai and
overseas Jewish communities
Kim Cunio — 36

Chapter 4
Thirty years of Australia-China encounters in
ethnomusicology — A personal memoir
Yang Mu — 44

iii

CONTENT (CONT.)

Part Two
Socio-cultural Perspectives

Chapter 5
Researching Kam minority music in China
Catherine Ingram   63

Chapter 6
'The Asian Björk'— Is Sa DingDing the voice of the 'New China'?
Tony Mitchell   81

Chapter 7
"Sounds Chinese": Musical meetings with China in contemporary Australia
Nicholas Ng   92

Part Three
Artistic Reflections

Chapter 8
Stylistic development and performance practice: From unpublished Chinese folksongs to new Australian compositions
Shan Deng   113

Chapter 9
琴 Qin
Tony Wheeler   116

Chapter 10
Musical encounters in The Wide Alley
Erik Griswold and Vanessa Tomlinson   125

Chapter 11
My performance pieces — a self-reflection
William Yang   130

CONTENT (CONT.)

Part Four
Conversations

Chapter 12
Conversations with Gao Ping and John Huie
Transcribed by Michael Barkrnchev   137

Chapter 13
Conversations with Anne Boyd and Julian Yu
Transcribed by Jaret Choolun   153

Chapter 14
Conversations with Larry Sitsky and John Curro
Transcribed by Jaret Choolun   166

Chapter 15
Conversations with Ash Dargan
Transcribed by Nicholas Ng   181

Biographies   185

Acknowledgements

My deepest thanks and gratitude go first and foremost to Professor Huib Schippers, Director of Queensland Conservatorium, Griffith University, for his unending guidance and support. Without his vision and patience, this volume, and the four-day event that inspired it, would never have eventuated.

I am eternally grateful to the authors, who participated in *Encounters: Musical meetings between China and Australia* (6–9 May 2010) and contributed to this volume with great forbearance and understanding.

My sincerest thanks go to the peer-reviewers for their conscientious and diligent assessment of the papers included in this volume. In addition too, I would like to acknowledge the selfless dedication of Jaret Cholun, Michael Bakrnchev and Clare Said in the transcription and proofreading process.

Special individuals include Emeritus Professor Colin Mackerras, for his collegial support with our project; Stephan May, and the staff of Australian Academic Press, for their generosity and patience; and William Yang and Sharka Bosakova, whose photographic images, taken during the time of *Encounters*, have significantly enhanced this publication's visual presentation. I am also grateful to the National Library of Australia for the use of their historical images.

Finally, I would like to convey my utmost feelings of appreciation to my family, colleagues, and friends, for their limitless tolerance and understanding in the preparation of this volume.

Dr Nicholas Ng
Queensland Conservatorium, Griffith University
December 2011

Encounters: Musical meetings between Australia and China is one of the signature events of Griffith University strategic investment 'Music, the arts and the Asia-Pacific' (2009–2013), which explores the shape and role of music and the allied arts in the Asian Century. It is the third in a series of four major events bridging scholarship, creativity, elite performance and community engagement. Earlier editions of this award-winning initiative explored meetings with Aboriginal culture (2005) and the Asia-Pacific (2007). This volume is an outcome of the 2010 focus on China (2010). In 2013, India will be centre of over seventy events including symposia, exhibitions, and performances.

Foreword

Since Australia and China established diplomatic relations in 1972, bilateral relations have become of major importance in Australia and more significant in China than one might expect for a country like Australia that is so much smaller in population and political power and younger in its culture. In the political realm, Australia-China relations have been mainly very good but with periods of instability. However, in the economic and cultural fields they have advanced very quickly indeed, trade and educational exchanges advancing much more rapidly and thoroughly than could have been imagined. In music, which is the realm of concern in this book, Chinese-Australian encounters have developed rapidly and become common, widespread and interesting.

It is to the credit of Queensland Conservatorium Griffith University that they have taken the initiative to push these encounters forward. In particular, I pay tribute to Professor Huib Schippers, Conservatorium Director, and Dr Nicholas Ng, a specialist in Chinese music, for their successful attempts in holding a major performance and academic forum in May 2010 entitled Encounters: Musical meetings between Australia and China. Professor Schippers has very broad and deep musical expertise, including in a range of ethno-musicologies. Dr Ng can play the erhu and other Chinese instruments, and has made major studies of various forms of Chinese music.

It is said that music is a kind of universal language and that it can link peoples in ways that other forms of intercommunication cannot. In some ways this suggestion is open to challenge. We have seen in several chapters, including the introduction, that many Australians have found Chinese music very difficult to listen to, especially opera. My personal observation is that such images are still easy to find. This being the case, perhaps music is not universal.

On the other hand, music can form a valuable bridge between peoples and can help promote understanding. People who make music together, people who try to understand the musical culture of another nation or ethnic group, assist in international understanding greatly. Australia has certainly become more multicultural over the last few decades. I would like to think it has also become more tolerant and accepting of unfamiliar musics. In any case, musical encounters not only exemplify but also assist in cross-cultural familiarity and understanding. In this sense, music is or at least can become a universal language.

We can see many examples illustrative of multicultural engagement and tolerance in the sort of cross-cultural encounters represented by the Australia-China musical meetings of May 2010. We see examples of Chinese who have attempted to present Chinese music in Australia, sometimes to Chinese resident in Australia, sometimes to non-Chinese Australians. At the same time, Australians have visited China to study the music of China, including that of peoples like the Kam, an ethnic minority known as Dong to the Chinese. The emphasis is on China's musics and their influence in Australia, but there is also attention given to the way the West and Australia have impacted on China.

One point that struck me strongly about these encounters is their diversity. They exist on many levels. There is academic discussion of the history of Chinese music in Australia, a very important aspect of encounters. There are also highly practical encounters involving performance of various kinds. And finally there are talks with individuals who have worked in the two countries, either Australians who have given performances or undertaken musical practice in China or the other way around.

For this book one might highlight the academic symposium on Chinese music and the "conversations." The reason is that a book can reproduce papers given at an academic symposium and interviews or conversations with specialists in a way that it cannot do for performances. There are several themes that come through the papers and interviews that are of interest more general than what applies to Australia-China musical encounters. They include intercultural creativity and the dichotomy between tradition and innovation. The "conversations" highlight the views and insights of people with particular expertise and experience worth sharing.

No matter which way one looks at it, these musical encounters show the past and present richness of cross-cultural musical relations between Australia and China. Many of the examples are very little known, and Queensland Conservatorium, Griffith University, Professor Schippers, and Dr Ng have done an excellent job in revealing them to the scholarly and general public.

Emeritus Professor Colin Mackerras, AO
Griffith Business School, Griffith University
October 2010

Introduction

Musical meetings

Nicholas Ng

> Let them whose good fortune has preserved them from auricular acquaintance with Chinese harmony, imagine a band of serenaders whose instruments should be tubs, tin pans, bars of iron, and bones, with a fiddle of indescribable shape and tone, and when these are beaten, banged and scraped till every nerve in the listener's system is quivering with torture he will have a faint conception of the concert which the surrounding inhabitants have to endure every evening ... (Mount Alexander Mail, 1858).

Unsavoury impressions of Chinese music were widespread in the goldfields of nineteenth century Australia. Newspapers such as the *Mount Alexander Mail* reported on the unceasing cacophony of percussion and unusual vocal timbres. For the entertainment of the fast-growing Chinese community, operatic and circus troupes from Southern China began performing in Victorian tents and town halls from the 1850s (Lyndon, 1999; Farrell, 2009, p. 20) and numbered from thirty to fifty by the early 1860s (Love, 1985). The performers brought with them all the intrigue and mystery of the orient including props, opium-addicted lead performers, female impersonators and "dandies" (Farrell, 2009, pp. 20-25; Love, 1985. pp. 80-81). Although Europeans came to Chinese shows, many were not accustomed to, nor appreciative of the noise and din of Cantonese opera. The performance of this musical genre, coupled with a clash of cultural values and work ethics (Rolls 1992), may be attributed to European resentment of the Chinese in the area. This disharmony eventually culminated in an outbreak of civil violence and brutal massacres (ibid).

Music is a revealing and significant area of exploration when examining the relationship between the western world and China. Australia, unequivocally a western nation situated in the Asia Pacific, has grappled to define and redefine its connection with the "Middle Kingdom" since the earliest times of Chinese migration. Interestingly, historians reveal that the intelligentsia of China were aware of the great land mass to the south centuries prior to European exploration: the northern Australian coast line was frequented by Chinese-employed Makassar fishermen in the search for *bêche-de-mer* (a potent aphrodisiac), while the great fifteenth century Ming Admiral Zheng He allegedly directed his fleet to the northern coastal line of Australia using the brilliant star Canopus for navigation (Rolls, 1992, 1996; Langton, 2011).

The implementation of the infamous White Australia policy (1901-1973), ironically concurring with the 1901 celebration of Australia's Federation, saw to the restriction of Chinese movement into Australia (Rolls 1996, Giese 1995). There are many accounts of the damaging ramifications of this policy on the lives of Chinese émigrés and their descendants, particularly in terms of social justice and equality (Bagnall, 2009; Fitzgerald, 2007, pp. 117-116; York, 2005). Despite the repression of Chinese culture and language, a number of Chinese community centres and societies such as the Chinese Youth League, established in 1939, allowed for the continual preservation of homeland culture and arts. Early to mid-twentieth century White Australian interest or intrigue with the Orient is evident in the recording of the Melbourne Chinese Orchestra and various Tin Pan Alley productions including *Chu Chin Chow,* quite possibly the "earliest Australian musical play on the international stage" (Thomson, ND). There were also a number of compositions written in Orientalist style (Scott-Maxwell, 1997) while a variety of photographs and press clippings document the performances of the musical Chinn family in Victoria (Wang, 1997), Long Tack Sam's acrobatic troupe, and the 1950s all-female foxtrot band, Alma Quon and the Joybelles.

As the exclusivist policy wanned, Chinese language, arts, and music continued to flourish with the influx of immigrants from various parts of Asia. The result was a distinct diasporic flavour of Chinese secular and sacred community music unique to Australia (see Ng, 2009, 2010). The post-1958 remigration of the Chinese diaspora saw to the rejuvenation of the Chinese Australian population with new arrivals, of which a significant proportion was non-Cantonese speakers. For the first time, the Chinese population did not hail directly from southern China as Australia experienced a surge in the Australian-born Chinese population and the admittance of Chinese students from various countries through the Colombo Plan (Williams, 1999, p. 8). Publication of Chinese language newspapers resumed; Chinese communities established benefit and welfare institutions and voluntary organisations as immigrant support units, while older organisations such as the Chinese Chamber of Commerce were revived (Fitzgerald, 1997, p.158). Assimilationism was finally replaced by multi-culturalism in the 1970s and 1980s, and the Chinese community swelled (Williams, 1999. pp, 2, 8). The migrant body was joined by two types of new arrivals: refugee migrants from Indo-China (Vietnam and Cambodia) during the 1970s and economic migrants from Hong Kong in the 1980s and 1990s as the post-1972 equality of citizenship laws and family reunion immigration corrected the imbalance of the sexes, an issue in earlier migration periods.

Introduction

With the disastrous incident of the 1989 Tiananmen Square[1] incident came "historical drifters" or "late-comers." This included "many of the most brilliant Chinese intellectuals from the mainland" (Shen, 2001, p. 90) and a large number of mainland poets, authors, and artists. There were also families who came to rusticate on vegetable farms on the outskirts of western Sydney. Influential musicians who formed part of this significant 1980s migration wave include composer Julian Yu (composer), Chen Xuebing and Henry Cao (erhu), Dr Yang Mu (ethnomusicologist and senior lecturer at University of New South Wales), Dr Wang Zheng-ting (Director of the Australian Chinese Music Ensemble at Melbourne Conservatorium of Music), and Chai Changning (Head of Chinese Music at The Australian International Performing Arts High School). Migrants from Taiwan and Southeast Asian countries including Singapore, Malaysia and Indonesia also arrived during this time in the form of students or small families who later took up Permanent Residency and then Citizenship.

Today, metropolitan Sydney hosts a number of Chinese secular and religious institutions in the form of schools, temples, churches and clubs, some dating from the earliest time of immigration. These meeting places are still to varying degrees the same centres of ethnic cohesion that they have been since establishment. One example is the Yiu Ming Temple in the Sydney suburb of Alexandria, built in 1908 to support the community of "aliens", or Chinese market gardeners of Botany Bay. This temple provides spiritual guidance and customary religious milestone rituals of life that accompany birth, marriage and death. The Australian Catholic Chinese Community and The Australian Chinese Teo Chew Association are similar centres of social cohesion offering welfare services and a number of social and recreational events for its members. The annual Buddha Birth Day Festival in Brisbane, Sydney, Wollongong, Melbourne and Perth involve musical and cultural performances of diverse styles by local and international artists. This nation-wide festival one of many cultural programs organised by the Buddha's Light International Association, which aims to integrate its Chinese temple community with the wider non-Chinese government, business and community sectors (Ng 2009, 2010). Serving these communities is a vast array of local professional and community performance groups specialising in music, acrobatics and martial arts. These include the Shaolin Kungfu Guan, the Australian National University Classical Chinese Music Ensemble and the Sunshine Philharmonic Choir. In the local art music scene, the development of Liza Lim (composer) and arrival of Julian Yu has led to evolved in interesting ways as composers of Chinese descent were added to the Australian art music canon.

In modern day Australia, Chinese émigrés and their descendants remain identifiable in their new homelands as the "overseas Chinese", or in more recent applications, "Chinese overseas", a term perhaps more legitimate and apt since it does not imply an immediate connection to the mainland of China (Tan, 2004; Poston and Yu, 1990)[2]. The Chinese overseas are nonetheless still a very broad category, and it is interesting that these sojourners and their descendants have managed to retain a certain element of Chineseness despite becoming naturalised citizens in their respective countries of choice (Wen, 1985). In Australia, this may be the result of continual migration and continual "racialisation" that Chinese descendants face, and the lack of Australian-Chinese representation in the media, a fault of Australian multiculturalism that is in recent decades has been slowly regulated with figures such as Lee Lin Chin (world news presenter), Jeff Fatt (musician), William Yang (photographer), Annette Shun-Wah and Poh Ling Yeow (actors) and Benjamin Law (author)[3]. While the Chinese "down under" may be celebrate a distinct flavour of Chineseness, such as will be explored in the chapters to follow, we must acknowledge the plethora of diverse histories that make up the Australian Chinese population. Tan Chee-Beng (2004) reminds us that "[o]verall, the ethnic Chinese all over the world are really different communities, each shaped by different forces of change and by diverse responses" (p. 65). As Christine Inglis (1998) notes:

> Attempts to bring the plethora of [Chinese] groupings together within a unifying structure or umbrella at either the national or local level have so far been unsuccessful. The diversity of interests and backgrounds, as well as personal competition, has made it difficult to develop an organizational structure acceptable to all, and to identify individuals able to represent, or speak on behalf of, the Chinese community as a whole (p. 282).

The Australian Chinese community is certainly very disparate and comprises smaller groups of people with shared values and common lifestyles. To obfuscate matters more is the additional complication of differing individual history within each collectivity. Music is closely linked to the cultural and social practices of these groups bound either by religion, dialect and clanship or some form of common interest.

The saga of musical encounters between Australia and China continues to this very day. Here, one may find of stories of forbidden love, prejudice and deceit, of gestures of harmony and the fulfilment of dreams and wishes. Many such stories are encapsulated in a myriad of contexts in the pages to follow by contributors from diverse backgrounds whose careers have been built, or have touched on, various modalities of the Australia-China connection.

We are fortunate to have these contributions from *Encounters: Musical meetings between Australia and China* (6-9 May 2010), a four-day event consisting of musical and theatrical performances, lecture demonstrations, academic papers, film screenings, and a photography exhibition held at Queensland Conservatorium, Griffith University and in the vicinity of Brisbane's South Bank precinct. All activities were aimed at promoting collaboration, awareness and creativity in the realms of practice and theory.

Focussing on encounters between China and Australia from the earliest imaginings and representations to the latest cultural exchanges, the Encounters Symposium addressed the following themes:

- music and history
- tradition versus innovation
- cultural diversity/intercultural creativity
- music and the related arts

Ethnomusicologists, composers, performers, historians and cultural theorists alike participated in a series of lively debates exploring the past, present, and future of a long, complex and culturally rich interaction.

Part One of this volume engages with the past. Travelling back to colonial Australia and the decades to follow, Wang Zheng-ting explores the development of Cantonese opera on Australian soil. His study complements Aline Scott-Maxwell's explication of early twentieth century Australian impressions of China in popular music and theatre. Kim Cunio presents an exposition of a largely undiscussed topic in Australia-China relations: the Jews of Shanghai, and the legacy of their musical culture throughout the world and in present-day Sydney. Yang Mu's personal recollections on his longstanding career in ethnomusicology reveals a largely unknown Chinese link to Australia at the prestigious Central Conservatory of Music.

An ethnomusicological focus is assumed in Part Two with Catherine Ingram, working similarly as a participant observer, presents a reflexive piece on her work as an Australian studying Kam minority music on the Chinese mainland. Veering towards popular culture, Tony Mitchell analyses the music of Chinese diva Sa DingDing, whose appearance at WOMADelaide in 2009 sent sonic shock waves through the southern Chinese diaspora. My self-reflexive analysis links ethnomusicology and composition to issues of cultural identity as an Asian-Australian, issues quite possibly sparked by the cultural orientalism and imaginings of the Chinese "other" at the turn of the twentieth century.

Our musical sojourn assumes a practice-based perspective in Part Three as Shan Deng, lecturer in piano at Tasmanian Conservatorium, describes her inter-cultural metamorphosis of Chinese folksongs into new Australian art music compositions with composer Maria Grenfell. Tony Wheeler, one of few Australians who studied traditional Chinese music in China, writes on his introduction to this sound world at Queensland Conservatorium, which eventually led to his discovery and mastery of the qin (Chinese seven-stringed zither) and the development of his artistic voice and practice. Queensland Conservatorium's resident duo Clocked Out (Erik Griswold and Vanessa Tomlinson) explicate their decade-long absorption of Sichuan music in their improvisatory practice, involving pitched and unpitched percussion instruments. Working in that fertile space of hybridity, The Wide Alley melds traditional practises with contemporary sensibilities with a myriad of unpredictable results. Intimately unravelling the essence behind his performance pieces, William Yang extends this volume's focus to live theatre, in which music plays a seminal role.

Part Four includes edited transcriptions of three public conversations between Vincent Plush and iconic figures in Australian music during *Encounters*. Composers Anne Boyd, Julian Yu and Larry Sitsky speak of their connection with China, and of the Chinese influences in their compositions. John Curro reminisces on his conducting and curatorial work in the early days of the People's Republic of China, and the many Australian-Chinese musical pathways that were to follow. The interviews continue with two transnational figures whose musical lives bridge both Australia and China: Gao Ping, expatriate Chinese composer and pianist is now resident in

New Zealand but maintains valuable ties to Queensland Conservatorium, while John Huie's adventures in Shanghai Jazz and fusion music lasted nearly twenty years in post-revolution China.

It is a particular delight to have the thoughts, impressions and recollections of Ash Dargan included in this volume. An Indigenous Australian of Chinese heritage, Dargan is a world music and didgeridoo artist whom I had the fortune of engaging in New York City. Ash, running a didgeridoo business in Colorado wanted to honour his Indigenous Australian and Chinese bloodlines by performing with me in a composition commissioned by the Foundation for University Music (now known as the Society of Universal Sacred Music) in a bid to honour. Through his lineage and art, Ash represents a chapter of Australian history still not taught in our textbooks, that of the interaction between the early Chinese and Indigenous Australians (Figure 1).

This volume contains the discoveries, thoughts and reflections of key artists and scholars from a range of disciplines and practices. Their writings, so varied and diverse, celebrate a multiplicity of identities, and present a challenging array of research avenues and perspectives through which to view the Australian-Chinese connection.

Notes

1. The Tiananmen Square protests, otherwise known as the 'June-Fourth Incident' involved the mass slaughter of Chinese civilians (students, intellectuals and labor activists) at the hands of the People's Liberation Army. The protests were for freedom and democracy, and Communist party members who publicly sympathised were purged. Following the incident, The People's Republic of China was swift to conceal information and ban the foreign press, which led to international criticism (Wong, 1995).
2. This is a term coined by Tan Chee-beng for the ethnic Chinese worldwide as an improvement on the term huáqiáo, which according to Wang Gungwu implies connections to the Chinese mainland (1996). The term also suggests a permanent foreignness due to race through legal and symbolic association (Poston & Yu 1990, p. 480). Meanwhile, the popular label huárén ("Chinese person") does not indicate any sense of diasporicity. Hence, the preference for the term "Chinese overseas" in its description of ethnic Chinese in diaspora without reference to political loyalty.
3. The recent Indian Oceans Productions film, China to Australia, documents the lives of many prominent Chinese-Australians.

References

Bagnall, K. (2009). *A legacy of White Australia: Records about Chinese Australians in the National Archives*. Paper presented at the Fourth International Conference of Institutes and Libraries for Chinese Overseas Studies, Jinan University, Guangzhou China (10 May 2009). Retrieved from http://www.naa.gov.au/collection/issues/bagnall-2009/index.aspx#ftnlink1_9.

Farrell, R. (2007). Chinese acrobatics unmasked in Australian circus in the nineteenth century. *Australasian Drama Studies, 50*, 36–48.

Farrell, R. (2009). Foot fascination in performance in China and Australia in the nineteenth century. *Early Popular Visual Culture, 7*(1), 19–27.

Fitzgerald, J. (2007). *Chinese Australians in White Australia.* Sydney, NSW: UNSW Press.

Fitzgerald, S. (1997). *Red tape, gold scissors: the story of Sydney's Chinese.* Sydney, NSW: State Library of New South Wales Press.

Giese, D. (1995). *Beyond Chinatown: Changing perspectives on the Top End Chinese experience.* Canberra: National Library of Australia.

Inglis, C. (1998). Australia. In L. Pan (Ed.), *The Encyclopedia* (pp. 274-285). Singapore: Archipelago Press.

Langton, M. (2011). *Trepang: China and the story of Macassan-Aboriginal trade.* Melbourne, VIC: Centre for Cultural Materials Conservation - University of Melbourne.

Love, H. (1985). Chinese theatre on the Victorian goldfields, 1858-1870. In *Australasian Drama Studies 3*(2), 45-86. Brisbane: University of Queensland.

Mount Alexander Mail [newspaper]. (1858, October 1). VIC.

Lydon, J. (1999). *Many inventions: The Chinese in the Rocks, 1890-1930.* Melbourne, VIC: Monash Publications in History.

Ng, N. (2009). Domesticating the foreign: singing salvation through translation in the Australian Catholic Chinese community. In A. Chan & Nelson, A. (Eds.) *Sounds in Translation* (pp. 111-144). Canberra, ACT: ANU E Press.

Ng, N. (2010). "I love the starry-sky at night-time": Singing and signing in the Buddha's Light International Association, Sydney. In J. Russell and F. Wilkins (Eds.), *Musiké 5/6, III, 1 (Sacred singing and musical spirituality)* (pp. 19-54). Rome – The Hague: Semar.

Poston, D. L. & Yu, M. Y. (1990). The distribution of the overseas Chinese in the contemporary world. *International Migration Review, 26*(3), 4480-4509.

Rolls, E. C. (1992). *Sojourners: the epic story of China's centuries-old relationship with Australia.* St. Lucia, QLD: University of Queensland Press.

Rolls, E. C. (1996). *Citizens: flowers and the wide sea.* St Lucia, QLD: University of Queensland Press.

Scott-Maxwell, A. (1997). *Oriental exoticism in 1920s Australian popular music.* Perfect Beat, the Pacific Journal of Research into Contemporary Music and Popular Culture, *3*(3), 28-57.

Shen, Yuanfang. (2001). *Dragon seed in the antipodes: Chinese-Australian autobiographies.* Carlton, VIC: Melbourne University Press.

Tan, Chee-Beng. (2004). *Chinese overseas: comparative cultural issues.* Hong Kong: Hong Kong University Press.

Thomson, J. (ND). *Will 'The Freak' follow Chu Chin Chow onto the musical stages of Australia?* Retrieved from http://www.australianmusicals.com/article_willthefreak.htm.

Thring, F. (c1931). *Melbourne Chinese Orchestra selections* [video recording]. RCA Limited. Courtesy of Vincent Plush, National Film and Sound Archive.

Wang, Zheng-Ting. (1997). *Chinese music in Australia - Victoria, 1850s to mid 1990s*. Melbourne, VIC: Asia Australia Foundation.

Williams, M. (1999). *Chinese settlement in NSW: a thematic history: a report for the NSW Heritage Office of NSW*. Retrieved from http://www.heritage.nsw.gov.au/docs/chinesehistory.pdf.

York, B. (1995). The Chinese in Australia: Exclusions and admissions, 1901–1957. In P. Macgregor (Ed.), *Histories of the Chinese in Australasia and the South Pacific*. Melbourne, VIC: Museum of Chinese Australian History.

PART ONE

Historical Perspectives

CHAPTER

1

The Gangzhou Yueju Quyishe ("Gangzhou Society Cantonese Opera Group") in Melbourne, Australia

Wang Zhengting

Melbourne is the capital of the State of Victoria. This multicultural cosmopolitan city has become the home for a large population of migrants since the end of World War II. Many different national and cultural backgrounds are now represented in Melbourne (Maher, 1984), and the city is noted for its visible Chinese population. By 2001, Melbourne's population had increased to 3,366,549, of whom 55,562 were born in China, Hong Kong or Taiwan. Some 101,575 speak Chinese at home (Australian Bureau of Statistics, 2002). Consequently, there is, in Melbourne, a vibrant program of Chinese cultural activities including many Cantonese opera groups, such as *Yiqing Cantonese Opera, Qingfengxiang Cantonese Opera* and *Shengyi Cantonese Opera Association*.[1] Among the Melbourne-based Cantonese opera groups still in operation, the Gangzhou Society Cantonese Opera Group has the longest history. As an ethnomusicologist, who was educated in China and Australia, and with a particular interest in Chinese performing arts in diaspora, I have spent considerable time researching Cantonese opera during the gold-rush period in Victoria. Due to the paucity of primary sources, we do not know what type of Cantonese operatic repertoire was performed during this period. Much of this history has been lost — such was the ephemeral nature of Chinese performing arts in the pre-twentieth century diaspora. The main focus of this article, therefore, is to provide a narrative history on the Gangzhou Society Cantonese Opera Group from 1961 to 2001.[2] The group's initial establishment, its temporary decline, and its later re-establishment will be discussed. As a Chinese musician, director of the Australian Chinese Music Ensemble, and occasional composer, I will also make critical comments on the group's theatrical activities.

A Brief Background to Cantonese Opera and Cantonese Opera in Victoria

The purpose of this section is to provide some historical background on Cantonese opera, which will assist the comprehension of this article. The statistics concerning traditional opera in China since 1985 show that there are approximately three hundred and forty textant traditional Chinese operatic styles (Xia Zhengnong, 1989, p. 563). Cantonese opera is one of the main forms of Chinese traditional opera and is known as *Yueju*,[3] which took shape more than three hundred years ago (Lai Bojiang, 1988, p. 1). This style of opera uses the Cantonese dialect and it is the most popular regional opera in Guangdong province. It is centralised in Guangzhou and also prevalent in Guangdong and parts of Guangxi provinces, as well as in Hong Kong, Macao, Taiwan and other countries where there are large numbers of Cantonese-speaking people. Generally speaking, the opera provides Chinese people with entertainment, social contact, moral and ethical education. To Chinese migrants, the opera also provides the memory of their motherland culture. The performer in a professional Cantonese opera group needs many years of substantial training. However, such training is unnecessary in an amateur groups, particularly in the Chinese diaspora.

The history of Cantonese opera in Victoria can be traced back to the gold-rush years. During the Victorian gold-rush, Cantonese opera was popular with Chinese miners, the majority of whom were from Guangdong province or Cantonese speaking regions of China. During that time, opera was known as the Chinese 'tent theater', because it was performed in a big tent. Fourteen Cantonese opera companies applied for theatrical licenses between 1850 and 1870 (Love, 1985). Opera companies during this period operated as businesses. For example, over 700 Chinese people paid three shillings each to attend one of Lee Gee's theatrical opera performances in Beechworth in March 1863 (*Ovens and Murray Advertiser*, 1863). On another occasion the *Creswick and Chinese Advertiser* reported that in 1862 a Chinese opera troupe cleared £150 in its first week's performances at Creswick, and sold the second week's performances in advance to another Chinese for £100 (*Creswick and Chinese Advertiser*, 1862).

The popularity of the Chinese tent theatre was very much affected by the Chinese population. In 1857, there were approximately 40,000 Chinese living in Victoria, and most of whom worked in the gold-fields. However, after 1870, as the alluvial gold was exhausted, many Chinese left the mining towns. By 1871, the Chinese population of Victoria had decreased to only 17,000 and the tent theaters in Victoria were affected (*Victorian Review*, 1861), although some sources show that the opera still performed after 1870, Love found no evidence that any Chinese theatrical company applied for a license after 1870. Paul Macgregor, ex-curator of the Museum of Chinese Australian History, has however suggested that after 1870 some Chinese applied for circus licenses, rather than theatrical licenses, although they still played opera (Macgregor, personal communication, 1995). Cronin's summary of the census figures for 1861-1891 shows a dramatic decrease in the number of Chinese males employed in the entertainment industry: forty-eight Chinese men were recorded as musicians and actors in 1871, but only two in 1881 (1982). The Chinese tent theatres, once so popular on the goldfields, gradually decreased their level of activity.

There is no significant evidence for the performance of Cantonese opera in Victoria from the beginning of the twentieth century to the mid-1950s, however, I have been informed by Zheng Jiale, a modern drama organiser and actor in the Melbourne Chinese community from 1942 to 1943, that Cantonese Opera was performed in Melbourne by sailors from Hong Kong and Singapore during the Second World War (Wang, 1997). The history of Cantonese opera in Victoria in during this time has not been researched and is at risk of being lost due to a general lack of documentation and secondary material.

Reasons for the Establishment of the Group

The Gangzhou Society Cantonese Opera Group was established in Melbourne in 1961.[4] There were four main reasons for its establishment. First, the majority of the Chinese population in Melbourne came from Guangdong province, a region fond of Cantonese opera. Second, because of the restrictive White Australia Policy during that time, many Chinese people in Melbourne were unable to bring their families to Australia. For people accustomed to support from the family, living in a place where they had little to no relatives was very difficult. The establishment of the Gangzhou Society Cantonese Opera Group therefore created a place for social contact and support within the Chinese community, and provided an avenue whereby migrants could enrich their lives and compensate for the lack of family support to which they were accustomed. Third, many Chinese who came to Australia were sponsored by Chinese businessmen to work as labourers. Most, therefore, had no education, nor did they have a good understanding of English. In addition, during that period, broader employment opportunities were limited for the Chinese. This resulted in the majority of the Chinese living within the confines of the Chinese community with their social activities limited to the local Chinese network. Finally, gambling had taken a serious hold in the Chinese community. Thus, in an attempt to dissuade the local Chinese from gamble, and to provide them with an alternative cultural activity, the Gangzhou Society Cantonese Opera Group was established.

The Nature of the Group

The majority of the members of the Gangzhou Society Cantonese Opera Group were migrants from China migrants; while some were Australian-born Chinese. According to Huang Zhaonan, one of my interviewees, the local Chinese learned Cantonese opera mainly from Hong Kong sailors. In the 1960s, air tickets were relatively expensive. Sea travel from Hong Kong to Australia was comparatively cheap, so the Chinese usually travelled by sea. Huang Zhaonan pointed out that a ship named the Zhiwanyi came to Melbourne from Hong Kong approximately once every three months and usually stayed for one or two weeks. After a long and arduous journey, the sailors looked for local recreational activities. The sailors on the ship would play Chinese music and act in performances of Cantonese opera. Some of the crew were even members of a Cantonese opera association in Hong Kong. While in Melbourne, they consistently made contact with the local Chinese community, and taught local Chinese musical skills and opera performance techniques. They also played Cantonese opera with local Cantonese opera enthusiasts. Since the local Chinese were predominantly male, some roles were played by female impersonators.

The instruments played by members of the group were of both Chinese and western origin. Using both Chinese and western instruments was not the group's invention and did not occur because the group was situated in a western country. A review of Cantonese opera history indicates that many western instruments were adopted into the Cantonese operatic tradition of Hong Kong and mainland China in the early twentieth century. The Gangzhou Society Cantonese Opera Group's operatic practice was very much influenced by its counterpart in Hong Kong. As Huang Zhaonan remembers, the early musical instruments were donated by the Hong Kong sailors. Figures 1 and 2 give a general idea of the instruments used by the group during the 1960s. These included a *gaohu* (high pitched, two-stringed bowed lute), *yueqin* (Cantonese 4-string plucked lute), saxophone, violin, Hawaiian guitar, and percussion instruments.

The Gangzhou Society Cantonese Opera Group's first opera, *Hubugui*, was performed at Cathedral Hall in Fitzroy in 1961. The plot concerned a faithful and loving couple. The wife was ill-treated by her mother-in-law and left the family while her husband was in the army. When the husband returned home and discovered what had happened to his beloved wife, he immediately left to look for her. Eventually, the couple was reunited. In 1962, the group performed this opera at the Russell Street Theatre which,

FIGURE 1 — The Gangzhou Society Cantonese Opera Group rehearsal in 1960.

FIGURE 2 — Instrumental Ensemble of the Gangzhou Society Cantonese Opera Group during a performance in 1961.

at that time, was one of the main theatrical venues in Melbourne. Other operas from the classical repertoires performed by the group included *Birongtanjian*, *Wangbaochuan*, *Yibacunzhongjian* and *Yiqufengqiuhuang*.

Unlike many of the Cantonese opera companies during the gold-rush period, the Gangzhou Society Cantonese Opera Group was not a business, but an amateur organisation. Audiences were almost all Chinese, and the group only performed to celebrate Chinese festivals and for charities, especially those raising funds to build the Chinese Nursing Home. In the late 1960s, the Australian Government eased restrictions on the immigration of non-Europeans. Therefore, family members still in China were able to come to Australia to be reunited with their families. The members of the group became re-involved with their family duties, resulting in less time for their involvement in opera. Consequently, the Gangzhou Society Cantonese Opera Group became inactive in the early 1970s (Kong Chew Society, 1985).

In 1973, the Australian Government abolished the migration policy based on racial quotas. The Minister for Immigration, Al Grassby, declared Australia a "multicultural society" (reference: I suggest Williams, 1999). With more liberal immigration laws now in place, many overseas Chinese started arriving in Australia from countries that included Vietnam, Hong Kong, Malaysia, Taiwan, Cambodia, and Laos. Among these new arrivals were Cantonese opera enthusiasts, many of whom knew how to act in Cantonese opera and perform Chinese music. Having found a lifestyle that provided greater security, they sought outlets for their Cantonese opera skills. This situation created a positive atmosphere for the re-establishment of Cantonese opera within the Chinese community in Melbourne.

The 1980s to 2001

In the 1980s the Gangzhou Society Opera Group rallied its forces. Local Cantonese opera enthusiasts held a performance in 1985 with the help of their Sydney counterparts and this performance laid the foundation for the re-establishment of the group. By 1987, local Cantonese opera performance was instituted in the Gangzhou Society with the assistance of Huang Zhaonan. According to Huang, the group did not have an official name at the outset. However, people in the Chinese community knew it as "Cantonese opera" attached to the Gangzhou Society. In late 1994, according to Mai Jianghua (a core member of the group), it became known as *Gangzhou Yueji Quyishe*.

The Gangzhou Society Cantonese Opera Group performs both Cantonese opera and *yuequ*, a folk art form from Guangdong province. Its performers favour *Yuequ*, which is less extravagant, has fewer players and is more economical to stage than Cantonese opera. As Huang Zhaonan pointed out, if the group performs Cantonese opera, it has to include more people and even invite additional performers from Sydney, making it quite an expensive production for an amateur grouip. Thus, the association usually performs and presents *yuequ* and highlights from Cantonese operas.

The group performs an entirely traditional Cantonese opera repertoire including stories of ancient China. Huang Zhaonan explained in an interview why the group never wrote its own plots: there were plenty of traditional repertoires that could be selected, and moreover, most of the members were too busy to write new ones (personal communication, 12 November, 1993). The first half of Huang's statement is true because there are more than ten thousand Cantonese operas in the repertoire (Liang Peijing, 1985, p. 8). The second part of Huang's second statement is also true, because as an amateur organisation, members of the group were busy with their work and family commitments. In addition, I believe that the group had the ability to write its own repertoires for due to two factors. Firstly, there were a few well educated members who knew Chinese literature very well would have been able to write the plot. Secondly, the structure of the operatic arias contains *banqiangti* (a metrical structure system) and *qupaiti* (a fixed tune system). *Bangzi* and *erhuang*, which belong to the metrical structure system, are the two main theatrical singing styles in the opera, although some narrative singing styles are also absorbed. The fixed tune system includes the *paizi* (title) and the *xiaoqu* (small tune) (Lai Bojiang, 1995, p. 1307). The former was mainly absorbed from *kunqu* (*Kun* opera, a southern style of opera) and *yiyangzhuqiang* (a type of theatrical singing style). The latter consists mainly of "traditional folk or urban tunes of obscure origin popular in the Guangdong area, some of which are regularly played as instrumental ensemble music" (Yung,1989, p.129). There is a difference between western opera arias and Chinese opera arias: the former are composed while the latter may be selected from the existing tunes or developed from the existing tunes. So if the group wanted to write its own repertoire, there were many existing tunes that could be selected. I believe that the group might try to keep and preserve their operatic tradition rather than developing new works. During my time in the field in 1999, I saw a notice on the wall of the rehearsal room, which indicated that popular songs were prohibited in the group. Generally speaking, the members of the group are over 40 years old, which might be one of the reasons why they favour ancient Chinese stories and refrained from writing new plots, and why modern songs were not performed. This might also be one of the reasons why audiences are predominantly middle aged and older Chinese migrants.

The purpose of the re-establishment of the group was to foster local Chinese interest in Cantonese opera and to create a social centre for Cantonese opera enthusiasts to meet and to compare notes, as well as to enrich their lives. The group is still a non-profit organization, and sometimes performs for fund-raising purposes. For instance in February 1994 the group gave two performances at the Gangzhou Society Assembly Hall. The funds raised were donated to the Chinese Nursing Home Welfare Foundation in Victoria and to the Heavenly Queen Temple Society Incorporation, Melbourne (Heavenly Queen Temple Society Inc., 1994-1995). In the two performances, the group played highlights from operas which included *Shihouji, Anyu, Guangxuhuangjifei, Zhaojunchusai, Huanjuelihentian,* and *Dengjieshicui*. Of the musicians, Huang Zhaonan played the *daruan* (large-sized, four-stringed plucked lute), Xu Caiping played the *erhu* (two-stringed bowed lute), Tang Xiongshan played the violin, Ren Xiafei played percussion and Peng Chunkui played the *guangdongyueqin* (Cantonese 4-string plucked lute).

In 1997, the group was invited by the Museum of Chinese Australian History to perform for the Museum's fundraising efforts. The selection for this performance included *Shijiuxirenxin, Shibaxiangsong, Weiqi* and *Huanjuelihentian*. The actors and actresses were Huang Zhaonan, Hu Qinyuan, Mai Jianghua, Ye Liqing, Deng Qunying, Chen Huiqin and Gu Shaoqiong. The musicians were Zhou Chikai, Wu Yongchang, YuanYuxin, Luo De, Li Darong, Shen Yinghua, Lei Qiuguang and Huang Zhaonan. In addition, two musicians from Sydney assisted at this performance. The afternoon performance took place on 19 January, 1997 at the Box Hill Town Hall in Whitehorse Road, Box Hill, a suburb of Melbourne where there is a substantial Chinese and East Asian population.

The information I have gathered on these performances reveals that the personnel of the group had changed significantly. For instance, only Huang Zhaonan's name was listed as a musician on the 1994 and 1997 programs. Xu Caiping had left the group and set up a new performing group. At the fundraiser for the Museum of Chinese Australia History in 1997, Tang Xiongshan was not listed in the instrumental ensemble; instead, his name appeared on the list of stagehands, even though he now sometimes still performs during the weekly rehearsals. Unlike the relatively stable, professional music and theatrical organisations of mainland China, constant changes of personnel is a common occurence for Chinese theatrical organisations overseas.

On 25 and 26 March, 2000 the Gangzhou Society Cantonese Opera Group mounted a Cantonese opera performance to celebrate the 40th anniversary of the establishment of the group. At Huang Zhaonan's suggestion, a few professional Cantonese opera performers from China were invited to perform with the group for this event. The income from the performance was donated to the Victorian Elderly

FIGURE 3 — Headquarters of the Gangzhou Society. Photograph by Wang Zhengting.

Chinese Welfare Society. Although the Gangzhou Society Cantonese Opera Group is still a non-profit making organisation, it is financially beneficial to its musicians. In recent years, singers had to pay musicians for accompanying services, but they did not have to pay the organisation. Paying artists for musical accompaniment resulted in more Cantonese opera enthusiasts migrating to Melbourne from Hong Kong before Hong Kong was handed over to mainland China in 1997, because this phenomenon is common practice in Hong Kong. The duet is the most common combination for a rehearsal; each piece normally lasts 20 to 30 minutes, and the two singers share the fee. The cost for singing is cheap for the rich, but expensive for the poor. A woman singer was asked why the group did not have more rehearsals each week, and she replied that it would be too expensive for her. Her position probably represents a common situation for many financially insecure Cantonese opera enthusiasts.

Today, there are many Cantonese opera groups in Melbourne. On the one hand, if the Gangzhou Society Cantonese Opera Group wants to be competitive, charging a fee for singing during the rehearsal has a positive value because it might attract and encourage competent musicians to join or stay with the group. If the singers perform with a better standard of musician, this will improve the singer's artistic level and advance the outlook of the group. On the other hand, charging a fee for singing during the rehearsal might decrease the number of the people able to afford to sing. To a certain extent, charging a fee for singing is contrary to the group's purpose of increasing access to Cantonese opera. Thus the organiser of the group needs to deal with this situation cautiously, lest the group lose support from the people.

The Group's Rehearsals

In order to gain a better understanding of the Gangzhou Society Cantonese Opera Group, I attended some rehearsals and interviewed group members in 1999. During rehearsals, the actors and actresses sang one after another. Whilst waiting, they would sit on chairs and listen to the others sing, or practise movements from the opera. If a singer forgot the words or sang out of tune, the musician or other singers would help by singing the same tune. After each piece, they would discuss any problems as a group. Most of the musicians could play more than one instrument, and some of

Figure 4 — A zhongruan photographed at a rehearsal and played by Huang Zhaonan, 1994.

them could even sing the opera. Moreover, some of the singers could play an instrument. Unlike China in the 1960s, most of the singers today are female and some of them sing the male parts.

Two types of musical notation included in music scores used by the group were *jianpu* (numbered notation) and *gongchipu* (traditional Chinese musical notation). The different uses of the two notation systems were probably the result of Cantonese opera musicians being from different musical backgrounds. On the one hand, it would seem that musicians from mainland China are more familiar with *jianpu*. This is because *jianpu* is the most popular notation for Chinese traditional operas in mainland China and generally speaking, *gongchipu* has not been employed for many decades in mainland China. Meanwhile, musicians from elsewhere are more familiar with *gongchipu*, because the traditional Chinese notation was commonly used by Cantonese opera musicians out of mainland China.

The most common instruments used by the musicians in the group included a *gaohu, guangdongyueqin, zhongruan* (medium-sized, four-stringed plucked lute),[6] *yangqin* (struck zither or hammered dulcimer), a western violin, and Chinese percussion instruments. The *zhongruan* used by the group was fitted with a *daruan* string, and an electronic amplifier was used to augment the sound (Figure 4).

This results in a distinct timbre in the instrumental ensemble. During the group's rehearsal on 14 November 1999, when visiting the group's rehearsal, I noticed that an electronic keyboard was used. The sound of the keyboard is incongruent with the Chinese instrumental character. Moreover, the heptatonic scale used in Cantonese opera did not match the keyboard's twelve-tone equal temperament. As Bell Yung (1989) pointed out in his book, *Cantonese Opera Performing as Creative Process*:

> The music in Cantonese opera uses a heptatonic scale; its seven tones in the octave, or scale degree, named *ho, si, yi, saang, che, gung*, and *faan* (romanized according to the Cantonese dialect ...) are roughly equivalent to the tones of the western major diatonic scale. Even though the tones do not imply absolute pitches, the general practice in Cantonese opera today is to equate the seven tones approximately with the following absolute pitches on the piano: G (below middle C), A, B-, C, D, E and F+ respectively. B- refers to a pitch halfway between B and Bb, and F+ refers to a pitch halfway between F and F# (p. 15).

Yung's description indicates that the heptatonic scale in Cantonese opera is not the same as the equal tempered western major diatonic scale. For example, in the western diatonic scale, as played on the piano, the interval between the second note A and the third note B is two half notes in twelve-tone temperament. However, in the heptatonic scale, the interval between the second note A and the third note B- is smaller. In the western diatonic scale, as played on the piano, the interval between the third note B and the fourth note C is a half note. However, in the heptatonic scale, the interval between the third note B- and the fourth note C is larger than half a note from the twelve-tone temperament. Furthermore, the interval between the sixth note E and the seventh note F+, the seventh note F+ and the eighth note G in the heptatonic scale in different from their respective western counterparts. With other instruments not of fixed pitch such as the *erhu*, the experienced performer could adjust the pitch level and intonation to suit the scale used in the Cantonese opera by adjusting the finger positions. Because the notes on the keyboard are fixed, the Cantonese scale played by Chinese instruments and the western scale played by the keyboard resulted in an unintended bitonality.

A similar problem occurred more than half a century ago. Sometime in the early 1930s, some western instruments such as the violin, saxophone, trumpet, clarinet as well as the piano were adopted into Cantonese opera and Cantonese music. Because the notes on the piano were not flexible, it was unsuitable for performing in Cantonese opera and musicand was thus abandoned (Li, 1992, p. 13).

During my time in the field, it appeared that some members of the Gangzhou Society Cantonese Opera Group did not notice the contradiction between the scales at all. The electronic keyboard player said that she could not feel the difference between the scales. She really appreciated the bass line which created by the keyboard since the ensemble needed a strong bass sound she explained.[7]

The *guangdongyueqin*, as the player Peng Chunkui, called it, originally had four strings. However, he only fixed three strings on the instrument because he hardly used the lowest sounding string (Figure 5). Generally speaking, a professional or highly-trained musician wants an instrument with a broad tonal and pitch range. This gives the musician greater flexibility in varying the music while accompanying the singer. However, amateur musicians often try to keep their parts simple, with only minor variations. This is probably the case for the *guangdongyueqin* performer in the group.

In 1994, I found that the percussion instruments were not in tune and did not match acoustically. This really disturbed the audience. In particular, the *bo* (a pair of cymbals) was conspicuously discordant. After testing the cymbal, it was clear that the

FIGURE 5 — A *guangdongyueqin* photographed at a rehearsal and played by Peng Chunkui, in 1994.

pair of cymbals were not at the same pitch. This was not surprising since the quality of commercial instruments made in China cannot be guaranteed unless they are specially ordered. I discussed the problem of the percussion instruments with the musicians in 1994. However, five years later, the problem still existed. On 7November 1999, I went to the group's rehearsal and found that the pair of cymbals, which was tested in 1994, had not been fixed. What was more, the sound of discordant percussion on the day had become even more obvious. The reason in this case was because the percussion performer could not find one of the cymbals from the original pair, so she used another piece from a different sized cymbal set instead. Although, one musician noticed the difference, the percussionist concentrated on playing the cymbals without any visible signs of disturbance. This phenomenon reflected the amateur status of the group and the emphasis on social interaction rather than on musical integrity or professionalism. Despite some problems with the instrumental ensemble, the artistic level of the ensemble has improved since 1994 due to the involvement of more skilled performers.

Summary and Conclusion

Research on the Gangzhou Society Cantonese Opera Group shows that the Australian Government's policy on immigration and multiculturalism influenced community attitudes with policies that were more positive towards ethnic groups and ethnic diversity. This indirectly encouraged Chinese cultural activities in Australia over the years such as the performance of Cantonese opera, which was the most popular form of Chinese opera in Australia. Cantonese theatrical performances are culturally potent events that provide Chinese people with entertainment and social contact as well as the memory of their motherland culture. Although opera is traditionally important as an educational medium for morality and ethics, the content of ancient stories is incongruent with the reality of urban, western life, rendering the educational purpose of opera largely irrelevant. The Gangzhou Society Cantonese Opera Group's theatrical activities mainly focused on the local Chinese community, particularly to people who speak the Cantonese dialect. The group's repertoire, which comprises ancient Chinese stories, does not acknowledge modern trends, making it hard to arouse interest and support among the younger generation. Regardless, the members of the group continue to enjoy their activities in this non-profit organisation with weekly rehearsals given significantly more importance than their performances, which are few and far between. The social activity of the rehearsal is important in that the actors and musicians pay close attention to each other whilst maintaining seriousness in their art. As with many amateur groups, opera-making has more meaning for the performers than for the audience. Moreover, the group is a valuable leisure-time activity for the middle and older generation of Cantonese-speaking migrants who, after many years of residence in Australia, still find their contact with traditional opera potent and meaningful.

Notes

1. Apart from Melbourne, there are many Cantonese opera groups in Australia. For example, in Sydney, the *Chinese Youth League of Australia Cantonese Opera Group* was established in 1939, *Yiqingtian Cantonese Opera* was established in 1983, *Sydney Cantonese Opera* was established in 1992 and *Shengbao Cantonese Opera* was established in 1993. In Brisbane, the *Guotai Cantonese Opera Group* was established in 1992 and *Queensland Cantonese Opera Society* was established in 1998.
2. I will research the Gangzhou Society Cantonese Opera's activities after 2001 in a future project.
3. *Yue* is the abbreviated name for Guangdong Province while *ju* typically means "opera", "drama" or "play." *Yue* is also the pinyin romanisation for "music." It should be noted that these homonyms are entirely different Chinese characters.
4. In 1994, I was informed by the group that it had been established in 1960. However, the group's program notes in 2005 indicated that it was established in 1961. Huang Zhaonan, a musician, actor, and director of the Gangzhou Society, explains that although the group rehearsed together in 1960, there were not many members. This is why the group now claims that it was established in 1961.
5. The White Australia Policy is a generic term used to describe a collection of historical legislation and policies intended to restrict non-white immigration to Australia, and to promote European immigration from 1901 to 1973.
6. The *ruan* is a Chinese four-stringed plucked lute, which has more then 2000 years of history. The instrument was named after a famous Chinese musician, Ruan Xian. After the establishment of the People's Republic of China in 1949, the instrument developed into four different sizes. The *zhongruan* is a medium-sized *ruan* and is the most commonly used of this family.
7. When I visited the group in 2001, the electronic keyboard was not being used.

References

Australian Bureau of Statistics. (2002). *2001 Census of population and housing-classification counts.* Canberra: Australian Bureau of Statistics

Blacking, J. (1977). Some problems of theory and method in the study of musical change." *Yearbook of the International Folk Music Council,* 9(1-26).

Creswick and Chinese Advertiser [newspaper]. (1862, April 4). VIC.

Clifford, J. (1994). Diasporas. *Cultural Anthropology,* 9(3), 302-338.

Cronin, K. (1982). *Colonial casualties: Chinese in early Victoria.* Melbourne: Melbourne University Press.

Cohen, R. (1997). *Global diasporas.* UK: University College London Press Limited.

Department of Immigration and Ethnic Affairs. (1978). *1788-1978 Australia and immigration.* Canberra: Australian Government Publishing Service.

Falk, C. (1997). Migrant music in Australia. In Bebbington, W. A. (Ed.), *The Oxford companion to Australian music* (pp. 375-381). Melbourne: Oxford University Press.

He Shishang. (1994). Yuequ Juyizai Melbourne [Cantonese Opera in Melbourne]. *Yueju Quyi Yueka* [*Cantonese Opera Monthly Magazine*], 14, 8-9. Hong Kong: Dongyue Xiongdi Ziliao Yanjiu Chubangongsi.

Heavenly Queen Temple Society Inc. (1994-1995). *Zhengxinlu* [*Solicited Articles of Essays*]. Melbourne: Heavenly Queen Temple Society Inc.

Huang Jingmin. (1989). Yueju [Cantonese Opera]. *Zhongguo Minzu Yinyue Daguan* [*The Chinese National Music History*]. Shenyang: Shenyang Chubanshe.

Huang Kunzhang. (1998). *Aodaliya Huaren Huaqiaoshi* [*History of the Chinese People in Australia*]. Guangdong: Guangdong Gaodeng Jiaoyu Chubanshe.

Kong Chew Society [Gangzhou Society]. (1985). *Gangzhou Tongxianghui Tekuai* [*Gangzhou Society Special Issue*]. Melbourne: Gangzhou Society.

Kartomi, M. J. (1981). The processes and results of musical culture contact: A discussion of terminology and concept. *Journal of the Society for Ethnomusicology*, 25(2), 227-249.

Lai Bojiang & Huang Jingming. (1988). *Yuejushi* [*The history of Cantonese opera*]. Beijing: Zhongguo Xiqu Chubanshe.

Lai Bojiang & Huang Yuqing et al. (1995). Yueju [Cantonese opera]. *Zhongguo Xiqu Juzhong Dacidian* [*Dictionary of Chinese Traditional Operas*] Ipp. 1305-1308). Shanghai: Shanghai Cishu Chubanshe.

Li Ling. (1992). Guanyu Zhongguo Yinjie Wenti [Issues with regard to the Chinese scale]. *Renmin Yinyue* [*People's Music*], 9, 13-15. Beijing: Zhongguo Wenlian Chubangongsi.

Li P. S. K. (1987). *Cantonese opera in Toronto* (Master's Thesis, York University, Toronto, Canada).

Li Tian. (1999). Dui Yueyue Sangewentide Pouxi [An analysis of three issues regarding Cantonese music]. *Renmin Yinyue* [*People's Music*], 10, 10–12. Beiling: Zhongguo Yinyuejiaxiehua Zazhishe.

Lian Bo. (1989). *Zhongguo Minzu Yinyue Daxi-Quyi Yinyuejuan* [*The Chinese national music-music of folk art forms*]. Shanghai: Shanghai Yinyue Chubanshe.

Liang Peijing. (1985). *Yueju Lumu Tongjian* [*Cantonese opera repertoires*]. Hong Kong: Joint Publishing Corporation.

Lo, J. (2000). Beyond Happy Hybridity: Performing Asian-Australian Identities. In I. Ang, S. Chalmers, L. Law & M. Thomas (Eds.), *Alter/Asians Asian-Australian identities in art, media and popular culture* (pp. 152-1682). Australia: Pluto Press Australia Limited.

London, H. I. (1970). *Non-white immigration and the "White Australia" policy*. Sydney: Sydney University Press.

Love, H. (1985). Chinese theatre on the Victorian gold-fields, 1858-1870. *Australasian Drama Studies* 3(2), 45-86.

Maher, C. A. (1984). *Melbourne...a social atlas*. Australia: Division of National Mapping and Australian Bureau of Statistics.

Mbuyamba, L. (1992). World music: musics of the world. In M. P. Baumann (Ed.), *World music, musics of the world: Aspects of documentation, mass media and acculturation* (pp, 69-87). Wilhelmshaven: Florian Noetzel Verlag.

Nettl, B. (1978). Some aspects of the theory of world music in the twentieth century: Questions, problems and concepts. *Ethnomusicology* 22(1), 123-136.

Ovens and Murray Advertiser (1863, March 7). VIC.

Qiu Kunliang, ed. (1981). *Zhongguo Chuantong Xiqu Yinyue* [*Chinese traditional regional opera music*]. Taibei: Yuanliu Chubangongsi.

Riddle, R. (1983). *Flying dragons, flowing streams: Music in the life of San Francisco's Chinese*. Westport: Greenwood Press.

Schramm, A. (1982). Explorations in urban ethnomusicology: Hard lessons from the spectacularly ordinary. *Yearbook for Traditional Music* 14, 1-14.

Victorian Review [newspaper]. (1861, March 1). VIC.

Wang, Kunzhang. (1998). *Aodaliya Huaqiao Huarenshi* [*A History of Overseas Chinese in Australia*]. Guangdong: Guangdong Gaodeng Jiaoyu Chubanshe.

Wang, Yiyan. (2000). Settlers and sojourners: Multicultural subjectivity of Chinese-Australian artists. In I. Ang, S. Chalmers, L. Law & M. Thomas (Eds.), *Alter/Asians Asian-Australian identities in art, media and popular culture* (pp. 107-122). Australia: Pluto Press Australia Limited.

Wang, Zheng-Ting. (1997). *Chinese music in Australia-Victoria (1850s to mid 1990s)*. Australia: Australia Asia Foundation Melbourne.

——. (1999). Chinese music in mid-Nineteenth century Victoria, *Australasian Music Research* 2-3, 23-38. Melbourne: University of Melbourne.

——. (2007). Cross-cultural experiment, Melbourne, Australia. In R. Bandt, M. Duffy & D. MacKinnon (Eds.), *Hearing places: Sound, place, time and culture* (pp. 375-381). Cambridge: Cambridge Scholars Publishing.

——. (2007). Chinese music on the Victorian Goldfields in the nineteenth century, *Victorian Historical Journal* (Migration issue), 78(2), 170-186.

Williams, M. (1999). *Chinese settlement in NSW: a thematic history: a report for the NSW Heritage Office of NSW*. Retrieved from http://www.heritage.nsw.gov.au/docs/chinesehistory.pdf.

Wu, Guodong. (2001). *Minzu Yinyuexue Gailun* [*An introduction to ethnomusicology*]. Beijing: Renming Yinyue Chubanshe.

Xia, Zhengnong, ed. (1989). *Cihai* [*Chinese work-ocean dictionary*]. Shanghai: Shanghai Cishu Chubanshe.

Yung, B. (1989). *Cantonese opera performance as creative process*. New York: The Press Syndicate of the University of Cambridge.

Zheng, Su. (1993). Immigrant music and transnational discourse: Chinese American music culture in New York City. (Ph.D. Dissertation, Wesleyan University, USA).

Zhou, Weizhi (Ed.) (1994). *Zhongguo Xiqu Yinyue Jicheng-Guangdong* [*The Chinese traditional regional opera music-Guangdong province*]. China: Zhongguo Xiqu Yinyue Jicheng Bianji Weiyuanhui.

Glossary in Pinyin, Hanzi and English

Bangzi	梆子	theatrical singing style (bangzi is also a Chinese percussion instrument)
Banqiangti	板腔体	a metrical structure system
Bo	钹	a pair of cymbals
Daruan	大阮	large-sized, four-stringed plucked lute
Erhu	二胡	two-stringed bowed lute
Erhuang	二簧	theatrical singing style
Hanzi	汉字	Chinese character
Gangzhou Yueju Quyishe	冈州粤剧曲艺社	Gangzhou Society Cantonese Opera Group
Gaohu	高胡	high pitched, two-stringed bowed lute, the principal instrument in Cantonese opera
Gongchipu	工尺谱	traditional Chinese musical notation
Guangdongyueqin	广东月琴	four-stringed plucked lute; popular in Guangdong province
Guotaihui Yuejutuan	国泰会粤剧团	Guotai Cantonese Opera Group
Jianpu	简谱	numbered notation
Kunqu	昆曲	Kun opera, a southern style of opera
Kunshilan Yuequxuehui	兰粤剧	Queensland Cantonese Opera Society
Paizi	牌子	title
Qiaoqingshe Yuejutuan	侨青社粤剧团	Chinese Youth League of Australia Cantonese Opera Group
Qingfengxiang Yuejuquyishe	庆凤祥粤剧曲艺社	Qingfengxiang Cantonese Opera
Qupaiti	曲牌体	fixed tune system
Shengbao Yuejutuan	声宝粤剧团	Shengbao Cantonese Opera
Shengyi Yuejuquyishe	声艺粤剧曲艺社	Shengyi Cantonese Opera Association
Xiaoqu	小曲	small tune
Xiniyuejuquyiyuan	悉尼粤剧曲艺团	Sydney Cantonese Opera
Yangqin	扬琴	struck zither or hammered dulcimer
Yiqing quyishe	怡情曲艺社	Yiqing Cantonese Opera
Yiqingtian Yuejutuan	义擎天粤剧团	Yiqingtian Cantonese Opera
Yiyangzhuqiang	弋阳渚腔	a type of theatrical singing style
Yueqin	月琴	four-stringed plucked lute with a full moon-shaped sound box
Yueju	粤剧	Cantonese Opera
Yuequ	粤曲	a folk art form in Guangdong province
Zhiwanyi	芝万宜	the name of a Japanese ship, phonetically transliterated
Zhongruan	中阮	medium-sized, four-stringed plucked lute

Cantonese Opera Repertoire in Pinyin and Hanzi

Anyu	庵遇
Birongtanjian	碧容探监
Dengjieshicui	灯街拾翠
Huanjuelihentian	幻觉离恨天
Hubugui	胡不归
Guangxuhuangjifei	光绪皇祭妃
Shibaxiangsong	十八相送
Shihouji	狮吼记
Shijiuxirenxin	仕九戏人心
Wangbaochuan	王宝钏
Weiqi	慰妻
Yibacunzhongjian	一把存忠剑
Yiqufengqiuhuang	一曲凤求凰
Zhaojunchusai	昭君出塞

CHAPTER

2

Australian encounters with an imagined China in early musical entertainment

Aline Scott-Maxwell

European-Australian fascination with — as well as fear of — "the Orient" has been a continuous strand throughout the greater part of Australia's cultural history. From the mid-nineteenth century to the early twentieth century, especially, the persistence of exoticised oriental themes and "imagined", stereotypical representations in Australian-produced or consumed popular music and stage entertainment testified to this fascination.

Creative imaginings or representations of China and other "oriental" locales (such as Japan and the Arabian world) in Australian popular culture were part of a much larger-scale orientalist phenomenon imported to Australia from Europe and America via the popular stage, blackface minstrelsy, opera (then a widely popular form), silent cinema music, Tin Pan Alley-style popular song and other mediums.[1] Nevertheless, this was not simply a transplanted European or American cultural phenomenon. From a geographical perspective, the so-called Orient was not the far-away place for Australians that it was for Europeans, or even Americans.[2] Moreover, the nineteenth century Australian gold-rushes brought many Australians into direct contact with the large numbers of Chinese who came to Australia to share in the glittering wealth being extracted from the ground and waterways of the goldfields.

The sheer magnitude of Chinese immigration and resentment of their success in finding gold and competitiveness in commerce and other areas, along with unwelcome cultural differences, engendered considerable anti-Chinese sentiment. With the development of Australian nationalism from the 1880s, this sentiment evolved into a more generalised fear of "invasion" of Australia's empty land by the "yellow hordes" to the north — as futuristically imagined in Kenneth Mackay's 1897 novel *The yellow wave: A romance* *of the Asiatic invasion of Australia.*³ Yet there was also curiosity, amazement and even occasionally admiration for some aspects of Chinese culture, or perceived Chinese attributes such as industriousness and patience.⁴ Representations of China in locally-created stage productions and music were therefore informed by these local circumstances to some extent, and imported theatrical entertainment and music were localised in various ways or ascribed locally-produced meanings.

In the early decades of the twentieth century, Australians were able to experience a packaged "Orient" more directly through the Chinese performers who appeared regularly on Australian vaudeville circuits. These performers, as it were, represented themselves on the popular stage, though in ways that both furthered and subverted the stereotypes that were so familiar to Australians from other representational stage and popular music forms.

Much of the data for this overview of encounters with "China" in Australian popular music and theatrical entertainment from the mid-1800s to the 1930s is necessarily drawn from contemporaneous newspaper reviews and reports. Given the ephemeral nature of many of the entertainments described and the scarcity and — all too often — brevity of reviews, reports and other textual sources (with the notable exception of published song sheets), the article does not attempt to speculate on how music functioned to reinforce other parameters of these entertainments such as verbal or visual aspects. And the paucity of sources does not permit assessment of whether the representations discussed contributed negatively or positively to a broader engagement with China.

The article, instead, points to the complexity, ambiguities and multi-faceted nature of the history of Australian musical engagement with an exoticised China over this period: an engagement that constitutes a somewhat patchy theme in Australia's cultural history rather than a sustained narrative. This engagement involved changing theatrical and musical forms, technologies and influences, importation and local staging and creation of works, and variable modes of representation ranging from relatively direct (in the sense of involving Chinese performers, as such) to multi-mediated and highly diffuse. The article also highlights some of the ways that musical representations of China by non-Chinese intersected with Australians' direct experiences and perceptions of Chinese theatre and music, the distinction between "imagined" and "real" being further blurred by the Chinese musicians and other performers who entertained Australians on vaudeville stages in the early twentieth century. Representations or imaginings of China in early popular musical entertainment were frequently mediated by American or European forms and products and it is precisely for this reason that they need to be understood in terms of the specifically Australian circumstances in which they were produced and/or consumed.

The nineteenth century popular stage

In the nineteenth century, stage entertainments such as melodramas, pantomimes, burlesques and so forth frequently incorporated or sometimes even revolved around

Chinese characters or themes, providing many and varied opportunities for representing — or rather misrepresenting — Chinese people and culture. These shows invariably presented Chinese as comic characters or figures of fun, employing stereotyped racialised parodies of Chinese names, accents and supposed behavioural traits. Musical accompaniment and on-stage music were integral to all types of stage entertainment in this era. "Oriental" musical effects underpinned the action at appropriate moments, or were incorporated into China-themed musical or dance items, for example, the *Chinese Song and Dance* performed by Maggie Moore in the farce, *The Chinese Question*, in 1874,[5] or the "characteristic Chinese dance" and the vocal duet, *Pretty Little China Maid*, both featured in *The Mandarin*, an 1896 musical show, or "Chinese comic opera", created by Adelaide writer Harry Congreve Evans and musician John Dunn ("Musical and dramatic", 1896).

Plots and characters in locally-created or adapted stage entertainments often drew directly on local experiences of and encounters with Chinese, featuring opium dens, Chinese laundries, market gardeners, miners, and such like. Alfred Dampier's famous 1889 melodrama, *Marvellous Melbourne*, for example, included scenes featuring, respectively, a Chinese opium den and an impudent, cunning Chinese market gardener (Williams, 1983, pp. 152-153). The plot of *The Mandarin* revolved around an unreadable will and the efforts of the beneficiary Tin Khan (together with other characters given comic names such as How Ler and Swee Tee) to recover his inheritance, which consisted of a tenth share in a Northern Territory gold mine and Chinese laundries in Sydney, Melbourne and Adelaide.

Similarly, many European Australians had some familiarity with Chinese music as such either from witnessing Chinese street festivals or opera performances or from inadvertent proximity to these or other Chinese musical activity, or through the many, generally uncomplimentary reports and comments about the music that appeared in colonial newspapers.[6] And this direct or mediated exposure influenced how Chinese music was creatively represented on the popular stage and how it was received, since audiences were able to compare and evaluate the cleverness of the imitations, or delineations, or the sharpness of the parodies against what they knew about Chinese music, as the following quote from a review of a burlesque pantomime of Aladdin makes clear:

> …the incidental Chinese ballet, with Chinese music, will be recognised as a most accurate copy of an original which must be quite familiar to a good many persons in this city. ("The Academy of Music", 1877)

Local and imported blackface minstrel shows were also a locus for representations of, or at least allusions to, Chinese music in the form of the "Chinese fiddle." Later more commonly known as the Japanese fiddle, this instrument was generally not even an imitation Chinese or Japanese instrument but, rather, a Western-conceived novelty instrument also known as the one-string fiddle. Alison Rabinovici, who has researched these instruments extensively, states that — quite apart from their Chinese references — Chinese fiddle performances often parodied Western virtuosi (Rabinovici 2009). Nevertheless, the name alone clearly invited a comparison from an audience familiar with the original, as indicated in the following excerpt from a Perth review of a visiting blackface troupe, Harvey's English Variety Company:

> Mr C. Harvey played a couple of solos on a single-stringed Chinese fiddle, and the melody he managed to evolve out of the instrument would hardly be conceivable by those who have only listened to the Celestial making night hideous with his outrages on sound. ("Harvey's English Variety Company", 1890)

Sometimes, the two performance worlds — one of imaginary exotic artifice and creative representation, the other authentic — converged and even interacted in intriguing ways, as in the Chinese fiddle act from a minstrel variety show in Melbourne described below, which appears to have had Chinese in the audience:

> Chinese burlesque — Big Shang-high and Little Hong Kong — is a most diverting interlude, which has attracted the attention of some of the Mongolian[sic] residents of this city, who appear to appreciate Mr. Barlow's performance on the Chinese fiddle. ("Mr. Barlow's Entertainment", 1871)

Another example of convergence comes from an account of a public event in which delineations of Chinese music by non-Chinese musicians were heard alongside Chinese musicians playing their own music. The occasion was a mammoth multi-faceted fund-raising event for the Women's Hospital in Melbourne, part of which comprised a Chinese procession and mock battle supported and funded by local Chinese merchants. The procession involved over five hundred personnel including numerous Chinese bands and a local brass band of repute, for which the musical director had arranged imitation Chinese music:

> The display [i.e. the procession] will be, as far as it is possible to render it so, thoroughly Chinese, and the music as near an imitation of that of China as the musical director, Mr H. Warnecke, will be able to arrange. ("The Women's Hospital Bazaar", 1886)

Touring shows

The orientalist trend in popular theatre intensified from around the turn of the century with a string of big imported musical comedies from the United States or Great Britain, feeding Australian fascination with oriental-style exotica. Many of these shows had a Chinese theme. *A Trip to Chinatown* was staged in Australia in 1899, the British "Chinese" hit, *San Toy*, in 1901–2, and *A Chinese Honeymoon* in 1902. The appeal and expressive potential of oriental themes for those who produced this sort of work is alluded to in a review of *A Chinese Honeymoon* at Melbourne's Princess Theatre:

> Chinese local colour, both scenically and musically, is so tempting that musical comedy librettists and composers find it hard to get away from the Far East, and the new work, "A Chinese Honeymoon", ... was one more example of the effectiveness of the 'Celestial' motif... ("Princess's Theatre", 1902)

The massively successful oriental extravaganza, *Chu Chin Chow: a Musical Tale from the East*, written and produced by expatriate Australian actor, Oscar Asche, with music by English composer Frederic Norton, toured Australia from 1920 following its unprecedented five year London run (see Figure 1). A second production with Asche in the lead role was seen in Australia from mid-1922. In the program for the 1920-1 Melbourne Tivoli production, Asche describes *Chu Chin Chow* as "...a lifelike and stimulating vision of the romance, the splendour, the inscrutable mystery of the East", while local promotion for the show claimed that composer Frank Norton "has contrived to instill into his compositions something of the mysterious and sensuous beauty and charm of the orient..." ("Amusements: Tivoli Theatre", 1920, p. 28). The musical's story is in fact based on the tale of Ali Baba and the Forty Thieves but has the main protagonist (Abu Hasan) disguised as a Chinese (Chu Chin Chow). It therefore brings together the two principal "sites" of orientalist interest, so-called Araby and China. Photos inside the Tivoli's souvenir program show the female actors in bizarrely fantastic and revealing costumes that underline the erotic appeal of the Orient for Europeans. *Chu Chin Chow* was so popular in Australia that it spawned

FIGURE 1 — *Chu Chin Chow*. (cover of the program for the Tivoli Theatre production, Melbourne, 1920-1). Courtesy of the Rare Books Collection, Monash University Library.

local spin-offs such as a burlesque parody called the *Two Chinned Chow* ("De Luxe and Lyceum", 1921) or the *Chu Chin Chow One Step*, a medley arrangement of two of the musical's hit songs by Allan's music house arranger, Fred Hall. The complete vocal-piano score for *Chu Chin Chow, San Toy* and other locally-performed oriental-themed shows could be purchased at Allan's in Melbourne and other Australian music houses.

Oscar Asche's *Cairo* was also staged in Australia in 1922 and, as in *Chu Chin Chow*, Chinese characters featured alongside the "Arabian" characters in an indiscriminate oriental melange. The lyrics of *The Chinaman's Song* in *Cairo* use a parodic Chinese-English dialect of a type that was ubiquitous in popular representations of Chinese, as well as the common stereotype of Chinese as cunning and deceitful:

> Me welly good old Chinaman
>
> Me Wei San Wei
>
> ....
>
> Me flom Pekin, Me fullie sin
>
> Me foolie men, Me plenty yen
>
> Me buyie sell, Me cheatie Hell!
>
> Me Wei San Wei (*The Chinaman's Song*, c1920)

These lyrics are nevertheless marginally less derogatory than those of the *Chinese Song and Dance* in the play, *The Chinese Question*, from nearly half a century earlier, which represents Chinese language as pure gibberish:

> Esau waya tetu lunga
>
> Samsi wenga tahi tonga
>
> Oolong souchong hinga wenga
>
> Pinga linga ching ching chow chow chung (*Chinese Song and Dance*, c1879)

Australian theatre historian, Veronica Kelly, has argued that, as colonised subjects who were themselves constructed as "an Other within imperial hierarchies", Australians to some extent identified with orientalist spectacles such as *Chu Chin Chow* and *Cairo* and, further, that Asche, as an expatriate Australian who expressed strong sentiments for rural Australia in his autobiography, presented a visual "orient" which resonated particularly with Australia and Australians through the use of innovative lighting and colour effects, especially bright white light, saturated colours and panoramic openness (Kelly, 1993, pp. 33– 35ff). The music of *Chu Chin Chow*, on the other hand, neither had a similarly Australian inflection nor much "oriental" colouring (in contrast to the subject matter, sets, costumes and other visual effects), its style belonging squarely to "the realm of early twentieth-century English sensibility" (Everett, 2007, p. 295).

Silent cinema music

Notions of China constructed through popular culture were also disseminated widely and pervasively through silent cinema, which was always accompanied by live orchestral, piano or theatre organ music. "Oriental music" was a major category in the film music catalogues of this period, along with "mysteriosos", "hurries", love themes, and other mood-enhancing genres, and was used principally to create an appropriate atmosphere for scenes depicting oriental locations or characters. Since oriental characters were often portrayed as villains, the accompanying music was intended to reinforce this characterisation, as in Montague Ewing's piece *Oriental Shadows* (1927), which was to be used "For sinister Oriental scenes." So-called oriental music for film did not necessarily distinguish between, say, music used for Chinese and Japanese themes. Indeed, film music manuals of the period (which, though American, were widely consulted in Australia) differ on the need for this sort of particularity, creating confusion for Australian practitioners about how Chinese characters should be represented musically. For example, Erno Rapee in his *Encyclopedia of Music for Pictures* classes Chinese and Japanese music together because "the character of the two to our western ears is hardly different" (1925, p. 25), but another manual, by George Beynon, advises that "Japanese and Chinese music, though Asiatic and distinctly Oriental, should be separately classified" (1921, p. 24).

Cinema pianists and organists often improvised oriental-sounding moods, bridges and effects according to their own perceptions of what was appropriate (Whiteoak, 1999, pp. 63-69). But most of the music used to accompany silent film was drawn or arranged from classical or popular repertoire, or specially composed

Ah Sin	Fu
Chang	Goodbye Shanghai
Chang-An	Heathen Chinee
Chinese Allegretto	Hong Kong Gong
Chinese Characteristic	In a Chinese Tea Garden
Chinese Festival	In a Chinese Tea Room
Chinese Honey Moon	In Hong Kong Street
Chinese Japanese	Li Hung Chang
Chinese Lullaby	Ling Ting Tong
Chinese March	Mandarin
Chinese Moon	Pearl of Pekin
Chinese Prelude	Pekin
Chinese Recollections	Pekin Peeks
Chinese Serenade	Shanghai Dream Man
Chinese Tragedy	Shanghai Gesture
Chinese Wedding Procession	Song of Shanghai
Ching-A-Ling	Street of Pekin
Chop Suey	Voyage en Chine
Chung Lo	

"moods." Parts and scores were made available to Australian cinema orchestras through major lending collections, such as that of the former Sydney State Theatre.[7] This collection includes a large quantity of scores in the Chinese "oriental" category, as can be seen from the list of just some of the titles in the collection on the previous page.

Annotations on the scores recording loans by various theatre orchestras, indicate the extent of their use. For example, *Chow Mein: a Chinese Episode*, was lent out fifteen times between April 1924 and October 1925 to theatres as far flung as Cairns, Gympie and Launceston.

China was represented in these scores principally in two ways, one of these being the use of Chinese percussion. For example, the percussion part for *Pekin Peeks* calls for drums, gong, Chinese drum and tom tom. The specific requirements of scores such as this aside, cinema orchestra percussionists used their ingenuity and whatever worked best to get appropriate "oriental" effects. The other principal means of conveying Chineseness was by the use of stereotypical rhythmic, melodic, harmonic and ornamentational devices or formulae designed to contribute colour and a Chinese-inflected exotic effect. Common musical features of these scores include gapped pentatonic scales, heavy use of repeated or parallel fourths and fifths, repeated tones in stilted "click-clack" rhythms (e.g. repeated quavers or semiquaver/semiquaver/quaver patterns), simple melodic figures that recur at different pitch levels, and chromaticisms of various sorts. Some of these devices also functioned as generic "orientalisms" and were interchangeable into other film music oriental settings, such as "Araby" or even the Pacific.

Tin Pan-Alley style popular song

The same type of oriental musical effects were also prominent in the songs on Chinese themes that formed part of a sub-genre of Tin Pan Alley-style popular songs in the late 1910s and 1920s.[8] The early 1920s craze for "oriental fox-trot songs" and "oriental vocal waltzes" saw the sheet music of large numbers of these songs imported to Australia, mainly from the United States, or re-published under licence by local Australian publishers such as Allan's or Albert's.[9] Australian composers and lyricists also wrote songs in this genre, although in smaller numbers. Re-published songs were "plugged" by local artists, whose photos were often depicted on the sheet music cover. *China Girl*, for example, was re-published by Albert & Son, Sydney, and "plugged" at the lavish Ambassadors cabaret by local artist, Phyllis Du Barry (see Figure 2). Another publication of this song sheet has a photo of Mervyn Lyons and his Ambassadors Band on the cover. These songs were also frequently featured in local pantomimes and revues, as was also advertised on the covers. Examples include *From Here to Shanghai* (republished by Sydney publisher D. Davis), performed by Miss Maude Fane in J.C. Williamson's production of *The Boy*, and *Chong He Come From Hong Kong* (republished by Allan's), featured by Clarice Hardwicke in "Hugh D. McIntosh's successful revue 'Bran Pie.'" The cover of *The Chinese Blues* (republished by Albert's) includes a photo of a fantastically head-dressed and "Chinese"-garbed

FIGURE 2 — China Girl (sheet music cover), author's collection. The vocalist, Phyllis Du Barry, is shown wearing an elaborate 'oriental' headdress.

Thelma Raye, who performed the song in *Tivoli Blues*. Inevitably, many of these songs appeared in productions of *Aladdin*.

Like other Tin Pan Alley categories of popular music, oriental-style song sheets are characterised by snappy titles, strongly coloured and strikingly designed eye-catching covers, sentimental and/or superficial lyrics, and simple, singable melodies invariably framed within the standard popular song format of one to four verses plus chorus. Titles like *Down in Chinatown, Goodbye Shanghai, China Moon* and *China Girl* place the song in their exotic oriental setting of China or Chinatown. The setting is further reinforced by the song cover imagery, which features such things as lanterns, bamboo, temples and, often, depictions of demurely alluring Chinese women — archetypal stereotypical or caricatured imagery associated with popular representations of China. The lyrics range from being trivialisingly patronising of their subjects to, in some cases, quite viciously racist. They are replete with clichéd references to "sweet China maidens", "pretty almond eyes", or "dreamy Chinese moonlight", and so forth, and make plentiful use of the usual parodies of Chinese English. Chinese women are common subjects (as is clear from titles such as *China Doll, Chinee Girl*, etc), invoking an orientalist gendering of the East. The perspective is typically that of a Western male and the implication of a non-Chinese lover from "across the seas" is sometimes made explicit. Songs often present absurd depictions of China, or Chinatown, with frequent allusions to opium use, pigtails, cunning and devious behaviour, and such like. Some fall squarely into the comic song category. Interchangeability between representations of China and Japan, or perhaps simply confusion, is also evident in some of these songs. For example, the lyrics of *Shanghai: a Chinese Romance* reference the Japanese three-stringed shamisen lute (as in "Wind-bells, singing as of yore, Moontime and then you played your samisen"). In an attempt at verisimilitude, there is even a footnote stating that the instrument is "A frail form of Mandoline with three strings used by Chinese singing girls. Pronounced 'Sam-a-zan'" (*Shanghai*, c1925).[10]

Like the lyrics, the music is also highly conventionalised and cliché-laden with China represented by similar devices to those used in the silent film scores, such as pentatonicisms, chromatic ornaments, open fourths and fifths, simple rhythmic patterns insistently repeated for bizarre effect, and so forth. Performative aspects were another significant medium for enhancing oriental themes, whether in a playful or parodic way. Performance practices heard on recordings of these songs include use of an exaggeratedly sing-song vocal style, timbrally-altered vocals and Chinese woodblocks and other instruments.

Australian composed oriental-style songs from this period include *My Chinee Girl* with words and music by Vince Courtney, which featured in the 1917 home-grown musical, *The Bunyip*; *Somewhere South of Shanghai*, by Jack Lumsdaine; *I'll Spend a Week in Pekin* by Moritz Lutzen; *China Doll* with words and music by Alf Lawrence; and another song by Alf Lawrence (with lyrics by Harry Evans) titled *Mah-jongg*, that was used for promotional purposes (and perhaps even commissioned) by the bookstore Robertson & Mullens, from where sets of the game could be purchased (see Figure 3). While still relentlessly formulaic, they tend to be more diluted than their American counterparts: the stereotypes are somewhat less strongly drawn and the musical orientalisms are less pervasive and exaggerated. The lyrics from the chorus of *China Doll* illustrate the relatively benign if trite and sentimental character of these songs:

    Oh you China Doll

    When those black eyes roll

    I just long to bill and coo

    Like those Chinese people do

    On that Willow pattern bowl

    For I'm loving you with all my heart and soul

    And I reach love's goal

    When that big Pagoda nigh

    Only holds just me and my China Doll.[11] (*China Doll*, 191-?)

FIGURE 3 — *Mah-jongg* (sheet music cover). Rare Books Collection, Monash University Library.

Notwithstanding the rabidly nationalist xenophobia that preceded and was formalised by the 1901 Immigration Restriction Act (known as the White Australia Policy), most of the representations in these songs are not strongly connected with a perceived reality but, rather, are deliberately playful and absurd — hence perhaps their common use in pantomime.

Chinese performers in vaudeville

Opportunities for Australians to witness Chinese music and theatre performed primarily for Chinese consumption or at major public civic events first-hand were significantly reduced from the early twentieth century following the introduction of immigration exclusion laws and the gradual diminution of the permanent Chinese population in Australia. But, by this time, Chinese had also begun to represent themselves musically and theatrically on the international popular stage as professional variety artists. The successful development of Australian vaudeville circuits brought both visiting and local Chinese performers, acrobats and magicians into mainstream theatres in acts that used on-stage or accompaniment music and effects. Acrobats were the most common type of act but there were also Chinese musical acts and musical content within acts. For example, the *The Mercury* (Hobart) reported on Chinese vaudeville artists appearing at the National Theatre:

> ...the Five Lewins, a Chinese family, who have been specially engaged for a short season. The five artists are all girls, and from baby Lewin to the eldest of the troupe, each one is thoroughly skilled in her own particular line. Genuine Chinese costumes are used in the various turns, and the whole entertainment is said to be absolutely unique in the annals of vaudeville in Australia. The Lewins opening number, "A Shanghai wedding", introducing genuine Chinese music, is said to be especially fine. ("Chinese Entertainers", 1920)

Newspaper reports and reviews suggest that Chinese vaudeville artists often played to audience expectations of what Chinese performance and music constituted, reinforcing notions of a strange and mysteriously exotic East. On the other hand, Chinese artists did not confine themselves to Chinese-referenced acts and therefore, conversely, could be seen as demonstrating cleverness in their "imitation" of European music as well as subverting stereotypes and audience expectations. For example, the two daughters of world-famous Chinese-American acrobat, magician and performer, Long Tack Sam, who toured on the Australian Tivoli circuit numerous times, astounded audiences with their toe dancing and violin-playing ("Chinese Troupe at Tivoli", 1928), while the act of Chinese comedian Ben Nee One, began with a song in Irish dialect and closed with a Chinese one ("New Acts at the Tivoli", 1926).[12]

Both Long Tack Sam (in 1923) and another troupe, the Sun Moon Lee troupe (in 1927), which was advertised as coming direct from China, were billed in acts as featuring a "Chinese jazz band." A brochure for Sun Moon Lee's Melbourne season at the Westgarth Theatre, 15–17 August, indicates that his troupe's act also included more usual Chinese vaudeville fare in the form of juggling, magic, and so forth. It is most likely that the Chinese jazz bands in these troupes were playing some sort of burlesque on jazz, which was common for stage jazz acts in vaudeville in the initial years of the jazz age (see Figure 4). The Australian-published song sheet for the Tin Pan Alley oriental-style song, *Hong Kong Dream Girl*, announces on the cover that it was "specially featured by the Sun Moon Lee troupe during their Australian tour", a highly tantalising indicator that these jazz bands exploited the popularity of this genre in a self-orientalising fashion (*Hong Kong Dream Girl*, c1924). This is the only evidence to hand regarding these bands' repertoire. However, whatever they played was probably performed with Chinese inflections since, according to the advertising brochure for Sun Moon Lee's Westgarth Theatre performances, "To all the regular — and irregular — instruments played in Jazz, it has added those of China, with a result unusual and striking." Early jazz variety acts (such as "Australia"s First Jazz Band" (Whiteoak, 1999, pp. 171-180)) were often equated with novelty noise-making, and Chinese percussion instruments were marketed as "jazz," or novelty effects instruments. Moreover, traditional Chinese bands had also long been associated in the Australian

FIGURE 4 — Sun Moon Lee and his 14 Oriental Stars with the Chinese Jazz Band (cover of advertising brochure, Melbourne, 1927). Courtesy of the Rare Books Collection, Monash University Library. The 'Chinese'-inflected iconography is enhanced by the colour design of a yellow dragon on a bright red background.

public mind with noise-making. It is therefore not surprising that traditional ensembles were sometimes even described as jazz bands, as in the following 1926 report:

> Mr Henry Foo's Chinese jazz band, which has been playing at broadcasting station 2BL, Sydney, comprises six performers, who play a three-string violin, a two-string banjo, another two-string instrument, a trumpet (or something like it) a cymbal and a drum. ("Chinese Band", 1926)

Evolving Chinese-Australian musical encounters

By the end of the 1920s, when most Australians associated Chinese music with orientalist-style stage or popular musical entertainment, other forms of musical and non-musical engagement with China began to emerge. Overseas reports in Australian newspapers began to depict a culturally modernising China and newspaper accounts of Chinese community presentations of popular entertainment gradually appeared.[13]

As European-Australians gained increasing appreciation and understanding of Chinese music and theatre, creative musical engagement with China shifted away from the types of popular musical and stage representations that had previously fed Australian fascination with a Chinese "other." Nevertheless, they were kept alive for many more decades via cinema and, later, television — as well as oddities such as Adelaide composer Irene Tucker's 1940s composition, *China,* claimed as "a musical tribute to our [Chinese] Gallant ALLIES" and comprising faux-Chinese music, lyrics and instructions for a farcical novelty dance, *The Chinee Trot.*

The legacy of earlier perceptions of an exotic "oriental" China — as well as other sites of oriental imaginings — reside in extant sheet music, theatre programs, newspaper reports, reviews and advertisements, and many other artifacts such as sound recordings and piano-rolls. These historical artifacts reveal the persistent recurrence and diversity of representations of an imagined China through music and early stage performance. They also retain traces of how these representations were localised for Australian audiences and how, in some cases, the production and reception of these representations were informed by Australians' direct encounters with Chinese music and performers. Conversely, later Chinese performers on the vaudeville stage themselves engaged with the sorts of representations that Australian audiences were familiar with while, simultaneously, gradually transforming the way they represented themselves and were perceived. This interplay between an exoticised and an "authentic" musical China continues, perhaps, to work itself out in the various ways that Chinese music or Chinese-inflected music is presented in Australia to this day.

Notes

1. The literature on musical orientalism overwhelmingly considers exoticism in serious and light classical music, not popular music of the type or period considered here. Amongst the literature on orientalism in popular music are two significant studies focusing on representations of China in early American popular music culture: Moon's comprehensive monograph (2005) and Garrett's study of the Tin Pan Alley song, *Chinatown, my Chinatown* (2004). Chinese and other 'oriental' exoticism in Australian popular music is addressed in Scott-Maxwell (1997) with a focus on the 1920s and also in Scott-Maxwell (2011). 'Orientalist' as used here invokes Edward Said's critique of the European discourses and representational practices that contributed to the colonial project and its agenda of cultural imperialism.
2. Within the Australian context, the Orient referred not just to the Middle East (the principal site of the European orientalist gaze), the Indian sub-continent and the Far East (as it was called from a European perspective) but also the islands of the Pacific, imaginary or otherwise. All these sites provided a source of exotic settings and materials in popular music and stage performance, as discussed in Scott-Maxwell (1997).
3. In Victoria, for example, approximately 1 in 10 males were Chinese by 1857, or over 6% of the total Victorian population (see Cronin 1982, p. 140).
4. See for example a newspaper article titled "The Chinaman" in *The Queenslander* (1876), which also refers positively to other Chinese attributes such as their honesty in repaying debts, ingenuity with minimal resources, cleanliness and politeness; and Doggett (2008), who compares Australian admiration for Chinese opera acrobatics, costumes and embroidery with their strongly negative response to Chinese music.

5   *The Chinese Question* was an American play by Clay M. Greene that was commissioned by J.C. Williamson and staged and performed in Australia by the actor/entrepreneur and his wife, Maggie Moore (Dicker, 1974, pp. 32-33, 55ff).
6   See Love (1985), Doggett (2008) or Wang (1997, p. 24-34) for examples of first-hand descriptions and reports of Chinese music. Some newspaper reports were less about the music as such than about complaints of the 'noise' from nearby residents.
7   The State Theatre collection is held at the National Library of Australia.
8   The 'oriental' genre of Tin Pan Alley-style popular song in Australia is discussed more fully in Scott-Maxwell (1997). Tin Pan Alley is the name commonly used to refer to the song-writing and publishing industry centred on New York.
9   See Moon (2005) for an extensively researched list of American popular songs with Chinese subjects or themes (pp. 169-179).
10 Garrett describes the shamisen as an all-purpose signifier of Asia for Tin Pan Alley, along with the kimono, paper lantern and Asian-style font (2004, p. 140).
11 The verse of this song conflates a porcelain china doll and a Chinese woman and was no doubt influenced by the 1904 American musical play, *A China Doll* and its hit song, *My Little China Doll*, as described by Moon (2005, p. 124).
12 Their 1931 program was called 'Celebrity Vaudeville'.
13 Examples of reports of Chinese modernity include articles about the large number of jazz clubs in Shanghai and the popularity of jazz dancing in China ("'Jazz-Mad' Chinese", 1929; "The Orient Learns Modern Dance", 1936). Reviews of Chinese community popular entertainment include, for example, a program of Chinese vaudeville 'with real Chinese music and effects' presented before a large Chinese audience with proceeds going to the Australian Chinese School fund ("Chinese Vaudeville Entertainment", 1930).

References

"The Academy of Music." (1877, February 22). *The Argus* [newspaper] (Melbourne, VIC: 1848-1956), p. 5.

"Amusements: Tivoli Theatre", (1920, December 11). *The Argus* [newspaper] (Melbourne, VIC: 1848-1956).

Beynon, G. W. (1921). *Musical presentation of motion pictures*. New York: G. Schirmer.

China Doll [sheet music]. (191-?). Alf Lawrence (Lyricist & Composer). Adelaide: Jack Fewster Limited.

"The Chinaman." (1876, March 18). *The Queenslander* [newspaper] (Brisbane, QLD: 1866-1939), p. 13.

The Chinaman's Song [sheet music]. (c1920). Oscar Asche (Lyricist) & Percy Fletcher (Composer). London: Ascherberg, Hopwood & Crew.

"Chinese Band." (1926, October 28). *The Canberra Times* [newspaper] (Canberra, ACT: 1926-1954), p. 12.

"Chinese Entertainers." (1920, May 27). *The Mercury* [newspaper] (Hobart, TAS: 1860-1954), p. 8.

Chinese Song and Dance. (c1879). Charles Schultz (Composer). Melbourne: J. C. Williamson.

"Chinese Troupe at Tivoli." (1928, October 30). *The Argus* [newspaper] (Melbourne, VIC: 1848-1956), p. 16.

"Chinese Vaudeville Entertainment." (1930, May 26). *The Sydney Morning Herald* (Sydney, NSW: 1842-1954), p. 7.

Cronin, K. (1982). *Colonial casualties: Chinese in early Victoria*. Melbourne: Melbourne University Press.

"De Luxe and Lyceum." (1921, January 31). *The Argus* [newspaper] (Melbourne, VIC: 1848-1956), p. 9.

Dicker, I. G. (1974). *J.C.W.: A short biography of James Cassius Willamson*. Rose Bay, NSW: Elizabeth Tudor Press.

Doggett, A. (2008). "Strains from flowery land": responses to Chinese musical activity in mid-nineteenth century Ballarat. *Context: Journal of Music Research, 33*, 107-120.

Everett, W. A. (2007). Chu Chin Chow and orientalist musical theatre in Britain during the First World War. In M. Clayton & B. Zon (Eds.), *Music and Orientalism in the British Empire, 1780s-1940s* (pp. 277-296). Hampshire: Ashgate.

Garrett, C. H. (2004). Chinatown, whose Chinatown? Defining America's borders with musical orientalism. *Journal of the American Musicological Society, 57*(1), 119-173.

"Harvey's English Variety Company." (1890, April 26). *The West Australian* (Perth, WA: 1879-1954), p. 3.

Hong Kong Dream Girl [sheet music]. (c1924). Geo E. Springer (lyricist) & Harry Barris (composer). Sydney: J. Albert & Son.

"'Jazz-Mad' Chinese", (1929, March 11). The Argus [newspaper] (Melbourne, VIC: 1848-1956), p. 7.

Kelly, V. (1993). Orientalism in early Australian theatre. *New Literatures Review, 26*, 32-45.

Love, H. (1985). Chinese theatre on the Victorian goldfields, 1858-1870. *Australasian Drama Studies, 3*(2), 45–86.

Mackay, K. (1897). *The yellow wave: a romance of the Asiatic invasion of Australia*. London: R. Bentley.

Moon, K. R. (2005). *Yellowface: Creating the Chinese in American popular music and performance, 1850s-1920s*. New Brunswick, New Jersey: Rutgers University Press.

"Mr. Barlow's Entertainment." (1871, March 29). *The Argus* [newspaper] (Melbourne, VIC: 1848-1956), p. 5. "Musical and Dramatic." (1896, November 28). *Adelaide Observer* [newspaper] (Adelaide, SA: 1843-1904).

"New Acts at the Tivoli." (1926, March 2). *The Argus* (Melbourne, VIC: 1848-1956), p. 12.

"The Orient Learns Modern Dance." (1936, May 19). *The Argus* (Melbourne, VIC: 1848-1956), p. 3.

"Princess's Theatre." (1902, July 1). *The Argus* [newspaper] (Melbourne, VIC: 1848-1956), p. 6.

Rabinovici, A. (2009, September 26-28). *Bridging the gap: minstrel origins of the Japanese fiddle*. Unpublished paper contributed to Bridges, Transformational Journeys: 32nd National Conference, Musicological Society of Australia.

Rapee, E. (1925). *Encyclopedia of music for pictures*. New York: Belwin.

Said, E. (1978). *Orientalism: Western conceptions of the Orient*. London: Penguin.

Scott-Maxwell, A. (1997). Oriental exoticism in 1920s Australian popular music. *Perfect Beat, the Pacific Journal of Research into Contemporary Music and Popular Culture, 3(3)*, 28-57.

Scott-Maxwell, A (2011) Representation and Authenticity Intertwined: Early Australian Constructions of 'China' through Popular Music and the Popular Stage. In J. Cattermole, S. Homan & G. Smith (Eds.). *Instruments of Change: Australia-New Zealand Conference Proceedings 24-26 November 2010*. Melbourne: School of English, Communication and Performance Studies, School of Music-Conservatorium, Monash University, pp.117–123.

Shanghai: A Chinese Romance [sheet music]. (c1925). Ray Morelle (Lyricist) & Horatio Nicholls (Composer). Melbourne: E.W. Cole. London (copyright Lawrence Wright Music Co).

Wang, Zheng-Ting. (1997). *Chinese Music in Australia — Victoria: 1850s to mid 1990s*. Melbourne. VIC: Australia Asia Foundation.

Whiteoak, J. (1999). *Playing ad lib: Improvisatory music in Australia, 1836–1970*. Sydney, NSW: Currency Press.

Williams, M. (1983). *Australia on the popular stage, 1829–1929: An historical entertainment in six acts*. Melbourne: Oxford University Press.

"The Women's Hospital Bazaar." (1886, May 10). *The Argus* [newspaper] (Melbourne, VIC: 1848-1956), p. 7.

CHAPTER

3

By the Bund and beyond: Music-making in the Shanghai and overseas Jewish communities

Kim Cunio

Shanghai in the 1930s was a bustling cosmopolitan city, the fifth largest in the world. A centre for trade and commerce, Western powers like Britain and France controlled lucrative concessions. It was also home to a rich and varied Jewish community, Sephardics who'd arrived from Iraq as traders in the 1800s and Russian Jews who'd escaped the 1917 Revolution. Between them they'd built many grand homes and buildings, at least seven synagogues, Jewish hospitals and schools, clubs, restaurants, coffee shops and bookstores (Edmonson, 2002, para. 22).

In 2001, I wrote and compiled a commissioned music work for the Jewish Museum of Sydney's exhibition *Crossroads — Shanghai and the Jews of China*, an exhibition that illustrated the richness of Jewish life in Shanghai. The commission comprised newly composed works and arrangements of traditional pieces played and sung by the Jewish communities of Shanghai. The exhibition was staged in association with other museums (the Migration Heritage Museum, Australian National Maritime Museum, the Powerhouse Museum) and was linked with the Department of Semitic Studies, University of Sydney and the Department of Sociology, University of Technology, Sydney. The exhibition contained film, numerous photographs, oral and written history as well as music. A principal theme was the diasporic communities of Shanghai, and the story by which they came to Australia after the Second World War. Writing this commission led to a process of reflection on the unique Jewish history of Shanghai and China. The commission also required the sourcing of repertoire for a CD, which would be both a sound installation and a standalone soundtrack to the exhibition. Meetings with the curator established a list of the types of music to be represented, and it was decided that there was room to write new music based on the themes of the exhibition itself. It became apparent when meeting Jews from Shanghai that they remembered specific songs in specific concerts as well as radio broadcasts of popular music forms including jazz. Most of the CD is directly related to the memories of Shanghai Jews and is drawn from Baghdadi, Russian and Central European repertoires. Four new compositions respond to the intercultural themes of the exhibition, such as *Journey from Baghdad*, a solo maqam played on the seven-stringed baglama, *Refuge from Europe*, a duo for clarinet and tabla, and two works for string quartet, *Crossroads* and *French Concession*. There is one setting of a traditional Buddhist text, *Om ah Hung* accompanied by the koto, to represent the Japanese influence that pervaded China from 1937. After sourcing the music for the exhibition a concise picture of Jewish migration into China and later Australia emerged. The liner notes to the CD respond to this intercultural music world:

> Imagine briefly Shanghai's musical life in the 1930s and 1940s. Traditional Chinese music was played by and for the local community, in the distinctive pentatonic modes and scales that so fascinated Western composers such as Puccini and Debussy. A thriving cabaret and opera scene was buoyed by the successive arrival of European refugees. A strong Russian community translated and presented great works in Russian, while folk based music from Russia to Western Europe was played.
>
> Classical music was not ignored either, and the Shanghai Symphony Orchestra was established from European players and teachers, including conductor Maestro Pacci from Italy. New composers such as Vertinsky were writing prolifically, and the Piaf of Shanghai Rao Zemena was thrilling café crowds with Yiddish song, while the Baghdadi Jews were keeping alive their 2000 year old musical tradition. Popular music and jazz took over parts of Shanghai from the 1930's as American Radio gained a strong presence and artists such as Duke Ellington, George Gershwin and Hoagy Carmichael became well known figures" (Cunio, 2001, p. 2).

Mapping the diasporas

All modern Jewish communities are descended from a unified Jewish State that is recorded before the destruction of the first Jewish Temple in 586 BCE. This first great Jewish diaspora was formed during the destruction of the first Temple when Nebuchadnezzar took many of the elite Jews to Babylon, something that is well documented in the Psalm *Al Naharot Bavel* ('By the Rivers of Babylon') (Randhofer, 2004, p. 26). The period before the destruction of the Second Jewish Temple in 70 CE accelerated the process of divergence as large communities followed cultural and trade routes in search of greater prosperity and religious freedom, while the destruction of the Temple caused Jews to be scattered throughout the known world. Oral accounts speculate that Jews first reached China within a generation of the destruction of Second Temple, as they did many other territories — the myth is of a scattering of the peoples, literally ten of the twelve ancient tribes, something that recent research has started to document in India and Ethiopia.

Tiberiu Weisz (2007), a Jewish history and Chinese scholar, speculates that the first Jews entered China after the Babylonian exile of 586 BCE, traveling to China from North West India (Weisz, 2006, pp. xiv, 68–74). A remnant still identify as an ancient Jewish community in China. They testify of a Jewish presence from at least the Northern Song Dynasty (960 CE), and their records describe various fragmented Jewish practices and histories, best known at the steles of Kaifeng. Steles (decorated stone slabs), are not uniquely Jewish, but one erected in 1489 describes the building and commemoration of a Kaifeng synagogue in 1163, as well as listing famous Jews from Abraham to Ezra. Later steles describe Jews as showing boundless loyalty to the country and fighting for their Song masters (ibid). By the nineteenth century, this remnant community was in decline and had little formal identification with Judaism or religious practice.

As British influence in South East Asia became paramount in the eighteenth and nineteenth centuries, Mizrachi Jews from Iraq and India migrated to fill positions of trade and commerce. Many had learnt English in previous colonial administrations, and this class of Jewish educated traders was well received by British companies after the infamous 'Opium Wars' of the mid nineteenth century. Margaret Kartomi and Andrew McCredie (2004) surmise that the Baghdadi diaspora trade route was a parallel of an Old Silk Road Route from the eighteenth century, and that Baghdadi Jewish culture remained largely intact throughout South East Asia (2004, pp. 5, 13). My own oral history supports this; my father's family migrated to Shanghai from Baghdad and Turkey via Hong Kong, between the late nineteenth and early twentieth Centuries. Shanghai's most famous synagogue, the Ohel Rachel (which still stands today), was built to replace the Beth El Synagogue (1887) in the 1920s (Yating, 2004, p. 104). My father's grandfather Hacham Eliyahu Ben Yitzhak was the Rabbi[1] of Ohel Rachel for many years.

Around the turn of the twentieth century a modest Russian Jewish community entered Shanghai from Harbin, which remained stable until the Russian revolution of 1917. Large numbers of Jewish and non-Jewish White Russians migrated and the community grew until the 1940s. The Russian community included a highly educated intelligentsia. In 1928 the first Russian synagogue, (the Ohel Moishe), was opened, and by the mid 1940s the New Synagogue was opened, holding a congregation of 4,000 (Yating, 2004, p. 105). Russian Jews were absorbed into the life of Shanghai with little or no anti-Semitism, and the Ohel Moshe survived and is now administered by the Chinese government.

In 1937, the Japanese invaded China, and the relative equanimity the Japanese showed towards Jewish refugees was one of the unlikely wonders of the Second World War. Despite pressure from the Germans, including the East Asian Gestapo chief Josef Meisinger (popularly known as the Butcher of Warsaw), Jews led a relatively normal life. In a concession to German demands to kill all Jews, the Japanese placed all stateless refugees who arrived from 1937 in a ghetto in Hongkew, but the Japanese Vice Consul of Shanghai, Mitsugi Shibata, allowed Jews to leave the ghetto for work and warned Jewish leaders of German demands to set up death camps in the 1940s (Archer, 2001, p. 1).

The largest wave of migration took place from Central Europe; including Germany and Austria, between the *Kristallnacht* of November 9–10 1938, and the formal German restriction on immigration of August 1941. This wave of migration was significant. In addition to the estimated 25,000 Jews already in Shanghai, at least 18,000 refugees arrived in this period, including 12,089 Jews in 1939 alone (Utz, 2004, p. 123). It is also worth reflecting that many of these Jews were unable to receive passage to any other place, including Australia. Gertie Jellinek (2002) described her experiences vividly on the ABC Compass 2002 documentary *Shanghai Jews*.

> We had a border with us for the last five years that was an Austrian couple who lived with us for five years in an adjoining room and on the day of the 13th March 1938 which was the annexation of Austria he opened the door and we met in the corridor and he was dressed in full Nazi brown shirt uniform. In February 1939 he threw us out of our apartment he gave us one or two weeks notice and we had to leave him everything because we couldn't take it, the furniture most of the crockery and so on (para. 10).

Polish and Lithuanian refugees moved by the Japanese from Japan into China in 1941, comprised the last Jewish diaspora community. This community was welcomed by Baghdadis and Russians, worshipping in the synagogues of both communities (Yating, 2004, p.107).

Marcel Weyland (2002) described the extreme fortune by which Jews escaped Eastern Europe on the same Compass documentary. His family fled from Poland to Lithuania while it was still independent, contacting all the foreign embassies for help, but found that only the Japanese would help. The Japanese Consul Chiune Sugihara issued Japanese transit orders without any orders from Japan.

> We were one of the early bunch who obtained those visas. Soon after we obtained it, he (Sugihara) was told by the Japanese Government to stop issuing, that he has issued too many — I think they allowed him to issue 100, by that time he had already issued over 300, and they told him to stop. And he did not obey that order, and kept on issuing visas, working day and night, really, and even when he was finally recalled and he was sitting in the train, he had the window of the train was open, there was a crowd outside and he was leaning out of the window still stamping those visas, passports with the Japanese transit visa. So really we owe our life to him, and so did many other people. (Weyland, 2002, para. 18).

Suzanne Rutland, who has documented the experiences of Australian Jewish refugees from Shanghai, along with historical Australian attitudes to their arrival, notes that despite the general cosmopolitan nature of Shanghai, most European refugees saw Shanghai as a last resort. Shanghai was the only place Jews could go without a visa, and few outside of the Baghdadi community had any desire to stay (Cunio, 2001, p. 9). Jewish communities left China with remarkable speed after Chiang Kai Shek announced that all stateless people must leave China. Jews moved to Israel, the United States, Canada, and Australia. Andrew Jakubowicz (2002) described what happened when on ABC Compass 2002:

> At the end of the, the Second World War, the Jewish populations of Shanghai had a lot of different reactions to what was going to happen to them. Some of them, like the Sephardic Jews, basically wanted to stay in China and most did often, later moving to Hong Kong. The Russian Jews, some returned to the Soviet Union, in 1947, Stalin sent a couple of boats to Shanghai to pick them up, and they had a fairly drastic experience

after their return. But many stayed in, in Shanghai. For the European Jews, the question was "What next?" (para. 43).

Kirtstie Archer described the end of Jewish life in Shanghai, with a particular relevance to the treatment of refugees in modern Australia. Suzanne Rutland's interview on ABC Compass 2002 makes it clear that Shanghai Jews were demonized in a similar manner to recent boat arrivals in Australia. Only 2000 were allowed into Australia before the passage of refugees was disallowed in 1947. The first boat, the Hwa Lien, left Shanghai in 1946 leading to hysteria within sections of Australian society. She describes a report form the Australian Consul General in Shanghai who described Shanghai Jews as undesirable people who have "lived by their wits by selling their services to the highest bidder" (Rutland, 2002, para. 47).

> The Jewish community's fortunes changed when Japan lost the war. Chiang Kai Shek announced that stateless refugees would be expelled. For most people repatriation was not an option and the future was uncertain. It is disturbing to remember that after World War II, Jewish refugees were unwelcome nearly everywhere. The first major exodus to Australia took place in 1946, but officials halted the flow in mid-1947 when a report from the Australian Consul-General in Shanghai, quoted in the exhibition, described the city's Jews as people with "pasts unknown and unspeakable, their intentions obscure." Nonetheless, those Jews carrying British passports had no trouble traveling to Australia (Archer, 2002, p. 1).

On ABC Compass, and in her published work, Rutland (2002) also notes political parallels between the Jewish refugees of Shanghai and the Middle Eastern refugees contained in recent boats arrivals, such as the Tampa in Australia.

> There were only 330 refugees — the Tampa only had 400 refugees, the parallels are astounding. The hysteria across Australia for Calwell allowing a boat load of Jewish refugees, which was on this steamer that was totally unsuited for sailing, it was in a terrible condition. But there were alarmist newspaper articles — Jews were bringing in counterbound jewellery on that boat, they were smuggling all sorts of things, they should not be allowed in ...(para. 51)

> So from the RSL point of view and from a general Australian perception, most Jews were Communists and as such security risks, and if they were not Communists, they were terrorists, or they were wealthy or they were generally undesirable. So all of these things were used against Jews, and these were typical, anti-Semitic stereotypes. In Europe the Jews were the Communists, they were also the capitalists — the Nazis developed all of those images, and ironically it was those same types of images which were highlighted in the anti-Jewish hysteria in the Australian press (Rutland, 2002, para. 45).

Shanghai Jews have played a prominent role in business, the arts, and the growth of Australian multicultural culture. Notable examples include the composer Larry Sitsky, and the businessmen Harry Triguboff (Meriton Apartments), Henry Roth (developer), and Hans Mueller (Lowes Menswear), and Sam Moshinsky (international accountancy). Thinkers include Harbin born journalist Mara Moustafine, and Professor Andrew Jakubowicz — a child of Shanghai refugees who has been an active scholar in the study of Australian Chinese connections (Encel & Rutland, 2008, p. 148). Jewish Australians from Shanghai now appear to look back on that time with greater fondness, documented by ABC Compass in 2002, which drew parallels between Australia and Shanghai for openness tolerance, and vibrant real world multiculturalism, told through the memories of three Shanghai Jews.

Music-making

Between 1937 and 1947, most of the major music traditions of Judaism flourished in Shanghai. The religious community contained religious and reform Jews who were following the latest trends in Jewish sacred music, such as the incorporation of a harmonium into services at the Eastern and Broadway theatres in Shanghai, the innovation of women's ensembles, and liturgical musical events within the Synagogue. Secular musicians were an important part of the internationalisation of Shanghai performing, teaching and promoting folk and art music concerts and events.

Until the Second World War, great Western artists visited Shanghai as part of a great Eastern tour incorporating British colonies such as India, Burma, and the International Concessions of Shanghai. British and foreign schools had active Western music programs, which many Jews attended, and most Jews had an awareness of Western art music in addition to a knowledge of their own sacred and secular repertoire. The waves of migration into Shanghai had obvious musical consequences, and Europeans particularly sought to continue the support of live music performances.

The fact that the music of these communities sustained and flourished in the face of catastrophic change is a testimony to the artistic disposition of many of the immigrants and refugees. While many musicians were not originally professional, some turned to music due to a limitation on the jobs many European Jews were able to take in the years leading up to the Second World War. Ashkenazi Jews explored music in Shanghai in order to preserve their own culture, as well as for entertainment and fund raising (Cunio, 2001, p. 3). Wolfgang Fraenkel, a Jewish string player, composer and conductor taught composition at the national Vocational Music School (now the Shanghai Conservatory), as well as conducting Chinese musicians and reflecting on the future of Chinese music (Utz, 2004, p. 120). A number of Australian Jewish Chinese immigrants were exposed to Western art music training from Frenkel and other teachers, and they continued to replicate concert programs originally presented in Shanghai after migration to Australia (Cunio, 2001, p. 6). A thriving concert scene combined with a burgeoning radio presence saw Jews name Shanghai the 'Paris of the East', as it was possible to hear new Western modernist music alongside opera, chamber music, jazz, cabaret, Middle Eastern maqam, Chinese opera and traditional music.

Both Russian and Central European communities provided music for their own events. Musicians included instrumentalists, conductors, singers and composers. Choirs were formed in all the Ashkenazi synagogues; most were all male, as is the case in Orthodox Judaism, but offshoot women's choirs were seen from the 1940s. Yating writes that in Rosh Hashanah 1940, the first solo woman's voice was heard in the Eastern Theatre, accompanied by a women's vocal ensemble (Yating, 2004, pp. 106–107), something which announced the mainstream arrival of Liberal Judaism.[2]

Most surprising is the relative isolation of each community, which had little cultural similarity to sister congregations. This was due to the fragmented nature of their respective migration histories, which did not encourage Jews to mix culturally and musically to the degree that they do in modern Western democracies. Each community sought to live and make music at concerts, recitals, cafes, worship services, community festivals and cultural events. In order to understand this, it is necessary to reflect that the stereotypes of the European world were largely replicated in Jewish communities. Russian and other central European Jews had little knowledge of the music of the Baghdadi community and Germanic Jews arrived with a self contained musical culture (Jacobs, 2001. p. 3),

Language was a significant player in the relative autonomy of these communities. Many Central Europeans spoke German, Polish and Yiddish (although some did also speak English and French). Russians spoke Russian and sometimes other European languages, while the Baghdadis spoke Arabic, Ladino (Judeo Espagnole), and often English (Cunio, 2001, p. 7). As time went on, the languages of English and French became important. Ellis Jacobs recalls that English was heard by many and spoken extensively in the Baghdadi community (2001, p. 5), and musical influences such as American Radio (including Radio GI) became paramount to younger refugees and locally born Shanghai Jews. Jazz itself was regularly seen on the streets of Shanghai, alongside cabaret, Yiddish folk song, and Western art music.

Australian musicologist Fiona Berry has catalogued the details of numerous instrumental and Para liturgical performances which shows that all Shanghai Jewish communities saw music as a functional part of life, as well as a vital part of resettlement and other activities. Concerts from 1939 include fundraisers for organisations such as the American Joint fund (January 25, 1942), poor Jewish children (February 7, no year), or general charity concert (Berry, 2009, pp. 1–5). Many concerts featured specific music types such as Yiddish Folk Song, chamber music, comedy and variety, new compositions based on the work of local poets, traditional Chassidic Songs, concerts of mixed cantors, and recitals of arias and German lieder (Berry, 2009, pp. 1–5; Yating, 2004, pp. 110–116).

From the history surveyed in this paper, it is quite evident that much cultural activity has accompanied the Jewish people wherever they have travelled. Of the many bridges linking Australia with China, the Jewish connection is certainly one worth investigating in the years to come. Certainly, much cultural expression by these émigrés has been through the medium of western music, but it is the eclectic bricolage of sounds filling the minds of composers such as Larry Sitsky that continues to inspire me in my own negotiation of cultural identity.

Notes

1. Referred as hacham by Baghdadi Jews and taken to mean rabbi (minister), chazzan (service leader) and mohel (circumciser).
2. This gave women a greater role in services, including singing sacred texts, leading prayers, and in recent decades the right to be Rabbis.

References

Archer, K. (2002). *Dissecting room: A celebration of Chinese and Jewish history.* The Lancet 359 (9307), 715–716.

Berry, F. (2009?). Cultural counterpoint: The musical activities of Central and Eastern European Jewish refugees in Shanghai, 1939–1947 (Honours Thesis, Sydney Conservatorium of Music).

Berry, F. "Cultural Counterpoint: The Musical Activities of Central and Eastern European Jewish Refugees in Shanghai, 1939–1947." Conference presentation at the Musicological Society of Australia 2009.

Cunio, K. (2001). Crossroads: Shanghai and the Jews of China. *Sydney Jewish Museum*, 1–8.

Cunio, Nissim. (2001). Interview with author on 8 May 2001 (for the Crossroads Exhibition at the Sydney Jewish Museum). Sydney [Cassette in possession of author].

Edmonson, M. (Producer). (2002). *Shanghai Jews.* [Videotape]. Australian Broadcasting Corporation. Retrieved from http://www.abc.net.au/compass/s712283.htm.

Ehrlich, A. (Ed.) (2008). *The Jewish-Chinese Nexus:* A meeting of civilizations. Routledge.

Encel, S., & Rutland, S. D. (2008). Australian Jewry, its Relations with China and the First Steps in Jewish Studies. In A. Ehrlich (Ed.), The Jewish-Chinese Nexus: A Meeting of Civilizations (pp.135–151). London: Routledge.

Jacobs, Ellis. (2001). Interview with author on 8 May 2001 (for the Crossroads Exhibition at the Sydney Jewish Museum). Sydney [Cassette in possession of author].

Jakubowicz, A. (2002). Interview. In Edmonson, M. (Producer). *Shanghai Jews.* [Videotape]. Australian Broadcasting Corporation. Retrieved from http://www.abc.net.au/compass/s712283.htm.

Jellinek, G. (2002). Interview. In Edmonson, M. (Producer). *Shanghai Jews.* [Videotape transcript]. Australian Broadcasting Corporation. Retrieved from http://www.abc.net.au/compass/s712283.htm.

Kartomi, M., & McCredie, A. (2004). Introduction: Musical outcomes of Jewish migration into Asia via the northern and southern routes c. 1780–c. 1950. *Ethnomusicology Forum*, 13(1), 3–20.

Weyland, M. (2002). Interview. In Edmonson, M. (Producer). *Shanghai Jews.* [Videotape transcript]. Australian Broadcasting Corporation. Retrieved from http://www.abc.net.au/compass/s712283.htm.

Randhofer, R. (2004). By the Rivers of Babylon: Echoes of the Babylonian Past in the Musical heritage of the Iraqi Jewish Diaspora. *Ethnomusicology Forum*, 13(1), 21–45.

Rutland, S. (2002). (2002). Interview. In Edmonson, M. (Producer). *Shanghai Jews.* [Videotape transcript]. Australian Broadcasting Corporation. Retrieved from http://www.abc.net.au/compass/s712283.htm.

Weisz, T. (2007). The Kaifeng stone inscriptions revisited. *Covenant — Global Jewish Magazine* 1(3 October). Retrieved from http://www.covenant.idc.ac.il/en/vol1/issue3/kaifeng-stone-inscriptions-revisited.html.

Yating, T. (in association with Dreyfus, K.) (2004). Reconstructing the vanished musical life of the Shanghai Jewish diaspora: A report. *Ethnomusicology Forum*, 13(1), 110–118.

CHAPTER

4

Thirty years of Australia-China Encounters in Ethnomusicology — A Personal Memoir

Yang Mu

In October 1978, two years after the end of the notorious "Cultural Revolution" following the death of Mao Zedong,[1] I arrived in Beijing from my home town in southeast China, to begin my studies at the Central Conservatory of Music (CCM) (Figure 1). I did not realise then that I was embarking on a journey in the course of which I would witness, and play an active role in, the introduction and development of contemporary ethnomusicology in the People's Republic of China (PRC) — and subsequently in Australia-China encounters in ethnomusicology. Being a personal memoir, this narrative is based on my own experience, so is naturally not comprehensive; it does not record all such encounters. Still, because I am the only ethnomusicologist to have participated in these encounters throughout the entire period of thirty-odd years, my account may provide an insightful and reasonably adequate picture for readers, especially since there is no other report of this kind available.

In 1978, for the first time since 1966, when the Cultural Revolution overturned the educational system throughout the PRC, the CCM resumed its conventional schooling. It admitted students nationwide through conventional examinations, conducted in late 1977 and early 1978. After three consecutive examinations in the form of a knock-out competition, I won a position as one of the twenty-one applicants finally admitted to the Department of Musicology. According to official statistics (ZYXYB 1990: 124), the CCM admitted a total of 213 students in this way. As the top conservatorium in the PRC at that time, the CCM had a staff of almost triple this number to cater for these students (see List of the 1978 CCM Staff in Chen and Liu 1990: 158-205; also see Yang 1988a). Selected competitively from 17,000 applicants

FIGURE 1 — Myself at the front gate of the CCM, Beijing, October 1978.

(ZYXYB 1990: 124), a pool of candidates that had accumulated nationwide during the period of twelve years since 1966, the students finally admitted were generally of much better academic quality than those normally selected from high school graduates in any single year. They were older than usual for first-year undergraduates, many having been in the work-force for some years before their admission. They were therefore more knowledgeable and mature academically, musically, and in social experience. This explains a later phenomenon: in contrast to any other single year since their graduation, most of this cohort have become China's leading figures in the fields of composition, (ethno)musicology, and music performance. Some of them have also become well-known internationally (Figure 2).

To this day, PRC scholars have not reached unanimity on the question when and by whom the contemporary Western term and concept of "ethnomusicology" was first introduced to mainland China. Since the mid-1980s, when "ethnomusicology" began to become a fashionable catchword among music researchers in the PRC, an academic symposium held in Nanjing in June 1980 has generally been identified as the first ethnomusicology conference in that country and as a milestone marking the formal establishment of contemporary ethnomusicology there. However, the reality is rather different. The name of the Nanjing symposium was *Minzu Yinyuexue Xueshu Taolunhui*, which translates as "Symposium on the Study of Music of Chinese

FIGURE 2 — The twenty-one students of the Department of Musicology at the CCM, spring, 1979. I am second from the left in the back row. More than half of them are now leading figures in (ethno)musicology in the PRC.

Peoples." Furthermore, all of the sixty-nine papers presented at the symposium (see Yuan Jingfang 1980 and NYXX 1980) followed conventional Chinese approaches in music study, which are very different from those of Western ethnomusicology for dealing with traditional Chinese music. Indeed, all but one of the papers indicate a complete lack of awareness of the Western term, concept, and approaches of ethnomusicology. The one exception is Gao Houyong's paper reviewing the study of Chinese traditional music during the period from 1925 to 1979 (Gao 1980). In it he mentions the English term "ethnomusicology" and briefly refers to this Western discipline. To judge from his paper, Gao's understanding of Western ethnomusicology was far from adequate; he simply equated ethnomusicology with the PRC's then existing study of Chinese music. Nevertheless, this was the first time that the English term "ethnomusicology" had ever appeared in a PRC publication. On this basis a couple of Gao's students have declared publicly that it was Gao and they themselves who first introduced this discipline into the PRC.[2]

I will not enter into the discussion about who actually was the first person to introduce ethnomusicology to the PRC. In this paper I am instead telling a story never told before, of how an Australian student introduced the term and concept of ethnomusicology to students and scholars at the CCM in 1979, the year before the above-mentioned Nanjing symposium and paper.

At that time the CCM was the top institute for music teaching and research in the PRC, and the only one in Beijing. It was also the institute that had gathered the largest number of scholars in music research in that country. According to my investigations, at that time no one at the CCM had ever heard the term "ethnomusicology." In the Department of Musicology at the CCM, the duration of undergraduate study was unusually long: five years. The curriculum included standard courses on Chinese traditional music, Western (including Russian) classical theory of composition technique, music analysis, and Western historical musicology. Except for these, nothing about non-Chinese music was taught. In addition, what we were taught about Western theory and the Western academic situation was limited to knowledge and information that had been preserved from the time before the establishment of the PRC in 1949. Since then the country had been self-isolated from the outside world for about thirty years under the extremist Maoist "closed-door" policy, blocking information from the outside. We had never heard of Jaap Kunst, Alan Merriam, or Mantle Hood, names known to every student of ethnomusicology in the West during the late 1970s.

In the CCM this situation continued until late 1979, when an Australian student, Marion H. Gray from Adelaide, began postgraduate study in the Department of Musicology at the Conservatory.

From its establishment in 1950 to the beginning of the chaotic Cultural Revolution in 1966, the Department of Musicology at the CCM had admitted only three foreign students (Chen and Liu 1990: 48, 64). Marion was one of the first two foreign students admitted to the CCM after the Cultural Revolution. In China she was known by her Chinese name Ge Zhenshu 葛榛树. The other student, a young woman from Japan, was known in Chinese as Ou Huihong 欧惠红. According to my investigations, they were also the first two foreign students to attend any music institute in the PRC after the Cultural Revolution. Marion had first visited China in December 1976, a couple of months after the end of the Cultural Revolution, in a study tour organised by the Adelaide Branch of the Australia-China Society (an Australian non-government organisation later renamed Australia-China Friendship Society 澳中友好协会). She already had a BA degree in Chinese from the University of Adelaide. In September 1977, on a two-year scholarship provided by the Australian Myer Foundation, she went to China again, this time studying advanced Chinese successively at the Beijing Languages Institute (now the Beijing Language and Culture University) and Liaoning University (in Shenyang) for one year and Chinese philosophy at Beijing University for another year. Her subsequent study at the CCM was as an exchange student funded by the New Zealand government, as she was born in New Zealand so had dual citizenship.[3] Marion began her study in the Department of Musicology at the CCM in September 1979 as a postgraduate student in traditional Chinese music. At that time the CCM had only undergraduate courses, so special arrangements were made for her. She was assigned two supervisors who taught her individually, and for one course she joined an existing undergraduate class in traditional Chinese music, in which I was majoring, so we became classmates.

As in all tertiary institutes in the PRC, at that time all students and almost all staff members of the CCM boarded on campus, in very basic dormitory style accommodation. Together with the music high school attached to the Conservatory, we were all jammed into just five very old, two- and three-story buildings and a few bungalows in a small campus. All the teaching-learning and living facilities were there. Six students shared each dormitory room of about eighteen square metres with double-decker bunks, and each staff member and family was assigned to just one or two rooms. We all had to share public toilets in the buildings, eat in the only two communal canteens, and use just one small shower hall. In using the showers, we had to follow a roster, with each person allowed only one shower per week, even during the hot sweaty summer. These were our living conditions throughout the five years of my study at the CCM. I vividly remember how, in 1980, a group of American professors visiting the CCM were so appalled at our crowded and poor living conditions that some of them actually cried in front of us.

Although few in number, the students were from all over China. Like myself, most knew no-one in Beijing when they moved into the CCM. In effect, the campus was our home during the years of our study, and the teachers and fellow students were our family. The bright side of this situation was that teaching, learning, and exchange of information and ideas between us were not confined within the classrooms and within teaching hours but extended to all times and occasions. After classes the students and teachers spent time with one another like family members at home or next-door neighbours. Nobody had a telephone, and there was no need to make appointments before visiting. You just came along and knocked on the door of anyone's room whenever you felt like it. In such a small, close-knit community any piece of news or information that anyone obtained would immediately spread across the entire campus. This was the community that Marion joined. Like the other students, she also lived on campus. However, she and Ou Huihong, as the only foreign students, received special treatment. The two of them were given one room, very small but large enough to accommodate

FIGURE 3 — Students and a few teachers of the Department of Musicology at the CCM, October 1980. Marion is at the left end of the front row.

two single beds, a luxury envied by us Chinese students (Figure 3).

In 1979, ordinary Chinese, suffering deeply in the aftermath of the Cultural Revolution, were still blocked from any foreign contact and information. Eager to learn about the outside world, I immediately became good friends with Marion. On learning that I was majoring in musicological study of traditional Chinese music, she immediately introduced me to ethnomusicology. Before long my classmates and professors in the Department of Musicology heard about this, and the information provided by Marion set off a wave of excitement among interested teachers and students there.

I had learnt English at high school. During the Cultural Revolution I continued improving my English by self-learning, though very slowly under the unfavorable and harsh social environment of that time. Consequently, my English reading ability was fairy good, and Marion happily shared with me all the English reading materials she had brought with her, generously lending me her copies to read. In addition to articles on ethnomusicology, they included Mantle Hood's book *The Ethnomusicologist* (1971). I read them all. The concept and methodology of this discipline, which I had never heard of previously, greatly appealed to me. Impressed, I began enthusiastically introducing them to my classmates and teachers. Some professors in my Department, such as Jiang Jing (now retired and living in Denver, USA), also became very interested, pursuing the subject further and discussing it with their students and colleagues.

I was wishing that more people in the PRC knew about the concept and methods of ethnomusicology, and believed I could do something to bring that about. Marion's collection included articles discussing Alan Merriam's approach. Personally I prefer Merriam to Hood, but unfortunately Marion did not have Merriam's *The Anthropology of Music* (1964) apart from photocopies of parts of the book. So I came up with the idea of translating Hood's book into Chinese and getting it published in China. At that time we were not allowed to contact foreigners privately. So I contacted *Renmin Yinyue Chubanshe* (The People's Music Publishing House) in Beijing, the top government-run publisher of music books in the PRC, for assistance. I was hoping they would be interested in my proposal and would contact Hood for copyright clearance. I was also hoping they could even get a copy of Merriam's book through official channels. However, they replied saying they had no idea what ethnomusicology was or who Hood and Merriam were, and that they saw no benefit in, and therefore no justification for, translating and publishing such books. Dismayed, I gave up my translation idea. (*The Ethnomusicologist* has still not been translated into Chinese; *The Anthropology of Music* was translated only recently, being published in April 2010.) Instead, I did my best to spread the news by word of mouth among relevant scholars in the CCM and elsewhere in Beijing. I frequently discussed the concept and methodology of ethnomusicology with my fellow students and professors, recommending that they read copies of the publications that Marion had provided me with. Her collection was regrettably small, but did give us something to go on. Marion's information, her introduction, and my efforts soon had some effect. At least half a year earlier than the above-mentioned Nanjing symposium, my classmates and relevant scholars at the CCM had already been introduced to the discipline of ethnomusicology, and had gained a reasonable idea of what this discipline was. Later a lecturer in my Department at the CCM, who had been interested in our discussion of ethnomusicology and subsequently found more information through other means, wrote and published an article introducing the Western discipline of ethnomusicology. This brief article was the first published in the PRC that focused entirely on introducing this discipline (Yu Renhao 1981).

Marion left China in July 1981, before ethnomusicology had become fashionable nationwide among the music research communities there. She left me all her English materials on ethnomusicology, including her copy of *The Ethnomusicologist* — unaware of her contribution to introducing this discipline to the PRC.

In following years, more articles dealing with this discipline were published in China. A heated debate took place on several issues: an appropriate Chinese translation for the English term "ethnomusicology"; the definition and scope of this discipline; and whether the existing study of Chinese music in China was equivalent to and should be labeled "ethnomusicology." This debate kept the PRC community of relevant scholars busy for at least a decade (for details see Yang 2003a).

In September 1983 Mantle Hood visited the CCM and gave a seminar there, introducing the Western discipline of ethnomusicology. In question time I asked him a few questions about his book. He appeared surprised that a student in mainland China possessed a copy of his book and was familiar with it. After our discussion he kindly signed my copy: "For Yang Mu, with my personal wish for his success in researching the rich heritage of China and the world" (Figure 4). I am happy that Marion's gift to

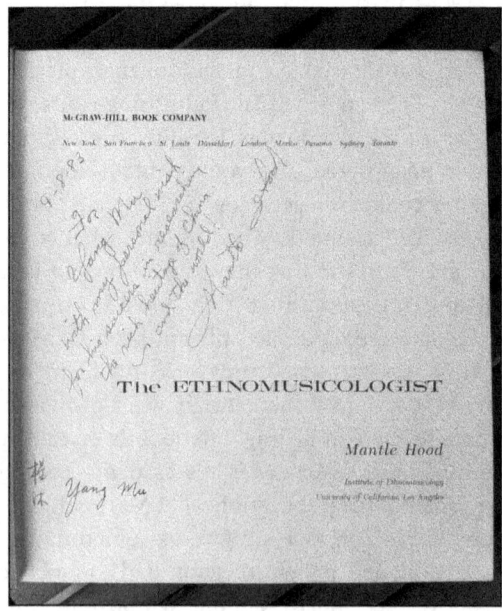

FIGURE 4 — Hood's inscription in my copy of his book.

FIGURE 5 — Friends at Marion and Julian's wedding, most of them CCM graduates, and two professors. Beijing, 1984. Marion and Julian are seated in the middle of the second row; I am at the left end of the back row.

me has become a memento of early exchanges between China and the outside world in the field of contemporary ethnomusicology. It is a reminder to me of her contribution to Australia-China encounters in this discipline.

After my graduation from the CCM in 1983, I investigated how I could go overseas for PhD study in ethnomusicology, partly because no institute in the PRC offered postgraduate study in this discipline, so I could not learn much about it there. Financially, the only way I could study abroad was to gain a scholarship from overseas; but at that time the PRC authorities still forbade private contact with foreign organisations, including universities. Information about studying ethnomusicology in Western universities was scarce and difficult to find. In 1984 Marion came to Beijing again to work with the New World Press, translating into English a comprehensive dictionary of Chinese musical instruments (Yuan Bingchang 1986), and in the same year she married Julian Yu, then a young lecturer at the CCM and now an internationally acclaimed Australian composer (Figure 5)[4]. While I secretly contacted some universities in the USA, she contacted a few Australian universities on my behalf. I eventually gained admission to several universities in both countries. Among them were an assistantship at Florida State University in the USA and a full scholarship, the Ernest Singer Scholarship for postgraduate research, at the University of Queensland, Australia. I decided to go to Australia.

I arrived in Brisbane on 4 June 1985, and began my postgraduate research for the MA degree in ethnomusicology under the supervision of Dr. Gordon Spearritt, then Reader and head of the Department of Music at UQ. With an Australian scholarship and under the supervision of an Australian scholar, I thereby became the first PRC student, whether within China or outside it, to pursue postgraduate study in ethnomusicology. For my research and thesis writing, the UQ library generously offered me excellent assistance in doing library searches and obtaining interlibrary loans worldwide. A large part of the references I needed could be obtained only from the PRC, so the UQ library approached the PRC national library for interlibrary loans. This was the first contact between these two libraries; and for the PRC national library it was the first international interlibrary loan they had ever done. My requests for interlibrary loans were frequent, and consequently so too were the contacts between these two libraries. A few years later, the librarian in charge of interlibrary loans at UQ told me: "It was because of your interlibrary loan requests that we initiated, and have now firmly established, contact with the PRC national library. In Australia we are now in the lead in exchanges with the PRC, and we really appreciate this." Apparently, both Australian and PRC libraries have benefited from those encounters.

In mid-1987 the UQ postgraduate committee approved the upgrading of my MA research to PhD research. For that reason I declined scholarship offers from overseas, including admission and a scholarship for PhD research at the University of Cambridge, and admission and a scholarship from New York University for PhD study there. By then Gordon Spearritt had retired, but I received further supervision and/or consultation from a group of musicologists, ethnomusicologists, and China studies experts within and outside UQ, including Dr. Rod Bucknell, Dr. Stephen Wild, Professor Noël Nickson, and Professor Philip Bracanin. I completed my PhD thesis at the end of 1989 and was awarded the degree the following year. I thus became the first person from the PRC to obtain a PhD in ethnomusicology, whether within China or outside it. This was itself an outcome of Australia-China encounters. Since then I have pursued an academic career in Australia, and this career has continued to interweave with Australia-China encounters in ethnomusicology.

During the period of my PhD research at UQ, Stephen Wild, a leading ethnomusicologist in Australia, introduced me to the wider community of ethnomusicologists in this country. From 1987 I began participating actively in activities of this community, thus further contributing to Australia-China encounters in this field. In 1987 I went to Canberra to participate in hosting the visit of Chen Yingshi, a professor from the Shanghai Conservatory of Music and a leading researcher in the study of Chinese classical temperamentology and ancient music transcriptions. The visit was initiated by Coralie Rockwell, an established Australian ethnomusicologist who had studied for a period at the Shanghai Conservatory of Music in the mid-1980s and carried out research into ancient Chinese music manuscripts; and the visit was sponsored by the Canberra Branch of the Musicological Society of Australia. This was the first time a PRC scholar specialising in Chinese music research had ever visited Australia. During Chen's visit I had intensive discussions with him on the difficult Chinese-English translation of ancient Chinese terminology for his paper on temperamentology. We achieved some helpful results, which were later applied in his English-language article published in *Musicology Australia* (Chen 1988-89).

In 1988 the MSA hosted the Symposium of the International Musicological Society in Melbourne from 28 August to 2 September. The MSA intended to sponsor a leading scholar from the PRC to present at the Symposium. I was consulted on this matter since outside of mainland China I was the person most familiar with the relevant scholarly community there. On my recommendation, the MSA invited Jiang Jing, a professor at the CCM and a leading researcher in traditional Chinese music in the PRC. She accepted the invitation and presented a paper at the Symposium. After the Symposium she accepted further invitations from the Canberra School of Music and the Department of Music Education at the University of New South Wales. Accompanied by myself she visited both institutes and gave seminars there.

During the 1980s the music research community in the PRC was eager to develop the newly introduced Western discipline of ethnomusicology, but there was a serious lack of relevant information and knowledge. They had extremely limited access to foreign publications and few opportunities for scholarly exchange with overseas scholarly communities. Consequently, any information provided by the few colleagues returning from overseas visits was highly appreciated. On their return to China, both Chen Yingshi and Jiang Jing shared their overseas experience with the PRC community, through their seminars, lectures and publications there.

Aware of the needs of the PRC community and of the lack of mutual exchange and understanding between the PRC and Western academic communities, I began to contribute actively to bridging this gap between the PRC and the outside world. The major part of this effort consisted in academic publication. In the late 1980s my Chinese articles focused mainly on sharing my Australian experience with the PRC community (e.g. 1986, 1987, 1989); but since 1990 I have switched to introducing Western theories of contemporary anthropology, ethnomusicology and cultural studies and their application in Chinese music research (e.g. 1993a, 1998a, 2001a, 2001b, 2006a, 2006b, 2009). I also raised and discussed issues concerning academic studies in general in the PRC, and the influence of my publications there has therefore extended to scholarly communities nationwide. For example, I was the first scholar to publicly and explicitly discuss in the PRC the shortcomings of classical Marxist methodology and its domination of academic studies there (e.g. 1997a), and to openly criticise the Han-ethnocentric practice in academic studies there (e.g. 1997b, 2000a). (The Han ethnic group comprises the overwhelming majority of the Chinese population.) At the same time I have, during my frequent field trips to China, been active in giving related seminars in many music institutes there.

Furthermore, because of an early article of mine (1988b) and my follow-up articles (e.g. 2000b, 2007) raising issues and discussing the situation regarding academic norms for scholarly study and writing in the PRC, I have been generally acknowledged there as having initiated the nationwide campaign combating academic corruption and promoting academic norms in that country. This campaign aroused heated discussion nationwide which continued throughout the 1990s and the following decade. It resulted in the construction and implementation of PRC government stipulations in this area (see reports, e.g. Zhou 2003, Wang 2009).

By the early 1990s I had obtained Australian citizenship, so my above-mentioned activities represent another aspect of Australia-China encounters. Among Western ethnomusicologists, I have become the one who has given the most seminars and produced the most publications in the PRC to promote ethnomusicological study and research in that country. At the same time, a number of my publications in English are also dedicated to examining and discussing the PRC situation and issues not previously examined in the West (e.g. 1988a, 1994, 1996, 1998b, 2003a, 2003b), thus helping to fill the above-mentioned gap in mutual understanding between scholars in the PRC and the West.

Australia-China encounters in ethnomusicology have not been confined to scholarly research and exchange. They have also happened in the area of traditional Chinese music performance. For example, the Queensland Conservatorium Chinese Orchestra was established as early as 1980. It was initially organised and directed by

FIGURE 6 — Program of the PEGS Chinese Orchestra 1997 performing tour of China, hosted by the Chinese Musicians' Association of the PRC and the Shanghai government.

Dr. Dale Craig, then a lecturer at the Conservatorium, and in the mid-1980s it was directed by Deng Wei, a musician from China. The directorship was taken over by Julian Yu in 1987 while he and Marion were pursuing further study in Brisbane, and I myself assisted in the orchestra's practice and rehearsals while I was in Brisbane in the late 1980s.

After leaving Brisbane early in 1990 to teach a semester of ethnomusicology at Monash University in Melbourne, I successively carried out two projects in 1990 and 1991. These were projects for applying ethnomusicological approaches in music education in Australian schools, and developing Chinese music learning in school curricula. To assist in carrying them out I was awarded two grants from the Australia-China Council, an Australian government council within the Department of Foreign Affairs and Trade. Direct outcomes of these projects included the publication of two audio cassettes, a two-hour video film, and a text-book introducing Chinese musical instruments (Yang 1992, 1993b, 1993c), and the establishment of Chinese music ensembles at two schools in Melbourne: Collingwood College and Penleigh and Essendon Grammar School. The latter, now the PEGS Chinese Orchestra sponsored by the school, has since remained active under the management of James Wu, the head of languages at the school, and with Sheng Pangeng as the conductor and artistic director. It has not only given concerts in Melbourne and Sydney but also accepted invitations to perform in Beijing, Shanghai, Nanjing, Taiwan, and Singapore, and it has appeared on television there (Figure 6).

Since the 1990s Australia-China encounters in ethnomusicology have reached a new level. Several academic projects deserve mention. In 1990, Noël Nickson, emeritus professor at UQ, accepted an invitation to Shanghai initiated by the above-mentioned Professor Chen Yingshi. There Nickson conducted the performance of the suite *The Emperor Destroys the Formations* 秦王破阵乐, for which he had prepared a first, justified score from unedited transcriptions of ancient manuscripts preserved in Japan. This was a significant outcome of the project *Music from the Tang Court*. Initiated in 1981 and led by Dr. Laurence Picken at Cambridge University until his death in 2007, this project aimed at reconstructing and transcribing the corpus of Chinese Tang dynasty entertainment music of the 7th to 9th centuries preserved in the Japanese *Tōgaku* (Tang dynasty music) tradition. Picken himself was also invited and presented the event in Shanghai. The suite was performed by an ensemble consisting of professors and students from the Conservatory, on Chinese musical instruments including exquisite replicas of Tang instruments made by the Suzhou Manufactory of Chinese Musical Instruments. Nickson is also the co-editor of Picken's seventh volume of Music from the Tang Court (Picken and Nickson 2000). Two other Australian ethnomusicologists have also participated in research into the ancient notation and transcription of the music from the Tang court: Professor Allan Marett at the University of Sydney, who is also a member of the Cambridge team for this project, and Dr. Steven Nelson, then a professor at Hōsei University in Tokyo. In 2005, both of them presented research papers at the International Symposium on Ancient Transcriptions from East Asia hosted by the Shanghai Conservatory of

FIGURE 7 — Li Minxiong (centre of front row), Yu Hui (right end of middle row), and myself (second from right in front row), with Australian Chinese musicians and four members of the Canberra Chapter of MSA.

Music. At the same symposium, Wu Guowei, a Chinese from Hong Kong doing his PhD under Marett's supervision, also presented a paper.

In 1993 the Coralie Rockwell Foundation was established in Canberra, in memory of Coralie Rockwell, who died in 1992. The main aim of the Foundation is to promote Chinese music teaching and research in Australia. In the year of its establishment the Foundation published the above-mentioned textbook of mine on Chinese musical instruments. Jointly with the Australia-China Council, the Foundation invited and sponsored a visit by the renowned Chinese percussionist Li Minxiong, a professor at the Shanghai Conservatory of Music, and Yu Hui, who was then a young lecturer at the Conservatory. (Yu Hui later obtained his PhD in ethnomusicology from Wesleyan University in the USA, and is now a professor and the director of the Institute of the Arts at Ningbo University in China.) For eight weeks they visited the Canberra School of Music at the Australian National University, the Queensland Conservatorium at Griffith University, and the Music Department of the University of New England. They gave seminars and observed and compared notes with Australian counterparts. Both sides benefited greatly from this exchange. During their visit to the Canberra School of Music, the School organised a special concert of Chinese music. I convened a group of top Chinese musicians residing in Sydney and Melbourne to form a Chinese ensemble; with Li Minxiong as the leading performer, they gave the concert (Figure 7). After his return to China, Yu Hui published an article there in Renmin Yinyue (The People's Music), the music journal that had the largest readership in China at that time, reporting their experience in Australia and their afterthoughts (Yu Hui 1994).

FIGURE 8 — Four of the students from the 2000 study group on the CCM campus, with Liu Hongzhu, head of the CCM office for foreign exchanges, at far right, and Philippa, second from the right.

From 1999 to 2001 Philippa Roylance, then senior lecturer at the Central Queensland University, carried out her project Asianising the Curriculum, a teaching-research project testing cross-cultural approaches to music education with three collaborating institutes in China: the Department of Music at Shandong Normal University in Jinan, the Central Conservatory of Music in Beijing, and the Department of Music at the Capital Normal University in Beijing. The project received a large grant of AUD$150,000 from the Australian government's Department of Education, Training and Youth Affairs. I accepted Philippa's invitation to serve as consultant for the project. Over the three years, the project sent three groups of Australian students respectively to these three institutes for a period of study (Figure 8). During their stay, these students mingled with Chinese students every day: staying in the same dormitories; eating in the same school canteens; attending the same seminars, concerts and discussions; exchanging ideas; and learning from one another as well as experiencing an active social life in China. Both Australian and Chinese students and teachers benefited greatly. For all the Australian students these study trips were their first China experience and have had a great effect in their lives. Many have since visited China again, some more than once; some later worked there for up to two years; one has returned there and has been working there for an Australia-China school education exchange program on a permanent basis; one has married a young Chinese ethnomusicologist whom she met on our group's first study trip to Beijing. Philippa herself has visited China many times. Subsequent to the project, in the second half of 2005 she was invited by the CCM as a visiting professor and taught for a full semester there in the Department of Musicology. Not only students but also some professors in the Conservatory attended her lectures during that semester.

Most recently, in 2009, the Australian government awarded Tsanhuang Tsai, assistant professor from the Department of Music at the Chinese University of Hong Kong, an Endeavour Research Fellowship to carry out his project *Chinese Musical Instruments in Australia*. For that project Tsai has visited Sydney, Melbourne, Bendigo and Brisbane, examining Australian collections of Chinese musical instruments and investigating relevant historical and sociocultural details. Subsequently, he obtained a 2011 visiting fellowship from the Humanities Research Centre at the Australian National University, to carry out in Australia another project developed from the previous one: *Relational Instruments: How Bendigo's Past Soundscape is Shaping its Present and Future*. He has since been preparing for the research, and expects to visit Australia again in 2011.

As Australia-China encounters in ethnomusicology develop, there will be more exchanges and collaborations between the two countries in this area. The international symposiums, *Preserving Tradition, Facing the Future* hosted by the Sydney Conservatorium of Music in April 2010 and *Encounters III* hosted by the Queensland Conservatorium of Music in Brisbane in May of the same year, marked the beginning of a new phase in these encounters. Both symposiums put considerable emphasis on Chinese music research and exchange between Australian and Chinese communities of music and music research. The numbers of researchers and performers from mainland China, Hong Kong and Taiwan presenting at the symposiums have been larger than at any music conference previously held in Australia. Looking back over the past thirty years, beginning with one Australian student's encounter with a music institute in the PRC, one sees how that initial encounter has developed into a series of large-scale encounters between scholars and communities of ethnomusicologists from the two countries. Such encounters can be expected to continue flourishing and yielding valuable fruits well into the future.

Notes

1. The "Cultural Revolution" began in May 1966. Following Mao Zedong's death on 9 September 1996, the "Gang of Four", led by Mao's widow Jiang Qing, were arrested on 6 October 1996 by the Chinese Communist Party's new Central Committee. This marked the end of the Cultural Revolution.
2. The entire situation concerning relevant issues is much more complicated than what I have succinctly introduced here. For details one may refer to a relevant article of mine (2003a). For a typical PRC scholar's view in this regard, one may refer to the English translation of a Chinese article (Shen 1999 [1996]) and the translator's note (Stock 1999).
3. My thanks to Marion Gray for checking the details given here.
4. Marion and Julian now live in Melbourne, where Marion works at Victoria University. I thank them for giving their consent to publish with this article a photo taken at their wedding.

References

Chen Yingshi. 1988-89. "Temperamentology in Ancient Chinese Written Records." *Musicology Australia* 11-12: 44-64.

Chen Yonglian and Liu Zhenbi, comp. 1990. *Zhongyang yinyue xueyuan xiaoyou lu* [List of the Alumni of the Central Conservatory of Music]. Beijing: Zhongyang Yinyue Xueyuan [The Central Conservatory of Music]. Internal publication.

Gao Houyong. 1980. "Zhongguo minzu yinyuexue de xingcheng he fazhan" [The Origin and Development of the Study of The Music of Chinese Peoples]. *Nanjing Yishu Xueyuan Xuebao* [Journal of the Nanjing Institute of the Arts] (2): 9-22.

Hood, Mantle. 1971. *The Ethnomusicologist*. New York: McGraw-Hill Inc.

Merriam, Alan P. 1964. *The Anthropology of Music*. Bloomington: Indiana University Press.

NYXX (Nanjing Yishu Xueyuan Xuebao [Journal of the Nanjing Institute of the Arts]). 1980. "Minzu yinyuexue xueshu taolunhui lunwen mulu" [List of Papers at the Nanjing Symposium on the Study of the Music of Chinese Peoples]. *Nanjing Yishu Xueyuan Xuebao* [Journal of the Nanjing Institute of the Arts] (2): 151.

Picken, Laurence, and Noël Nickson, eds. 2000. *Music from the Tang Court*. V.7. UK: Cambridge University Press.

Shen Qia. 1999 [1996]. "Ethnomusicology in China." Trans. Jonathan P. J. Stock. *Journal of Music in China* 1: 7-36.

Stock, Jonathan P. J. 1999. "Ethnomusicology in China by Shen Qia: A Response." *Journal of Music in China* 1: 37-38.

Wang Heping. 2009. "Xueshu guifan jianshe ershi nian: zongguan yu fansi" [Twenty Years of Construction of Academic Norms: Review and Reflection]. *Guangxi Minzu Daxue Xuebao* [Journal of Guangxi University of Nationalities] (2): 175-180.

Yang Mu. 1986. "Aodaliya yinyue xuehui di shiyi jie nianhui ji yuhui duanxiang" [The Tenth Conference of the Musicological Society of Australia and Some Afterthoughts]. *Yinyue Yanjiu* [Music Research] (4): 112-15.

———. 1987. "Aodaliya yinyue xuehui di shiyi jie nianhui ji qita" [The Eleventh Conference of the Musicological Society of Australia and Other Matters]. *Yinyue Yanjiu* [Music Research] (4): 116-19.

———. 1988a. "Some Problems of Music Education in the People's Republic of China." *International Journal of Music Education* 11: 25-32.

———. 1988b. "Woguo yinyuexue wenlun xiezuo zhong de yixie wenti" [Some Problems of Academic Writings on Musicology in China]. *Yinyue Yanjiu* [Music Research] (4): 67-72.

———. 1989. "Guoji yinyue xuehui 1988 nian xueshu yantaohui ji yinyuejie zongshu" [Comments on the 1988 Music Festival and the Symposium of the International Musicological Society]. *Zhongyang Yinyue Xueyuan Xuebao* [Journal of The Central Conservatory of Music] (1): 103-05.

———. 1992. *Introduction to Chinese Musical Instruments*. Video (140 minutes) with *Teacher's Guide*. Melbourne: Education Resources Centre Media Service, University of Melbourne, Australia.

———. 1993a. "Danzhou Diaosheng yanjiu" [Research into Danzhou *Diaosheng*]. *Zhongyang Yinyue Xueyuan Xuebao* [Journal of The Central Conservatory of Music] (4): 3-13.

———. 1993b. *Chinese Musical Instruments: An Introduction*. Two audio cassettes (120 minutes). Canberra: Coralie Rockwell Foundation, The Australian National University.

———. 1993c. *Chinese Musical Instruments: An Introduction*. Canberra: Coralie Rockwell Foundation, The Australian National University.

———. 1994. "Academic Ignorance or Political Taboo? Some Issues in China's Study of Its Folk Song Culture." *Ethnomusicology* 38 (2): 303-20.

———. 1996. "Music Loss among Ethnic Minorities in China—A Comparison of the Li and Hui Peoples." *Asian Music* 27 (1): 103-31.

———. 1997a. "Dangdai renleixue yu yinyue yanjiu er san ti" [A few Issues in Contemporary Anthropology and Music Research]. *Zhongyang Minzu Daxue Xuebao (Shehui Kexue Ban)*

[Journal of the Central University of Chinese Nationalities (Social Sciences Edition)] (6): 25-31, 38.

———. 1997b. "Ye tan 'Huizu minjian yinyue'" [On "Folk Music of the Hui People"]. *Zhongyang Yinyue Xueyuan Xuebao* [Journal of The Central Conservatory of Music] (1): 47-56.

———. 1998a. "Dangdai renleixue zhong youguan yinyue yanjiu de ji ge wenti" [Contemporary Anthropological Issues Relevant to Music Research]. *Zhongyang Yinyue Xueyuan Xuebao* [Journal of The Central Conservatory of Music] (1): 6-15.

———. 1998b. "Current State and Methodology of Chinese Music Research in Mainland China." *Tongyang mak (Journal of the Asian Music Research Institute, Seoul National University)* 20: 19-38.

———. 2000a. "Zhongguo yinyue xingtai lilun jianshe yu Hanzu zhongxinlun wenti" [Constructions of Chinese music morphology and issues of Han-centrism]. *Yinyue Yanjiu* [Music Research] (1): 87-93.

———. 2000b. "Zaitan xueshu guifan yu wende wenfeng" [Further Discussion on Norms, Style and Ethics in Academic Writing]. *Zhongyang Yinyue Xueyuan Xuebao* [Journal of the Central Conservatory of Music] (1): 19-30.

———. 2001a. "Houxiandai lilun yu yinyue yanjiu (1)" [Postmodern Theory and Music Research (1)]. *Zhongyang Yinyue Xueyuan Xuebao* [Journal of the Central Conservatory of Music] (1): 3-14.

———. 2001b. "Houxiandai lilun yu yinyue yanjiu (2)" [Postmodern Theory and Music Research (2)]. *Zhongyang Yinyue Xueyuan Xuebao* [Journal of the Central Conservatory of Music] (2): 41-51.

———. 2003a. "Ethnomusicology with Chinese Characteristics?—A Critical Commentary." *Yearbook for Traditional Music* 35: 1-38.

———. 2003b. "Government Policy and Traditional Performing Arts in the People's Republic of China." *Journal of Chinese Ritual, Theatre and Folklore* (English edition, Taiwan) 141: 55-94.

———. 2006a. "Xing'ai yinyue yanjiu—yi Hainan Lizu wei shili (1)" [Research into Erotic Musical Activity—a Case Study of the Li people on Hainan (1)]. *Zhongyang Yinyue Xueyuan Xuebao* [Journal of the Central Conservatory of Music] (3): 71-82.

———. 2006b. "Xing'ai yinyue yanjiu—yi Hainan Lizu wei shili (2)" [Research into Erotic Musical Activity—a Case Study of the Li people on Hainan (2)]. *Zhongyang Yinyue Xueyuan Xuebao* [Journal of the Central Conservatory of Music] (4): 83-91.

———. 2007. "Cong guji zhengyin tan jiejian xifang xueshu guifan" [On Borrowing from Western Bibliographical Standards: a Discussion Focusing on Citation of Ancient Chinese Texts]. *Xinhai Yinyue Xueyuan Xuebao* [Journal of the Xinhai Conservatory of Music] (1): 51-55.

———. 2009. "Kuajin 21 shiji de yinyue renleixue—guoji chaoliu yu Zhongguo shijian" [Ethnomusicology into the 21st Century: International Trends and Chinese Practice]. *Xinhai Yinyue Xueyuan Xuebao* [Journal of the Xinhai Conservatory of Music] (4): 1-19.

Yu Renhao. 1981. "Minzu yinyuexue jieshao" [Introducing Ethnomusicology]. *Yinyue Yanjiu* [Music Research] (4): 96-97.

Yu Hui. 1994. "Aodaliya yinyue jiaoyu jianwen" [Observations on Music Education in Australia]. *Renmin Yinyue* [The People's Music] (10): 36-38.

Yuan Bingchang et al., eds. 1986. *Zhongguo Shaoshu Minzu Yueqi Zhi* [The Musical Instruments of the Chinese National Minorities: A Dictionary]. Beijing: Xin Shijie Chuban She [The New World Press].

Yuan Jingfang. 1980. "Ji zai Nanjing zhaokai de minzu yinyuexue xueshu taolunhui" [Notes on the Symposium on the Study of National Music in Nanjing]. *Zhongyang Yinyue Xueyuan Xuebao* [Journal of the Central Conservatory of Music] (4): 63-64.

Zhou Xiangsen. 2003. "Xinjiu zhongxi de chongtu: guanyu xueshu guifan taolun de sikao" [Conflict of the New and the Old, China and the West: Thoughts on the Discussion on Academic Norms]. *Shixue Yuekan* [History Study Monthly] (10): 98-107.

ZYXYB (Zhongyang Yinyue Xueyuan Yuanshi Bianjibu [Editorial Office of the History of the Central Conservatory of Music]), ed. 1990. *Zhongyang Yinyue Xueyuan yuanshi (1950-1990)* [History of the Central Conservatory of Music (1950-1990)]. Beijing: Zhongyang Yinyue Xueyuan [The Central Conservatory of Music]. Internal publication.

二

PART TWO

Socio-cultural Perspectives

CHAPTER

5

Researching Kam minority music in China[1]

Catherine Ingram

"That's the perfect song for you to sing," Kam friends and teachers stated emphatically in conversations on innumerable occasions. "It really suits you, and how you came from so far away to live with us and sing with us here."

I often received such comments in relation to my performance of a particular Kam song from the *ga nya* (river song) genre.[2] The song, *Nai dao jong der ma men* ("Now we are both together under the clouds"), was the second *ga nya* that I had learnt. It had been taught to me by my three teachers in the Kam village in southwestern China where I lived while conducting most of my recent doctoral and postdoctoral research. Whenever an appropriate occasion arose during sung dialogues or other types of performances, my teachers or other Kam friends invariably encouraged me to sing the song, and the performance was always warmly received. The lyrics to the song make much use of metaphor, a feature considered to be the hallmark of any song's quality. As evident from the translation of the lyrics below, they also incorporate praise — an expected part of Kam etiquette within both sung dialogues and everyday interactions:

> Now we are both together under the clouds [here on earth]
>
> Why are you in your own village?
>
> We are both children of Jang-lyang [a mythological ancestor][3]
>
> Why are you in your own place?
>
> When we are each in our own village we never meet
>
> When we are each in our own village we never meet
>
> Today we meet each other and have this love

> Now I look at your face, as white as cotton
>
> As shiny and fresh as a sharpening stone
>
> Eyebrows small and beautiful
>
> Like the flowers of a tree blossoming[4]

When Kam people I knew responded to or interpreted my singing of this song, they seemed to emphasise how it directly communicated a commonality between us that transcended both cultural difference and residential distance, as well as joy in our interaction and a sense of shared respect. Both the song and my singing of it within a Kam cultural context were, I believe, appreciated because they focussed upon the concrete point of contact between us made possible through my physical presence in Kam villages, my willingness to learn the Kam language, and my ability to communicate — at least to some degree — through the medium of song. For me, being taught this song and encouraged to sing it in such contexts was a privilege, and an important way of expressing my feelings towards my Kam friends, teachers and hosts.[5] The response I received gave me a greater sense of personal connection with Kam people, and of Kam support of my research, than it might have been possible for me to feel simply through everyday discussions.

There are two reasons why I begin this essay about musical research by describing Kam people's reactions to my singing of a Kam song. The issues that were raised through both Kam interpretations of these song lyrics and Kam people's enthusiasm for my performance of the song — issues such as direct communication, commonality across difference and distance, and joy and respect in personal interaction — were similarly important in my experience of researching Kam minority music in China. I also begin with this description to emphasise that the views of cultural custodians regarding the interactive process of undertaking research are an important dimension that complements what is, in the case of this essay, only one individual's perspective on how that research unfolded.

In this chapter I present and discuss the doctoral and postdoctoral research I have conducted within rural Kam communities over almost twenty-four months since 2004. Below, I give a brief introduction to Kam people and culture, and a description of how my involvement in those communities gradually developed. I then discuss my research focus, the main aspects of my methodology, and Kam involvement within and support of my research. To date, this research constitutes one of a very few instances of in-depth musical contact between Australia and China that has taken place within the context of mainland China. As noted in the final section of this paper, such research enriches relations and understanding between the two countries.

Kam people and Kam culture

The Kam are one of China's fifty-five officially recognised minority groups, and are known in Chinese as *Dongzu* 侗族. They have a registered population of over 2.9 million (*2000 nian renkou*, 2003, p. 3), most of whom live in southeastern Guizhou province and

Researching Kam minority music in China

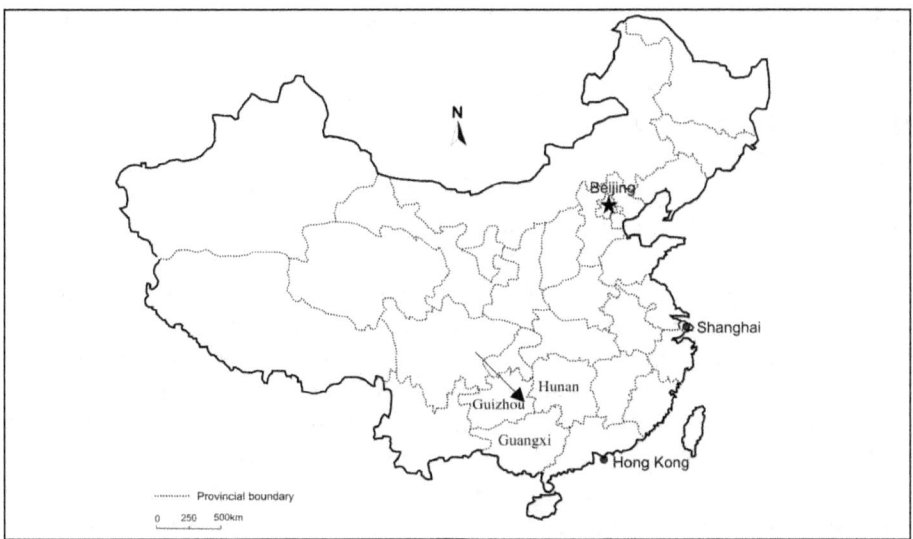

FIGURE 1 — Map of China, showing major cities and the two provinces (Guizhou and Hunan Provinces) and one autonomous region (Guangxi Zhuang Autonomous Region) where most Kam people reside. The approximate location of Sheeam, where the fieldwork described in this paper was mainly undertaken, is marked with an arrow. Map by Wu Jiaping.

the bordering areas of adjacent Guangxi and Hunan, as shown in Figure 1.[6] Many Kam people speak a dialect of Kam, a tonal language that has no widely used written form. The Kam language is classified within the Kam-Sui branch of the Tai-Kadai language family, and is thus quite different from the various dialects of Chinese.[7]

The last two decades have seen massive sociocultural changes in rural Kam areas, leading also to major cultural changes. The three sociocultural changes that have had the most significant influence upon contemporary Kam culture are the absence of almost all youth for work or study outside Kam villages, the promotion of Han Chinese education, and the inception and subsequent great popularity of television viewing. The absence of almost all younger people (and many middle-aged people) during most of the year has had particular impact upon systems of musical transmission, and thus many aspects of Kam music-making. Aside from the growing proportion of students amongst this absent population, the vast majority of these absent villagers become workers in eastern seaboard restaurants and factories. Besides some student visits home at weekends, and the return of married women for short periods prior to and following childbirth, most absent villagers make only occasional visits home for holidays or to help with rice planting and harvesting. In many respects, the effects of these recent changes upon Kam culture have been even more pronounced than the influences felt by the famines of the Great Leap Forward (1958–60) and the Cultural Revolution (1966–76). While some recent changes have led to a resurgence of interest in Kam singing — and especially interest in the Kam song genre usually referred to in English as "big song" — the present situation is complex and the future of Kam musical traditions is uncertain.

Despite these changes, many Kam villagers that I met during my research maintained various unique Kam customs, and sang many genres of songs in their local variant of the Southern Kam dialect. For example, people sang at weddings and engagements, or at celebrations after the building of a new house. When important guests visited for meals, praising them with suitable songs was still considered just as important as giving them food and drink. When groups of important visitors arrived or departed, people still blocked the road and engaged in a sung exchange of *ga sak-kun* (road-blocking song). In the procession and other ritual activities carried out in many Southern Kam villages at lunar New Year, singing was still used to honour the female deity *Sa* (Figure 2). Every day for over a week during the New Year celebrations, Kam opera performances or a type of circle, responsorial singing called *dor yeh* took place, as did performances of big song. Since the Kam language has no widely used written form, these various genres of Kam songs — especially big song — have been particularly important for recording and transmitting Kam history, philosophy and aspects of social structure. In 2006, the Chinese government recognised four Kam musical traditions as National-Level Intangible Cultural Heritage. One of these traditions, Kam big song, was inscribed on UNESCO's Representative List of the Intangible Cultural Heritage of Humanity in 2009.[8]

My research was conducted in the area where the Southern Kam dialect is spoken, and almost exclusively in the area from which big song originates. Residents of this area, who are estimated to comprise less than 4% of the Kam population, speak the

FIGURE 2 — Sheeam, February 2011. Villagers prepare to sing *ga yeh* (*yeh* songs) in *sak lan* (*lan* plaza) at the culmination of a large community New Year ritual honouring the female deity *Sa*. Photograph by Catherine Ingram.

second lect of Southern Kam.⁹ Despite the relatively small size of the genre's home region, big song has become the most widely promoted, researched and performed of all the many Kam song genres. Within state-sponsored cultural activities, such as staged Kam song performances and other types of cultural tourism promotion, big song is increasingly featured as a symbol of Kam identity.

Developing an involvement with Kam communities

My first visit to a Kam village in October 2004 marked the beginning of a two-month period of initial field research. During those two months I visited many different rural Kam regions and met many Kam singers. The contemporary local situation, which was barely documented in the Chinese scholarly publications I had previously read, gradually became clearer. As I met different Kam people in the various villages that I visited, I began to learn some basic Kam words and expressions. However, in grappling with the many differences amongst the Kam lect variants, I realised I would need to be based in one area in order to learn to speak Kam. I eventually decided to live in Sheeam (in Chinese, Sanlong 三龙), a small but well-known big-song-singing region with about 6,000 registered residents that is located in Liping county, southeastern Guizhou Province (see Figures 3 and 4).

Although I was welcomed in all the Kam areas I visited, within those first two months the people I met in Sheeam were amongst the few to explicitly extend an invitation to teach me and involve me in their music-making. At that time, Sheeam was also one of the few regions where big song singing occurred privately on a regular nightly basis, and where public performances were held at New Year. Only later did I learn of the legend of "See-yai carrying songs to Sheeam," widespread throughout Southern Kam areas, which suggests that Sheeam was the place of origin

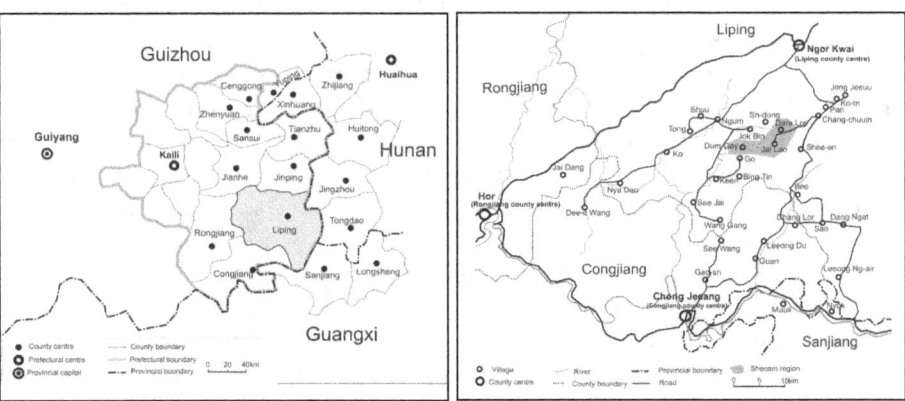

FIGURE 3 — Left: Map of Guizhou, Hunan and Guangxi showing Liping county (shaded) and other main counties of Kam residence. Right: Map showing the location of Sheeam in Liping county (shaded), and its position in relation to nearby Kam villages and county centres. Maps by Wu Jiaping.

FIGURE 4 — Left: January 2005. Looking down into the main Sheeam valley. Villagers must cross the mountain range seen here in order to reach Shee-en, the township centre and the closest local market. Right: Sheeam, July 2008. Looking down into the centre of the largest village, Jai Lao. The top of the main *dare low* (or "drum tower") can be seen left of centre. Photographs by Catherine Ingram.

or the main repository of many Kam songs.[10]

The other important factor prompting me to select Sheeam as a research base was that three of the main Sheeam *sang ga* (song experts) — Sa Lyang-kai, Sa Yuu-jin and Sa Yuun-yong[11] — could speak Chinese to varying degrees. This was particularly important when I first began to learn to speak Kam and sing Kam songs, as I was able to use Chinese to discuss the meanings of song lyrics and various issues associated with singing. Even later, when I had become more fluent in Kam, it was sometimes important for checking that I had accurately understood the deeper meanings of Kam song lyrics or complex aspects of Kam musical concepts. As detailed elsewhere (see Ingram et al., 2011a), in the 1950s and 1960s these three women had all had experience singing in Kam performance groups at county, provincial and national level, as well as in the village. Fortuitously, they had a wide range of friends throughout the broader big-song-singing region, wide knowledge of Kam song genres, and some experience of outsiders being interested in their music. They became my main Kam song teachers as well as very good friends, and I spent much time with them discussing and learning songs as well as working together in their fields and sharing meals.

I was invited to join various social and singing activities with my teachers and their friends and relatives, and countless evenings of singing. Not only did I come to know many other Sheeam women from sitting and singing together night after night, but through their invitations to join them in different activities I also came to know many of those women's relatives, meeting people from all villages in Sheeam and gaining firsthand understanding of local kinship structure. I sought out other female and male song experts and knowledgeable singers to discuss many aspects of music making, and also gained from informal conversations with anyone I met who was willing to share their views with me. In these experiences, food, friendship, singing, working together on the mountains, informal Kam language lessons and discussions about songs were invariably interwoven.

Just before my first visit to Sheeam I met Lyang-jyao,[12] a Kam middle-school student from the region. In a chance conversation after visiting her school in the county centre in October 2004, Lyang-jyao invited me to stay with her family (then consisting of her parents, three younger siblings and great-grandmother) when I went to her home village. Subsequently, I lived with Lyang-jyao's family in the largest village in Sheeam for a total of almost twenty-four months during four different periods: from the beginning of 2005 to March 2006, from February to July 2008, briefly in October 2009, and from December 2010 to June 2011. I was extremely fortunate to have such a welcoming and friendly family to eat, work, live and laugh with. Along with their many relatives, with whom I also spent much time, they assisted my research in countless ways, and we have become firm friends. Finally, during the periods I spent based in Sheeam I also made occasional research trips to other Kam areas or other parts of China (often in the company of members of Lyangy-jyao's family, my teachers, or other friends from Sheeam), and I joined my Sheeam friends in travels to other areas for singing performances.

When I first began research in rural Kam areas many people were nervous talking with me, and my interactions were restricted as I could only converse directly with people who spoke Chinese. It was clear that formal interviews would be uncomfortable and, at least initially, unlikely to be of much use.[13] Later, I gradually learnt this was because some people had no confidence speaking in Chinese, or were worried about how to speak politely to a foreigner (most Kam villagers had never met a non-Chinese person before, or possibly even someone of my height). Many more Kam villagers became active in developing friendships as I learnt to speak Kam, and as villagers got to know me and saw how I took part in all kinds of tasks (especially in physical, farming tasks that most outsiders disdained), how I valued the songs and knowledge that were shared with me, and how I generally conducted my activities and interactions.

My research focus and methodology

My doctoral research (Ingram 2010c) was an ethnographic study of Sheeam villagers' involvement in and views concerning big song singing. As I mainly drew upon data and understandings obtained using the methodology conventionally referred to as participant observation,[14] in this essay I focus on my research when based within Kam communities in China, and leave aside discussion of the various kinds of subsidiary research I also undertook.[15] During subsequent postdoctoral fieldwork over 2010 to 2011 I retained an ethnographic orientation as I continued to follow the many developments in villagers' big song singing, further expanding my understanding of the genre. I also had the opportunity to spend time investigating other Kam song genres in greater detail than was possible during earlier fieldwork periods, thus deepening my knowledge of various issues related to Kam music-making. Although I have learnt or discussed songs from all Kam song genres, my more detailed study of big song, and the greater promotion big song singing currently receives over other Kam song genres, has meant that the big song genre retains a central position in my research.

The many different songs now considered to be "big songs" are thought to be centuries old.[16] However, the identification of these songs within a "big song" genre dates only from the 1950s. At that time, researchers gradually came to refer to all the categories of Kam songs that involve two vocal lines and are sung in a particular New Year performance context by the Chinese name *dage* 大歌 ("big song"), from which the English name derives. The Chinese name derives from and is one of several possible translations of the Kam *ga lao*, the name of the main category of such songs.[17] Today, while the Kam name *ga lao* is sometimes also used to refer to all such categories of Kam song, the polysemous ambiguity of "*ga lao*" makes it problematic to refer to all songs with two vocal lines using this indigenous Kam term (see also Ingram, 2007, p. 88; Ingram, 2010c; Yang, 2008).

In the original village context for transmission of these songs, unmarried villagers would form fixed single-sex singing groups during the year, and arrange to learn the songs from one of their village's song experts. In the evenings during New Year celebrations, these singing groups would gather in one of the village's tall pagoda-shaped *dare low* (see Figure 5)[18] to carry out a sung exchange of these songs. Such systems of big song transmission and performance continue in Sheeam and nearby regions today, albeit with numerous significant alterations. As further detailed elsewhere (see Ingram 2010a, 2010c, 2011, 2012; and Ingram et al., 2011a), the most significant of these alterations have involved changes to the cohorts involved as singers, the social

FIGURE 5 — February 2008, Sheeam. The tallest of the three *dare low* in Jai Lao, the largest village in Sheeam. Photograph by Catherine Ingram.

interactions that occur through the song transmission and performance, and the structure of the song exchange.

Another significant development has been Kam villagers' involvement in staged performances of big song, which has recently escalated to an unprecedented level. During my research, I was not only invited to participate in big song performances within Kam villages as part of what I call the "village tradition," but I also joined Kam villagers in some of their now-numerous song performances onstage. The largest of these was 10,000 people singing big song, a performance at the Liping county Airport-Opening Arts Festival in 2005 that I also participated in. Besides participating in various big song performances, I also joined Kam friends in singing other genres of Kam songs at events within the village at New Year, at weddings or engagements, and to guests during meals.

My research involved extensive participation in singing activities — and especially big song singing — within the context of regular participation in all aspects of daily village life. Thus, not only did I learn to sing many songs but I also planted and harvested rice, attended social events such as marriages and engagements, went foraging for wild foods on the mountainsides and carried manure to hillside gardens, amongst other activities. My learning of Kam songs, which was essential preparation for my participation in singing events, sometimes took place in intensive sessions in my teachers' or friends' homes, or when having a rest while working together on the mountainside, or even while we were walking up the mountains to reach the place where we would be working. On other occasions, particularly when I joined friends in preparing for staged performances, I learnt the songs as my friends did by copying down song lyrics (using Chinese characters to represent the Kam language) and/or by reciting them over and over many times. Sometimes, I would *ao ga* or "get the song" — a reference to learning the song lyrics — from one person, and then other singers or friends would help to explain the lyrics and demonstrate how the song should be sung. As the one *sor* (a Kam term referring to a particular understanding of a song melody) is used for singing all Kam songs in the one genre or one category of a genre, my main tasks in learning each new song were understanding and memorizing the lyrics, and learning how to fit these with an appropriate rendition of the song's *sor*.[19] I often recorded my teachers or friends singing a song so that I could later learn it through repeated listenings, and so I would finally be able to join others in singing the song. Memorizing enough Kam song lyrics so that I could participate in singing without needing to resort to written notation was a challenge that remained constant throughout my research.

Kam villagers and I also made many recordings of singing events, of instrument making, and of various other traditional or distinctive Kam activities. Over the time I spent in Kam areas this process became increasingly collaborative. The musical events we recorded not only included village celebrations already part of the community's social calendar, but also performances that villagers staged — usually at their own instigation — especially for filming. As my relationships with Kam people developed, we also video-recorded an increasing number of formal interviews and

FIGURE 6 — Sheeam, February 2006. Villagers pause during a ritual procession that occurred as part of a community-instigated re-enactment of the inter-village visiting ritual known in Kam as *gan go-mao*. Photograph by Catherine Ingram.

specially organized group discussions that focussed on many music-related topics. Over the periods I spent in Kam areas I returned copies of all requested recordings to singers in many Kam areas, and viewing these VCDs and DVDs together with Kam friends gradually formed an important part of my research methodology.

These various recordings are amongst the approximately 180 hours of video recordings and 130 hours of audio recordings that, as authorised by Kam villagers, I am in the process of uploading into the Pacific and Regional Archive of Digital Sources in Endangered Cultures (PARADISEC).[20] Upload of this footage has allowed this important collection of recordings to be stored in a sustainable digital archive, and to my knowledge constitutes the first archive of Kam song recordings. Not only is the collection itself of significance, but the process of my collaboration with different groups of Kam people to create the recordings provided what was clearly a useful role in the revitalisation of local song traditions. For example, Kam villagers decided to re-enact previously abandoned lengthy ritual visiting activities involving performance of numerous song genres especially to create an audiovisual record (see Figure 6), and interest in making recordings motivated some singers to decide to revise (or even learn) and then record certain songs that are rarely performed today and not being transmitted to younger generations.

Finally, my research within Kam villages also involved collaboration with Kam singers in other contexts related to Kam music. I assisted with typing and translation of articles by Sheeam Kam song expert Gong Lyang-jyao[21] that were intended for local circulation. Five Kam female singers and I worked to collaboratively author a book chapter on rural Kam women and contemporary Kam "cultural development" (Ingram et al., 2011a). I worked with Sheeam song experts on a book chapter about cultural custodians and digital archive access (Ingram et al., 2011b), and on two conference papers about Kam singing. I also collaborated with Kam community members in promoting Kam song within different forms of media. Such collaborations included many interviews with visiting Chinese reporters and, in 2005, 2006 and 2011, involvement in the making of two 30-minute quasi-documentaries produced by Guizhou Province TV (directed by Bai Chuan). The film made from the 2005-2006 footage, entitled *Ga Lao My Love*, was awarded one of the "Ten Best Documentaries" in China in 2006.

The significance of this musical interaction

This musical ethnographic research, which constitutes of one of the few instances of in-depth musical contact between Australia and China that have taken place within the context of mainland China, may well be the first instance of an Australian becoming personally involved in the music-making of a Chinese minority group within mainland China to any extensive degree.[22] I believe that my research within Kam minority communities, and the musical interaction that it has facilitated, has been significant in several different ways.

This research and musical interaction demonstrates Australian engagement with and attempts towards understanding of Chinese music and Chinese minority society and culture — two facets of China that are relatively less explored by non-Chinese scholars working in China.[23] My focus upon the culture of part of China's minority population allows insight into an aspect of Chinese society that, aside from certain widely publicised exceptions, remains relatively overlooked within general and academic circles outside China (and also, to a lesser degree, within China itself). In the realm of musical scholarship, my research and publications that have been made possible through the willingness of Kam communities to teach me and to involve me in their music making has permitted a new perspective on Kam cultural traditions, greater involvement of Kam village song experts and singers themselves in representations of those traditions, and increased ability of those traditions to become noticed outside the Chinese-speaking context. As my methodology has involved relatively extensive participation in the actual traditions I have researched, and as my research has been conducted through developing some command of the Kam language (rather than only using Chinese), this research has facilitated important insights that have hitherto been largely unavailable within both Chinese and non-Chinese scholarship.[14] All these insights have significance not only to particular aspects of academic scholarship, but also to enhancing Australia's knowledge of China, one of our important neighbours.

The creation of an archive of recordings of Kam music and other aspects of daily life is also of particular significance given the uncertain future of these musical traditions, and because of the likelihood of ongoing socio-cultural change within rural Kam communities. Australian involvement in the process of creating valuable resources for future generations of Kam people and future scholars of China demonstrates that Australia is actively involved in promoting cultural research and cultural sustainability within the Asia-Pacific region, and enhances ties between these two countries.

The personal interactions within and beyond shared music-making that have been the basis for my research, and for the development of what I believe are long-standing friendships with many Kam villagers, also have significance.[25] As emphasised in Kam people's comments on my abovementioned performance of one *ga nya*, they provide a channel for direct communication and understanding. Several researchers have recognised the significance of direct musical communication to cultural understanding. For instance, Marina Roseman (1991) states that: "The body is the medium through which self is engaged with other. It is a reference point for our isolation and for our connection" (p. 179). Similarly, Steven Feld (1990) writes, "for me it was the physical sensations of vocalizing and drumming that brought me closer to the performance aesthetic and brought some Kaluli closer to talking with me about its inner dimensions" (p. 237). From a Kam perspective, personal engagement and musical involvement are not unusual: they form the core of proper social behaviour and are thus a most appropriate channel for allowing such cultural and personal interaction to occur. Many Kam villagers went to great lengths to support and become involved in my research, to teach me about Kam culture, and to assist with checking or further explaining various songs and Kam concepts. Not only did this include many different activities during the periods I spent in China, but also information and ideas shared through emails, posted letters, phone (and, more recently, video) calls and text messages during the times I have been away from Kam areas. I believe that many Kam friends' willingness to collaborate in or to support my research in these ways can be taken as evidence of how our musical meeting, and my role and actions concerning Kam singing, have been welcomed, valued and enjoyed by many Kam people.[26] These personal interactions directly enhance the development of understanding and relations between China and Australia at the personal or grassroots level.

The same sentiments were echoed in the choice of *ga nya* that Kam singers often sang, as is typical, to "reply" to my performance of the song described at the opening of this essay. The song usually chosen was *Deeuu kun nai ngai* ("This road is long"), a song with lyrics that emphasise development of a relationship that overcomes a great separation in distance. It concludes with the wish for a connection which, once built, will always remain:

> This road is long: I always call on you to make it closer
>
> These mountain valleys are deep: I always call on you to make them level
>
> If the mountains cannot be level, I will ask you place stones to fill the gaps
>
> If the road is difficult to traverse, I will ask you to build a bridge
>
> Build a wooden bridge, later it will rot
>
> Build a stone bridge, afterwards it will be standing forever [27]

Endnotes

1. I gratefully acknowledge the many Kam people without whose assistance my research could not have been conducted. In particular, I thank once again Wu Meifang, Wu Pinxian, Wu Xuegui and Wu Zhicheng; Nay Lyang-jyao (Wu Xueyun) and all her family; and the Kam community of Sheeam. I also acknowledge the financial support provided by an Australian Postgraduate Award and an Endeavour Australia Cheung Kong Research Fellowship, and by various grants and other support offered through the University of Melbourne (Faculty of Music, Asia Institute, and Writing Centre for Scholars and Researchers) and PARADISEC. Thanks also to an anonymous reviewer and to Nick Ng for helpful comments on an earlier draft of this essay.

2. The *ga nya* genre probably originated in the Kam villages of the Fulu river area of Sanjiang county, Guangxi, hence its name. As I have described elsewhere (see Ingram, 2007, 2010c), I transcribe Kam words using my own practical phonemic orthography that is based upon standard (Australian) English pronunciation. All song lyrics are translations from Kam, and all Kam words are transcribed from the Sheeam variant of the second lect of the Southern Kam dialect.

3. Jang-lyang (or Jang-lang) and his sister Jang-moy are considered by Kam people to be the primordial ancestors of the human race; see Ingram (2010c), Somsonge Burusphat (1996), Ruan Xing (2006, pp. 41, 185–86) and Geary et al. (2003, p. 215–18).

4. A translation of the lyrics to *Nai dao jong der ma men* ("Now we are both together under the clouds"), a *ga nya* (river song) from Sheeam. The full Kam lyrics are as follows: *Nai dao jong der ma men, nya mang gak sen nyao? / Jong lak Jang-lyang, nya mang gak dee fang? / Nai dao gak sen gak nyao, dao ben lyen song dong / Nai dao gak sen gak nyao, dao ben lyen song dom / See nai dom yao dom nya, lee dang nga bu lor / Say nang na nang nya ju, ee yang bark min yong / Nang na ju gen, lee nut din ban tee / Dyap da ju see, lee nut nuk may moong.*

5. In a similar vein, Gregory Barz (2006) comments that "Many of us — myself included — feel that in our privilege to share in and make meaning out of the musical lives of people around the world, we are the most fortunate of all storytellers" (p. 1).

6. As Wu Wanyuan (2000) notes, a small number of Kam people now also live in Hubei Province.

7. Significant English-language studies of the Kam language and the Tai-Kadai language family include Edmondson & Solnit (1988), Long & Zheng (1998), Sagart (2004), and Diller et al. (2008); see also OLAC's *Resources in and about the Southern Dong language* (2009). Within the period and geographical scope of my research, the romanised Kam orthography that was adopted in 1958 (see Yang & Edmondson 2008, p. 580–581) was not widely used.

8. Kam big song, Kam *beeba* (pipa) song, Kam opera and Kam *nuo* opera were recognised in 2006 (see Zhou, 2006, pp.104–106, 501–502, 517–518). In the 2009 UNESCO materials, the big song genre is referred to as "Grand Song": see *Grand song of the Dong ethnic group* (2009).

9. The Southern Kam dialect is considered to contain four distinct "lects" (Long & Zheng, 1998, pp. 180–181; Geary et al., 2003, p. 34; Yang & Edmondson, 2008, p. 579). Luo & Wang (2002) quote figures provided by the Chinese Academy of Social Sciences giving the population in big-song-singing areas as 100,000.

10. See Ingram (2010c) and Geary et al. (2000).

11. Their Chinese names are, respectively, Wu Pinxian 吴品仙, Wu Xuegui 吴学桂 and Wu Meifang 吴美芳.

12. In Chinese, Wu Jiaxian 吴家仙.

13. Although interviews often constitute an important research methodology, they are not always problematised. Some exceptions are Lancaster (1992, p. 109), who describes why he largely abandoned formal interviews, and Harris (2004, p. xx) who outlines why she continued with interviews but preferred not to tape-record them. Cornet (2010) clearly outlines the limitations of her research in another Kam village as a researcher reliant mainly upon interviews and unable to speak Kam.

14 On the difficulty of simultaneously attempting to combine both participation and observation, which in many contexts are two very different activities, and on other possible interpretations of "participant observation," see Stoller (1992, p. 214), Emoff (2002, pp. 11–12), Behar (1996, pp. 5–6), Herzfeld (1987, pp. 16–17), Fabian (1990) and Dirks (1994, p. 499).

15 Consequently, although archival sources, prior writings on Kam music and culture, online and audio-visual sources and interviews with certain Kam and non-Kam people living outside rural Kam areas helped to provide a context for my understanding of Kam village singing, I do not discuss them in this essay.

16 Given the lack of reliable written records on Kam history and culture prior to the 1950s (see Ingram 2010b, 2010c), the songs cannot be precisely dated.

17 *Ga* translates as "song," and *lao* can be variously translated as "big," "old," "main," or "important."

18 Kam villages are well known for their tall pagoda-shaped wooden towers (see Ruan, 2006). In the Sheeam dialect these towers are known as *dare low*, but in Chinese they are usually referred to as *gulou* ("drum tower/building"). As the Kam name makes no reference to drums, and as it is considered to solely refer to these important buildings, I have used it in its original Kam form.

19 In brief, I suggest that each *sor* is perceived as a "melodic habitus" (drawing upon the terminology of Bourdieu ([1972] 1977)), and the melodic choices possible for all songs sharing the same *sor* are loosely defined by that habitus. In the context of village performances the *sor* is rendered differently in each song, in performances of the same song by different groups and, to a lesser degree, in each group's performances of the same song on different occasions (see Ingram 2010c, 2012).

20 See http://www.paradisec.org.au, and Ingram et al. (2011b). Anthony Seeger (2008) has been one of the strongest advocates for such archiving practices as part of ethnomusicological research, writing that: "Preservation of audio and video-recordings should be of major concern to ethnomusicologists, and ensuring their survival and future usability is an important kind of public ethnomusicology. Even when community members make their own recordings, there is little likelihood these will be playable fifteen, thirty, or fifty years from now… Even when commercial recordings have appeared of the community's music, there is no guarantee that companies will take care of the masters" (p. 285).

21 In Chinese, Wu Zhicheng 吴志成.

22 Colin Mackerras is perhaps the most well-known Australian scholar to have investigated Chinese minority music (see, for example, Mackerras, 1984, 1985a, 1985b, 1995). Australian-based ethnomusicologist Yang Mu is also well known for contributions in this area (see, for example, Yang, 1990). Other scholars currently or recently based in Australia and who have conducted and published research that relates to the traditional music of Chinese ethnic groups (both Han and minority) include Anne McLaren (see McLaren, 2008), David Holm (see Holm, 1984, 1991), and Kao Ya-ning (see Kao, 2009). Perhaps because most of these scholars are not working within the field of ethnomusicology, they have not undertaken the kind of long-term participatory musical ethnographic study that formed the core of my research and is described in this essay. Consequently, their research and publications present a musical interaction between Australia and China that is significantly different from that I undertook and describe here.

23 According to recent statistics, more than 91% of China's population officially identify as the majority Han, and about 105 million people (approximately 8.5% of the population) identify as belonging to one of the fifty-five recognised *shaoshu minzu* 少数民族 or "minority groups" (*2000 nian renkou*, 2003, pp. 2–3). As Sara Davis (2006, p. 39) notes, these minorities occupy 60% of the nation's landmass.

24 To my knowledge, the vast majority of contemporary scholars writing (almost exclusively in Chinese) about Kam music are not Kam speakers, and/or have never been active participants in the traditional cultural activities of the communities they describe. Although Kam women now have the main roles as custodians of Kam song traditions, very few of the authors writing about Kam musical traditions have been women. This is significant because the gender distinctions in

both song performance and social interactions within Kam villages preclude male researchers from the experience of singing with or talking freely over long periods with these women; furthermore, as a large proportion of Kam women are essentially monolingual Kam speakers, many would be unable to communicate with monolingual Han Chinese researchers.

25 The politics of friendship and empathy in fieldwork have been discussed by a number of scholars, and in many cases critiqued as exploitative and appropriating the voice of those amongst whom research is conducted (see Lather, ([2000] 2009), Visweswaran (1996), Abwunza (1995), Parameswaran (2008), Skeggs (2001), Walter (1995), Wolf (1996), Stacey (1988), Abu-Lughod (1990) and Lassiter (2005)). Nevertheless, I suggest that while friendship or empathy with research participants, teachers and colleagues may sometimes invite exploitation, these can equally invite a greater concern for ethics, ethical representation, collaboration and understanding that can stretch across cultures, languages, belief systems, genders and generations. From a practical viewpoint, it would have been impossible for me to learn to speak Kam, to sing with Kam villagers, and to discuss aspects related to Kam music, without first building friendships with many Kam people; see Ridler (1996) for a somewhat similar perspective.

26 While Kam people's response to my research was, overall, very positive (as described here), it was not without complexities and reservations; see Ingram et al. (2011b) for a more detailed analysis, including statements from Kam song experts.

27 A translation of the lyrics to *Deeuu kun nai ngai* ("This road is long"), a *ga nya* (river song) from Sheeam. The full Kam lyrics are as follows: *Deeuu kun nai ngai, deeuu ben jum nya ao wair jin / Jim jin nai yum, deeuu ben jum nya ao wair been / Nu bao gay been, deeuu yuu jum nya ao nut deen dip cha / Nu bao kun gay lai da, deeuu yuu jum nya ga bu jeeuu / Ga bu jeeuu may, lun yuu moong / Ga bu jeeuu deen, mu dao jin bai ten wen nyin.*

References

2000 nian renkou. (2003). (Full title: *2000 nian renkou pucha Zhongguo minzu renkou ziliao* 2000年人口普查中国民族人口资料 [Chinese nationalities population materials from the 2000 population census]. Edited by Guojia tongjiju renkou he shehui keji tongjisi 国家统计局人口和社会科技统计司 [Department of Statistics of Population, Social Science and Technology, National Bureau of Statistics] and Guojia minzu shiwu weiyuanhui jingji fazhansi 国家民族事务委员会经济发展司 [Department of Economics and Development, National Ethnic Affairs Commission]. Beijing: Minzu chubanshe [Nationalities press].

Abu-Lughod, L. (1990). Can there be a feminist ethnography? *Women and performance: A journal of feminist theory* 5, 7–27.

Abwunza, J. M. (1995). Conversation between cultures: Outrageous voices? Issues of voices and text in feminist anthropology. In S. Cole and L. Phillips (Eds.), *Ethnographic feminisms: Essays in anthropology* (pp. 245–258). Ontario: Carleton University Press.

Barz, G. (2006). *Singing for life: HIV/AIDS and music in Uganda*. New York & London: Routledge.

Behar, R. (1996). *The vulnerable observer: Anthropology that breaks your heart*. Boston: Beacon Press.

Bourdieu, P. ([1972] 1977). *Outline of a theory of practice*. R. Nice (Translation). Cambridge, London, New York & Melbourne: Cambridge University Press.

Cornet, C. (2010). Fieldwork among the Dong national minority in Guizhou, China: Practicalities, obstacles and challenges. *Asia Pacific viewpoint*, 51(2), 135–147.

Davis, S. (2006). Dance or else: China's "simplifying project." *China rights forum* 4, 38–46.

Diller, A. V. N., Edmondson, J. A., & Luo Yongxian (Eds.). (2008). *The Tai-Kadai languages*. Oxford & New York: Routledge.

Dirks, N. B. (1994). Ritual and resistance: Subversion as social fact. In N. B. Dirks, G. Eley and S. B. Ortner (Eds.), *Culture/Power/History* (pp. 483–503). Princeton: Princeton University Press.

Edmondson, J. A., & Solnit, D. B. (Eds.). (1988). *Comparative Kadai: Linguistic studies beyond Tai*. Texas: Summer Institute of Linguistics and The University of Texas at Arlington Publications in Linguistics.

Emoff, R. (2002). *Recollecting from the past: Musical practice and spirit possession on the east coast of Madagascar*. Middletown, Connecticut: Wesleyan University Press.

Fabian, J. (1990). *Power and performance*. Madison: University of Wisconsin Press.

Feld, S. (1990). *Sound and sentiment: Birds, weeping, poetics, and song in Kaluli expression*. 2nd ed. Philadelphia: University of Pennsylvania Press.

Geary, D. N., Geary, R. B., Ou Chaoquan, Long Yaohong, Jiang Daren, & Wang Jiying. (2003). *The Kam people of China: Turning nineteen*. London & New York: RoutledgeCurzon.

Geary, N., Geary, R., & Long Yaohong. (2000). Kam singing. In *Proceedings of the international conference on Tai studies, held 29–31 July, 1998, at the Institute of Language and Culture for Rural Development, Mahidol University, Bangkok* (pp. 213–222). Bangkok: Mahidol University.

Grand song of the Dong ethnic group. (2009). UNESCO Representative List of the Intangible Cultural Heritage of Humanity. Available from http://www.unesco.org/culture/ich/index.php?RL=00202.

Harris, R. (2004). *Singing the village: Music, memory and ritual among the Sibe of Xinjiang*. Oxford & New York: Published for The British Academy by Oxford University Press.

Herzfeld, M. (1987). *Anthropology through the looking-glass: Critical ethnography in the margins of Europe*. Cambridge: Cambridge University Press.

Holm, D. (1984). Folk art as propaganda: The *Yangge* movement in Yan'an. In B. S. McDougall (Ed.), *Popular Chinese literature and performing arts in the People's Republic of China 1949–1979* (pp. 3–35). Berkeley & Los Angeles: University of California Press.

———. (1991). *Art and ideology in revolutionary China*. Oxford: Oxford University Press.

Ingram, C. (2007). "If you don't sing, friends will say you are proud": How and why Kam people learn to sing Kam big song. *Context: A journal of music research 32*, 85–104.

———. (2010a). A localized perspective on China's intangible cultural heritage: The case of Kam big song. *Proceedings of the Asian Studies Association of Australia 18th Biennial Conference, University of Adelaide, July 2010*. Available from http://www.adelaide.edu.au/asaa2010/reviewed_papers/Ingram-Catherine.pdf.

———. (2010b). *China's Kam minority: A short bibliographic outline of Kam-related research materials in the University of Melbourne library*. East Asian Library Resources Group of Australia newsletter, 56 (July 2010). Available from http://coombs.anu.edu.au/SpecialProj/NLA/EALRGA/newsletter1007/1007_ingram.html.

———. (2010c). *Hwun hwun jon ka* (Listen): Kam villagers singing big song in early twenty-first-century China. PhD diss., Music & Asia Institute, University of Melbourne, Melbourne.

———. (2011). Echoing the environment in Kam big song. *Asian Studies Review* 35 (December), 439–455.

———. (2012). *Ee, mang gay dor ga ey* (Hey, why don't you sing)? Imagining the future for Kam big song. In K. Howard (Ed.), *Music as intangible cultural heritage: Policy, ideology and practice in the preservation of East Asian traditions* (pp. 55-76). Farnham, UK & Burlington, VT, USA: Ashgate.

Ingram, C., with Wu Jialing, Wu Meifang, Wu Meixiang, Wu Pinxian, & Wu Xuegui. (2011). Taking the stage: Rural Kam women and contemporary Kam "cultural development." In T. Jacka & S. Sargeson (Eds.), *Women, gender and rural development in China* (pp. 71–93). Cheltenham, UK & Northampton, MA: Edward Elgar.

Ingram, C., with Wu Meifang, Wu Pinxian, Wu Xuegui and Wu Zhicheng. (2011b). Discussing "fair use" of archived recordings of minority music from the mountains of southwestern China. In N. Thieberger, L. Barwick, R. Billington and J. Vaughan (Eds.), *Sustainable data from digital research: Humanities perspectives on digital scholarship* (pp. 90–118). Melbourne: Custom Book Centre, University of Melbourne. Also available from http://hdl.handle.net/2123/7890.

Kao Ya-ning. (2009). Singing a hero in ritual: Nong Zhigao and his representation among the Zhuang people in China. PhD diss., Anthropology & Asia Institute, University of Melbourne, Melbourne.

Lancaster, R. N. (1992). *Life is hard: Machismo, danger, and the intimacy of power in Nicaragua*. Berkeley, Los Angeles & Oxford: University of California Press.

Lassiter, L. E. (2005). Collaborative ethnography and public anthropology. *Current anthropology* 46(1), 83–106.

Lather, P. ([2000] 2009). Against empathy, voice and authenticity. In A. Y. Jackson & L. A. Mazzei (Eds.), *Voice in qualitative inquiry: Challenging conventional, interpretive, and critical conceptions in qualitative research* (pp. 17–26). London & New York: Routledge.
Long Yaohong, and Zheng Guoqiao. (1998). *The Dong language in Guizhou province, China.* D. N. Geary (Translation). Dallas: Summer Institute of Linguistics and The University of Texas at Arlington Publications in Linguistics.
Luo Xiaoyan 罗晓燕, and Wang Xiaomei 王小梅. (2002). *Guniang xiaohuozi waichu dagong, Minzu geshou yanzhong duanceng, Dongzu dage chuancheng jixu guanzhu* 姑娘小伙子外出打工，民族歌手严重断层，侗族大歌传承急需关注 [Young people go to other areas to work, the traditional methods of song transmission are broken, the transmission of Kam big song must urgently be addressed], Renmin wang [People's net]. Available from http://unn.people.com.cn /GB/channel1265/267/807/200210/22/ 222158.html.
Mackerras, C. (1984). Folksongs and dances of China's minority nationalities: Policy, tradition and professionalization. *Modern China* 10(2), 187–226.
——. (1985a). Traditional Uyghur performing arts. *Asian music* 16(1), 29–58.
——. (1985b). Uyghur performing arts in contemporary China. *China quarterly* (101), 58–77.
——. (1995). *China's minority cultures: Identities and integration since 1912.* Melbourne: Longman Australia.
McLaren, A. (2008). *Performing grief: Bridal laments in rural China.* Honolulu: University of Hawai'i Press.
Parameswaran, R. (2008). Reading the visual, tracking the global: Postcolonial feminist methodology and the chameleon codes of resistance. In N. K. Denzin, Y. S. Lincoln and L. T. Smith (Eds.), *Handbook of critical and indigenous methodologies* (pp. 407–428). Los Angeles, London, New Delhi & Singapore: SAGE.
Resources in and about the Southern Dong language. (2009). [webpage]. Open language archives. Available from http://www.language-archives.org/language/kmc.
Ridler, K. (1996). If not the words: Shared practical activity and friendship in fieldwork. In M. Jackson (Ed.), *Things as they are: New directions in phenomenological anthropology* (pp. 238–258). Bloomington & Indianapolis: Indiana University Press.
Roseman, M. (1991). *Healing sounds from the Malaysian rainforest.* Berkeley and Los Angeles: University of California Press.
Ruan Xing. (2006). *Allegorical architecture: Living myth and archetectonics in Southern China.* Honolulu: University of Hawai'i Press.
Sagart, L. (2004). The higher phylogeny of Austronesian and the position of Tai-Kadai. *Oceanic linguistics* 43(2), 411–444.
Seeger, A. (2008). Theories forged in the crucible of action: The joys, dangers and potentials of advocacy and fieldwork. In G. F. Barz and T. J. Cooley (Eds.), *Shadows in the field: New perspectives for fieldwork in ethnomusicology* (pp. 271–288). 2nd ed. New York & Oxford: Oxford University Press.
Skeggs, B. (2001). Feminist ethnography. In P. Atkinson, A. Coffey, S. Delamont, J. Lofland and L. Lofland (Eds.), *Handbook of ethnography* (pp. 426–442). London, Thousand Oaks & New Delhi: SAGE Publications.
Somsonge, B. (1996). Surface indicators of storyline in the Kam origin myth. *Mon-Khmer studies* 26, 339–355.
Stacey, J. (1988). Can there be a feminist ethnography? *Women's studies international forum* 11(1), 2–27.
Stoller, P. (1992). *The cinematic griot: The ethnography of Jean Rouch.* Chicago & London: The University of Chicago Press.
Visweswaran, K. (1996). *Fictions of feminist ethnography.* Delhi: Oxford University Press.
Walter, L. (1995). Feminist anthropology? *Gender and society* 9(3), 272–288.
Wolf, D. L. (Ed.). (1996). *Feminist dilemmas in fieldwork.* Boulder (Colorado) & Oxford: Westview Press.
Wu Wanyuan 吴万源. (2000). Hubei E'xi Dongzu kaocha ji 湖北鄂西侗族考察记 [Records of investigation into the Kam of western Hubei]. In "Dongzu bai nian shi lu" bian wei hui 《侗族百年实录》编委会 ["Veritable records of one hundred years of the Kam" editing committee] (Ed.), *Dongzu bainian shilu (shang xia ce)* 侗族百年实录（上、下册） [Veritable records of one

hundred years of the Kam (2 vols.)] (pp. 726–732). Beijing: Zhongguo wenshi chubanshe [China literature and history press].

Yang Mu. (1990). Folk music of Hainan island – with particular emphasis on Danxian county. PhD diss., Music, University of Queensland, Brisbane.

Yang Tongyin, & Edmondson, J. A. (2008). Kam. In A. V. N. Diller, J. A. Edmondson, & Luo Yongxian (Eds.), *The Tai-Kadai languages* (pp. 509–584). Oxford & New York: Routledge.

Yang Xiao 杨晓. (2008). Nandong "ga lao" ming shikao – jianlun Dongzu dage yici de duozhong neihan "嘎老"名实考一兼论侗族大歌一词的多重内涵 [Research into the definition of the southern Kam "ga lao": Concurrent investigation into the multiple emphases of Kam big song]. *Zhongguo yinyuexue* 中国音乐学 [Musicology in China] (2), 10–19.

Zhou Heping 周和平 (Ed.). (2006). *Diyipi guojiaji feiwuzhi wenhua yichan minglu tudian (shang, xia)* 第一批国家级非物质文化遗产名录图典（上、下）[An illustrated register of the first series of National-Level Intangible Cultural Heritage] Beijing: Wenhua yishu chubanshe [Culture and art publishing house].

CHAPTER

6

'The Asian Björk'— Is Sa DingDing the Voice of the 'New China'?

Tony Mitchell

World music: Anxiety and celebration

World Music has been a problematic music genre since its inception as a category incorporating various forms of non-Western music. This occurred at a famous meeting of independent record company owners held at the Empress of Russia pub in London in 1987 (Frith, 2000, p. 305–306). It has essentially survived as a rather nebulous and highly flexible marketing term used to designate a genre of music which is widely used in music stores, by record labels and in the music press. It incorporates both traditional and popular music from non-Western sources which does not fit appropriately into existing genres of reggae, jazz, blues or folk. African, Afro-Caribbean, Latin American, South Asian, Arabic, Eastern European and various indigenous musics tend to predominate in the category, which leans toward traditional and folk music, often with "Western" beats and production overlaid or underpinned, rather than, say, more unashamedly pop forms such as Hong Kong Cantopop or Chinese Mandapop (see Mitchell, 2001).

This paper examines the case of Chinese singer Sa Dingding, a recent entrant from Mongolia into the field of World Music who has bypassed Mandapop and Cantopop in the interests of more globally-based marketing strategies which arguably correspond more to the global enterprise of the post-Beijing Olympics "new China." She has succeeded in fitting comfortably into the World Music genre while generating dilemmas of interpretation and reception which are similar to those of a number of artists who combine Western production values and musical styles with traditional "ethnic" elements (for example Paul Simon's *Graceland*, Deep Forest). Unlike her most noted Chinese predecessor, the Beijing-born, Hong Kong-based Faye Wong, who despite a considerable fan base outside the Chinese diaspora, seemed content to restrict herself to the domestic Mandarin and Cantonese-language markets of Cantopop and Mandapop, Sa Dingding has toured the world, and made considerable impact on international audiences through the World Music circuit.

One of the principal live performance networks for World Music is WOMAD (World of Music Arts and Dance) established in the UK in 1980 by singer Peter Gabriel. Gabriel also set up the Real World label in 1989, which has released albums by artists from all over the world, many recorded in the Real World studios in Bath, England. The current Real World catalogue runs to albums by some sixty artists from Australia to Finland. The fact that Gabriel, a former member of the British prog rock group Genesis, has collaborated with some of his artists, such as the Senegalese singer Youssou N'Dour, has sometimes drawn criticism for an inappropriate hybridisation of musical styles. Artificially constructed groups made up of artists on the Real World label such as the Afro-Celt Sound System, a combination of Irish and African musicians who produce a highly artificial mixture of traditional forms, have also been criticised. Sa Dingding is a recent recruit to the WOMAD circuit.

World Music has also generated numerous debates around issues of copyright and authenticity. An important precedent for these debates was a highly popular CD by Belgian producers Michel Sauchez and Eric Mouquet called *Deep Forest*. Released in 1992, this album contained a track entitled *Sweet Lullaby*, which sampled what were claimed to be UNESCO ethnographic recordings of "pygmy" [sic] chants over ambient-styled programmed keyboards and a drum machine. These chants, however, turned out to be uncredited recordings of musicians from the Solomon Islands. Prominent ethnomusicologist Steven Feld (2000, p. 156) in an important essay about the recording, referred to it as "primitivist caricature" in its appropriation and subsequent distortion of a song called *Rorogwela* by a female singer from the Solomon Islands, Afunakwa. Needless to say, no royalties were paid to the singer/composer, whose music is part of an oral tradition, by the Deep Forest artists. Feld asked the "anxious question": "Is World Music a form of artistic humiliation, the price primitives pay for attracting the attention of moderns, for gaining entry into their world of representation?" (2000, p. 166).

The term World Music has had many detractors (eg. Andrew Ford, who has railed against it on ABC radio) who have claimed it is vague, amorphous and even insulting, but it has survived as a useful shorthand music-industry term. Simon Frith (2000, p. 320) has made a distinction between "globalisation from above" and "globalisation from below" in relation to the genre, the former being a music-industry-imposed marketing strategy, the latter involving initiatives by musicians from different ethnic backgrounds who exchange musical traditions, styles and techniques in an innovative way. These two concepts roughly correspond to two contrasting viewpoints as to whether World Music is merely a form of exoticism or musical tourism which has contributed to the global homogenisation of ethnic musics, a frequent "anxiety"; or a vehicle for the proliferation and increased distribution of global musical diversity which has occurred on a grassroots level, and cause for "celebration." The terms "anxiety" and "celebration" come from Feld (2000, p. 151), whose work in the field has been salutory. In either case, the term World Music has persisted, and music from increasingly remote parts of the world continues to be released to Western audiences even if power relations between musicians and record labels often remain problematic.

"A Chinese pioneer"

Sa Dingding is the most recent figure in World Music to generate anxieties and celebrations both in her music and in her interviews. These have largely occured in the UK, where, like Icelandic singer Björk, she appears to have established her principal European base. London *Times* journalist David Hutcheon (2008) first interviewed her in London in 2007 when she was an unknown artist whose record label was testing the waters for a possible release in the west of her two million-selling "first" album *The Life of 10,000 Things*. It was actually her second album — again, like Björk, she has dismissed the pop-dance album she released at the age of 18 as 'childish'. Her title is oddly reminiscent of the very Westernised 1993 Cantopop album *100,000 Whys*, by her compatriot Faye Wong, sometimes referred to as "the Chinese Madonna", which contained Chinese versions of Tori Amos's *Silence All These Years* and Sting's *Da Do Da Da*.

In a 2008 article on Sa Dingding, Hutcheon stated: "If we can enjoy *Crouching Tiger, Hidden Dragon* and indulge the musical eccentricities of Björk, shouldn't there be a place on our shelves for a Chinese 'pioneer' such as Sa Dingding?" His cultural frames of reference for her music subsequently became one of her most widely-used marketing slogans, and she went on to employ one of Björk's (and Madonna's, U2's and Massive Attack's) producers, Marius De Vries, on her second official album *Harmony*, released in 2010. This includes a remix by British house music and "progressive trance" guru Paul Oakenfold (with an inane "we are the world"-style English chorus, "hey hey let's sing along, come on come on let's live as one") and *Lucky Day*, a spoken word track in thickly-accented English. The album received a diverse range of judgments in reviews in UK newspapers, covering a spectrum between outright condemnation (one star in the *Sunday Times* from Clive Davis (2010): "bombastic, electro-fuelled anthems that often resemble a wrestling bout between Björk and Kate Bush") to cautious celebration (four stars from Hutcheon (2010) in the *Times*: "[t]hough the album has been dressed up in the finest silks for Western consumption, Dingding's roots shine through"). Andy Gill (2010) was cautiously positive in the *Independent*: "the pop consciousness and economy has been upped, the songs sound ripe for samplers with their strange vocals or effects, and the little girl voice of the debut has given way to a more confidently experimental singer"). Other comments ranged from *Mojo*'s "Yoko Ono would be proud, sounds like the next Bond theme" (which turned out to be Hutcheon yet again), to Robin Denselow (2010) in the *Guardian*: "Why doesn't Sa Dingding record a more acoustic album to prove there's a real personality behind all the bombast?." The equation of acoustic music with "real personality" and, implicitly, authenticity is an interesting one, as it is difficult to ignore the "overproduced" aspects of *Harmony*, which tends to swamp most tracks in electronic special effects, somewhat in the manner of Deep Forest. On the other hand, this has led to the use of the term "trip hop" to describe her music, and comparisons with Bristol innovators Massive Attack via producer De Vries.

To backtrack from *Harmony*: Hutcheon's 2008 feature interview in the *Times* celebrated Sa Dingding's return to London in triumph, pursued by a media pack, riding the celebratory wave of the Beijing Olympics, and performing, in what *Sunday Times* reviewer Clive Davis described as a "schlock-ridden display" (2010), at the Royal Albert Hall. The occasion was her receiving the 2008 BBC Radio 3 World Music Award for the Asia-Pacific region. Her first album, re-titled *Alive* — one-word titles being cool, if somewhat bland in this case — had introduced her in its publicity as "an unprecedented and mysterious artist." To Hutcheon, she had all the visual hallmarks of a pop star worth celebrating: "unnervingly good-looking, with her long hair tied in a topknot, Dingding exudes the assured air of a pop star who refuses to be caught off duty, who views Kylie as a part-timer" (2008). This rather incongruous reference to Kylie was to re-emerge when she performed at WOMADeladie in Australia. The BBC Award duly became the crowning achievement of Sa Dingding's World Music career, and was used in her CV as a cultural endorsement legitimising and cel-

FIGURE 1 — Sa Dingding in self-created traditional Chinese mode (Daly, 2008).

ebrating her status on the worldwide WOMAD circuit, which is, after all, a very British institution with inevitable colonialist overtones.

There was one snag in her London triumph, however, which caused some anxiety. Asked by the British media for her views on Tibet, she answered "I am Chinese, so I definitely support our government policy on this issue." She later added: "[p]eople see me standing for Chinese culture, and it does not matter if this means Mongolian, Han, Tibetan or any other. They are all part of Chinese culture" (in Hutcheon, 2008). This led to the withdrawal of an invitation for her to perform at the 2008 Glastonbury rock festival, as he was considered too "controversial." As Hutcheon (2008) commented, "One wonders whether [US rapper] Jay-Z was interrogated about his thoughts on Iraq before being handed [the Glastonbury] headlining slot."

Linguistically *Alive*

Alive was released in the west through major label Universal on Wrasse Records, a British World Music label formed in September 1998 by Ian Ashbridge, formerly head buyer at HMV and marketing director of A&M (UK). The Wrasse roster is broad, including a slew of popular World Music African artists such as Ladysmith Black Mambazo, King Sunny Ade, Fela Kuti, Amadou and Mariam, along with the Italian singers Paolo Conte and Zucchero, and even US pop artists such as the Village People. The music of Sa Dingding, the label's first Chinese artist, was described on Wrasse's website as "Chinese electronica", a questionable claim if one compares her to largely British exponents of this genre such as Orbital, the Prodigy, Aphex Twin, the Chemical Brothers, Underworld and Massive Attack(prior to De Vries' production credit). The intention appears to market her as exotic but familiar, and not just confined to World Music, like Björk, some of whose music can be read as electronica, thanks to the producers and musicians she has worked with.

Alive features Dingding singing her own compositions in Sanskrit and her own "self-created" language as well as in Mandarin, in a rather child-like voice, comparable to Björk, as well as US harpist, "new folk" and indie music darling Joanna Newsom (Figure 1). She also plays the zheng (Chinese twenty-one-stringed zither), the Mongolian horse-head fiddle and some dense, echoing percussion, which is used to dramatic effect. As the BBC Radio 3 website added:

> ...folk melodies played on zheng, bamboo flute and ma tou qin (horsehead fiddle) mesh with electric guitars, keyboard washes and digital beats that suggest the influence of seminal trip hoppers Massive Attack one moment and Tibetan monks the next (Lusk, 2008).

Again, the use of a well-known Western musical reference point serves to cement her music in the familiar, misleadingly suggesting user-friendly dance beats mixed with exotic Asian chants. But the BBC Radio 3 website blurb also added a dissonant note: "[a]s with last year's Chinese nominee Dadawa, there's some controversy over Sa Dingding's use of Tibetan music" (Lusk, 2008). This degree of anxiety was no doubt important in polarising opinion about her and in encouraging her advocates to rush to her defence. Dadawa, a highly exoticised Chinese singer who first gained attention in the west in 1996 for her ambient, new-age Tibetan folk-inspired album *Sister Drum*, followed by *Voices from the Sky* (1998), had returned to the World Music scene after a long silence in 2006 with *Seven Days*. In this album her Tibetan folk influences had been purged and replaced with more orthodox Chinese melodies. Clearly Sa Dingding and her spin doctors had learned Dadawa's lesson and tried to play down the Tibetan influences—hence the "self created language" — although *Alive* does contain one song, *Holy Incense* in a "Tibet Version." On the other hand, her preference for mantras seems to reflect her Buddhist and dyana yoga interests as well as increasing the exotic new age factor attractive to many World Music devotees. The elegantly produced CD jacket of *Alive* plays up the hieroglyphic design aspects of the lyrics for the Western reader/listener, and features a series of highly exoticised photos displaying her own designer-modified traditional Chinese costumes. These are reminiscent of Faye Wong at her most fashion conscious, when she employed Björk's designer Alexander McQueen. Sa Dingding also wears Middle Eastern-style veils and headscarves in some photos, to emphasise a self-Orientalising sense of "mystery" as well as to enhance the "eye candy" factor (Figure 2).

She has explained that the invented language is there purely in the interests of authenticity, as the song *Lagu Lagu* comes from an ethnic minority in the Yunnan province, who are of Himalayan origin and speak a Tibetan-Burmese dialect. She felt

FIGURE 1 — Sa Dinging in self-Orientalising mode (Lusk, 2008).

it would be theft to appropriate their language, but wanted to promote their culture to a wider audience, most of who would be unaware of the existence of the Lagu. There are of course precedents for this kind of glossolalia: Björk's "wordless vocalisations", in which, as Nicola Dibben argues:

> The effect on listeners of singing without words is that it can suggest authentic emotional expression: non-lexical singing taps into a common cultural belief in the 'natural' and spontaneous character of the singing voice, in contrast to the perceived rationality (2009, p. 103).

Icelandic rock group Sigur Rós, enormously popular among indie rock enthusiasts worldwide, occasionally sing in "Hopelandic", an invented language, which Dibben distinguishes, rather contentiously, from Björk's wordless singing as a "refusal of language and naming that is part of the international language of rock." Dibben argues that "Björk's wordless singing often occurs at climactic moments in tracks, where it has a heightened expressive effect" (2009, p. 186). This is probably because Björk sings predominantly in English, whereas Sigur Rós's lingua franca is Icelandic. Arguably glossolalia has a similar effect in Sigur Rós' music, but it is difficult, if not impossible, for non-Icelandic speakers to distinguish between Icelandic and Hopelandic. Both they and Björk draw on the fact that the majority of their global audience do not understand Icelandic, just as Sa Dingding plays on the inability of most of her Western listeners to understand Chinese or its numerous dialects.

All appear to have drawn on the example of the British duo the Cocteau Twins, whose glossolalia was an integral part of their ethereal musical soundscape, which Simon Reynolds referred to as "oceanic rock": "Attracted to expanses (the sea, the sky, the desert, the tundra) in which self-consciousness evaporates as the borders of the self dissolve" (1990, p. 127). Faye Wong was similarly influenced by the Cocteau Twins, even recording with them, and also singing in her own invented language (see Mitchell, 2001). To make a slightly cynical observation, one of the advantages of singing in an exotic language such as Icelandic or Chinese, or an invented language, is that it leaves the audience "lost in translation", and free to immerse themselves in the sound of the language and let their imagination wander in a soundscape unimpeded by semantic meaning. One of the most dispiriting by-products of the World Music circuit is that many artists are persuaded to abandon their native language and sing in English, for largely commercial reasons, with often banal results which merely detract from the pleasures of the music.

"Deep China"

Sa Dingding has nominated her favourite Western influences as Deep Forest, Peter Gabriel and Björk, which situates her clearly in the World Music market, but with a pop-fashion orientation aimed at the hipper end of the Western market. So it comes as no surprise that at this point Eric Mouquet of Deep Forest briefly re-enters the picture. After working on projects entitled "Deep Africa" and "Deep Brasil [sic]", in 2008 he announces a collaboration with Sa Dingding to be called "Deep China." To date there are two tracks: the first was *Won't Be Long*, a soporific time-stretched ballad sung by Mouquet in English backed by keyboard washes, augmented by segments of Sa Dingding's highly dramatic-sounding vocalisations and echoing percussions. This was recorded in 2008, and was downloadable for one Euro "to help the Tsunami's victims in China." *Deep Love*, released in January 2010, is a slow song sung entirely by Sa Dingding, accompanied by clunky drums and piano and a Chinese flute, which sounds like any number of mediocre Cantopop releases of the 1990s. Despite the proclamations of "depth", the result is banality and superficiality of astounding proportions. Presumably (and hopefully) this will be as "deep" as the project gets. As Feld notes, "the existence and success of World Music returns to one of globalisation's basic economic clichés: the drive for more and more markets and market niches" (2000, p. 167).

Reception at WOMADelaide and beyond: Lost in translation?

For Sa Dingding's performance at WOMADelaide in 2009, the promotional blurb, penned by Nigel Williamson, was headlined "Diva with unique voice and mind-boggling frocks." It placed particular emphasis on the "eye candy" costume factor, reproducing a slightly garbled version of earlier British press releases, adding a "diva" factor:

> She's been called China's answer to Björk or Kate Bush and her music described as 'Crouching Tiger, Hidden Dragon scored by The Cocteau Twins'. Meanwhile, her extraordinary frocks excite almost as much comment as her remarkable voice. That Sa Dingding has that indefinable diva quality is evident in almost everything about her. Combining traditional Chinese folk music with Western electronica and other influences, she creates a richly layered ethereal tapestry of sound…As for those eye-catching frocks, they're all her own design, too (Williamson, 2009).

The "ethereal" connotations may have set off alarm bells in some, as would the reference to Kate Bush, who had previously also been closely associated with Peter Gabriel, suggesting something of an "Asian Enya." Clearly these anxieties could be partially alleviated by the visual spectacle, which was indeed extraordinary. Commenting after the event on 7 March 2009 in a podcast, Natalie O made the perhaps inevitable comparison with Kylie:

> … was wowed by Sa Ding Ding (she is like the Chinese Kylie Minogue, I tell you – so many costume changes and hot male dancers).

No anxieties here, just pure pop pleasure. Reviewing WOMADelaide for the US website *Pop Matters*, Deanne Sele commented that what set Sa Dingding apart from other performers at the festival was her apparent insistence that people sit and listen rather than dance to her music, since she had already provided the dance element:

> 'The D in WOMAD is for dance', is the line the announcers use. It usually works … Most of the musicians apparently preferred an audience who stood and danced or clapped, but not Sa Dingding. Why should she? What kind of dance could you do to this crooning, floating pan-Chinese electronica? You could wave your arms in ripples, look noble or thoughtful, drift gracefully sideways like a jellyfish, perhaps, but there'd

be no clapping, no jumping, none of those dances that go down well among masses of casual strangers. The only person who danced to Sa Dingding was Sa Dingding herself, in tandem with three men who came onstage with her, dressed in loose trousers and in strips of white gauze worn across their chests like bandoliers. Holding crimson fans as long as their forearms they performed acrobatics in formation, snapping the fans shut on the beat with a sharp ssssth-clack! as if a dozen umbrellas were being closed in unison (2009).

No anxiety here either, just contemplative pleasure in the visual and aural spectacle of a performance of "crooning, floating pan-Chinese electronica", a triumph of the ethereal factor. WOMADelaide is, after all, a haven for devotees of the spectacle of World Music, and as such a relatively anxiety-free zone where performances from anywhere in the world are always acceptable, the more exotic and spectacular the better.

For a subsequent performance in Australia at the Sydney Opera House, Sa Dingding was promoted as

> the exotic Sa Dingding … a richly layered tapestry of the ethereal, escapist, eclectic and simply unforgettable … with engaging beauty and graceful reverence, Ding Ding makes getting 'lost in translation' a wonderful experience in unexpected pleasure. Signed to Universal Music, she is a very special choice to lead China onto the world stage (*Sydney Opera House*, 2009).

The "lost in translation" reference may have set off alarm bells, but the reference to her "lead[ing] China onto the world stage" was a factor not emphasised in previous publicity. In Chinese-Australian photographer Anna Zhu's "Shutter Stutter" blog, staginess got the better of authenticity, and Dingding's imposed role as a musical ambassador for China was unconvincing:

> …everything just seemed a little too staged.
>
> From the choreography to the costumes, everything just screamed this is traditional Chinese, as if the audience wouldn't get it otherwise. She uses a mish-mash of Asian elements familiar to Westerners that don't quite add up — Kung fu performers (eastern China), pipa (east China), erhu (north-east China), she sings like a Tibetan, dances like a southerner, was born in Mongolia, uses some Sanskrit lyrics, and poses like a buddhavista [sic]. She is trying to embody all that is obviously Asian, and it doesn't sit true with me.
>
> I feel … that Ding Ding has very consciously and aggressively marketed herself for a global audience, and in the process has lost credibility. Sure, … everything's pretty to look at but the talent was somewhat lacking. Voices like Ding Ding's are a dime a dozen in China — check out the variety shows, those singers just haven't been marketed like she has.
>
> I think the real cringe moment was when she sang a tooth-melting ballad accompanied by her pianist — it sounded like it came straight from a Taiwan-pop songbook. [this song may have been 'Deep Love'].
>
> I was disappointed. I was expecting something a lot more authentic (Zhu, 2009).

Zhu's anxieties about Sa Dingding's authenticity relate to her perception of a homogenised "Asian mish mash" which amounts to little more than musical tourism. These were not shared, however, by Philippa Barr in her review in *Inthemix*, which saw the multicultural plurality of the Opera House audience as a reflection of the pan-Asian heterogeneity and multifaceted fabric of Sa Ding Ding's costumes and hybrid musical styles, and as an expression of the diversity of the "new China":

> Sa Dingding is new China…She weaves together traditional Chinese lutes and drums, multiple languages, and electronica, becoming a symbol of tradition, modernity and super hip styling. Her audience are as gathered as the seams of her multilayered costume. A few bohemians in long skirts, artistic women with bold red lipstick and conservative Chinese families. Dingding drew a surprisingly pan-Asian crowd, I saw many Indian families and heard conversations in Japanese and Indonesian as I waited to go inside. But it was mostly overseas Chinese who wanted to see Sa Dingding. … Sa Dingding's heterogenous style reflects Chinese cultural policy. Instead of a China where Han Chinese rule alone, Sa Dingding represents a China threaded through with many different cultures and languages (Barr, 2009).

Metaphors of weaving aside, "New China" seems apposite: a homogenised yet also heterogenous World Music pop star who can be associated with Björk as well as appeal to dedicated multicultural followers of more traditional forms of World Music. This may not be an especially "deep" reading of what "new China" may constitute, but it does suggest that Chinese pop music is shaking off the often embarrassing mantle of Cantopop and Mandapop. Sa Dingding may still ring false for some, in a similar way to the hyper-elevated antics of Kate Bush (let us not forget her mawkish venture into Australian Aboriginal music with Rolf Harris in *The Dreaming*), or the superficial chameleon fashion moves of Kylie. She may even match the exuberantly childlike, elfin vocal and visual excesses of Björk, but she makes up in musical and visual dexterity and imagination for what she loses in capitulating to sometimes banal Western electronica and pop influences. And therefore remains an intriguingly ambivalent figure, and a representative of the "new China", which like "World Music", has become essentially a marketing slogan, with its own anxieties and celebrations: "The New China: Opportunity or Threat?", for example, was the title of a discussion which took place on US public radio station NPR in July 2005 (Conan, 2005) emphasising the economic factors that underlie the continued existence of World Music.

References

Barr, P. (2009). Sa Dingding @ Sydney Opera House, Sydney (7/3/09). *Inthemix*, 12 March. Retrieved from http://www.inthemix.com.au/events/reviews/41915%20Sa_Dingding_Sydney_Opera_House_Sydney_07030.

Conan, N. (2005). The New China: Opportunity or Threat?. *NPR*. Retrieved from http://www.npr.org/templates/ zstory/story.php?storyId=4759625.

Daly, Marie Clare (2008). Sa Dingding stands out with her blend of cross-cultural influences. *Metro*. Retrieved from http://www.metro.co.uk/metrolife/238412-sa-dingding-stands-out-with-her-blend-of-cross-cultural-influences.

Davis, C. (2010, March 7). Review of Sa Dingding. *Harmony, Sunday Times*.

Denselow, R. (2010, 11 March). Review of Sa Dingding. *Harmony, The Guardian*.

Dibben, N. (2009). *Björk*. London: Equinox.

Feld, S. (2000). A Sweet Lullaby for World Music. *Public Culture* 12 (1), 145-171.

Frith, S. (2000). The Discourse of World Music. In G. Born and D. Hesmondhalgh (Eds.), *Western Music and its Others: Difference, representation, and appropriation* (pp. 305-322). Berkeley: University of California Press.

Gill, A. (2010, March 5). Review of Sa Dingding. *Harmony, The Independent.*

Hutcheon, D. (2008, April 27). Sa Dingding, The Asian Björk. *Sunday Times.*

Hutcheon, D. (2010, March 13). Review of Sa Dingding. *Harmony, The Times.*

Lusk, J (2008). Sa Dingding. *BBC — Awards for world music 2008.* Retrieved from http://www.bbc.co.uk/radio3/worldmusic/a4wm2008/2008_sa_ding_ding.shtml.

Mojo magazine, March 2010.

Mitchell, T. (2002). Learning to love Cantopop: Musical inbetweenness in the Chinese Diaspora. In D. Crowdy, S. Homan and T. Mitchell (Eds.), *Musical In be-tween-ness: the Proceedings of the 8th IASPM Australia-New Zealand Conference* (pp. 87-97). Sydney, N.S.W.: IASPM, Faculty of Humanities & Social Sciences, University of Technology.

Reynolds, S. (1990). *Blissed Out: The Raptures of Rock.* London: Serpent's Tail.

Sele, D. (2009). Review of Womadelaide. *Pop Matters*, 31 March. Retrieved from http://www.popmatters.com/pm/feature/72359-womadelaide-2009.

Sydney Opera House. (2009). Retrieved from http://www.sydneyoperahouse.com/About/09EventMediaRelease_Hemispheres.aspx.

Williamson, Nigel (2009). Sa Dingding. Womad. Retrieved from http://womad.org/artists/sa-dingding/

Womadelaide. (2009). Retrieved from http://www.womadelaide.com.au.

Zhu, A. (2009). *Shutter Stutter,* March 9. Retrieved from http://www.annazhu.com/blog/?p=823.

CHAPTER
7

"Sounds Chinese": Musical meetings with China in contemporary Australia

Nicholas Ng

When I turned 15, I experienced a terrifying moment of darkness while preparing to sit for the AMEB (Australian Music Education Board) diploma in piano performance. So traumatic was the ordeal that I can no longer recall the compositions I was practising again and again to Virgo-driven perfection. I was the typical Asian piano-basher — starting at age four and rising at incredible speed to complete my piano grades, to play the Australian National Anthem at every school assembly, and to compete in piano competitions and eistoddfods. I was the apple of my family's eye, and the source of much angst amongst my younger cousins and Asian friends.

But it was not long into my adolescence that the passion I had for music-making, or what I thought was music-making at the time, completely dissipated. Gone was that feeling of excitement and satisfaction that came with every performance, when I bedazzled the people in my world with how fast and furiously loud I could play the piano: I had fallen out of love with music. Plagued by a host of hormonal issues, I was in particular, experiencing the need to recreate myself, musically and culturally.

To the dismay of my parents, who by that time had spent thousands of dollars on private piano tuition, I insensitively, but with great sincerity and conviction, bemoaned the fact that I knew nothing much about my culture, had never learnt a Chinese instrument, and why did they send me to piano lessons in the first place? Why not *guzheng* (Chinese twenty-one-stringed zither), or *erhu* (Chinese two-stringed fiddle)? Why, as I had discovered by listening to vast quantities of Chinese music cassettes and CDs, was so much of so-called traditional or authentic Chinese music harmonised with western chords, and often in very derivative ways?

Little did I know it at the time, but my overactive teenage mind was starting to discern the concepts of appropriation, colonisation and Anglo-American musical hegemony, terms that did not enter my vocabulary until "Modern Asian History Module 1" at Sydney University many years later. I see this period in my education as the beginnings of my opposition to being an ethnic "Other" in contemporary Australia. It was this internal conflict fuelled that my recovery from the piano to create a unique, space and place for my art governed by a certain cultural in-between-ess. This process has taken several years to develop and

Touching on issues of migration, identity, hybridity and appropriation, this paper reveals how the disciplines of ethnomusicology and composition helped remedy my "cultural crisis" of sorts by enabling me to shift my focus from when I am "from" to where I was "at", in the words of Ien Ang (2001). The ethnomusicological component of this discussion draws on original fieldwork conducted between 2003-2008 in three Chinese communities in Sydney. I focus on Chinese-Australians who have chosen to create a new home in Australia as opposed to diasporans who might be classed as "cosmopolitans" in their constant movement from country to country. Applying certain cultural theories, I reveal how these ethno-specific centres, which function as loci of transformation in a fast-changing contemporary climate, have come to influence my artistic voice as a first generation Chinese-Australian composer. It is this ongoing passion for rediscovering, redefining and revitalising notions of Chineseness that in many ways led to my curatorship of the four-day event, Encounters: Musical meetings between Australia and China (6–9 May 2010).

Chinese encounters

Not long after departing from the piano, I quickly picked up the *erhu* (Chinese two-stringed bowed fiddle) at the recommendation of Clive Lane, my high school music teacher. It was a decision that changed my musical life forever.[1] Lessons were conducted in Mandarin and English in the living room of Chen Xuebing, a notable performer from the mainland of China who immigrated to Australia as part of the late-1980s intellectual mass exodus. Ms Chen's name was familiar to me as a student of composition through her involvement in Nigel Westlake's *Roads to Xanadu* (1989-1990) project. I found the entire cognitive and cultural context of learning a Chinese instrument completely foreign to me, but I was happy to re-create myself in this new space as the erhu seemed to resonate with a certain familiarity within the core of my being in a way that I can only describe as primordial and innate/inherent. Playing what is regarded as a Chinese popular helped me claim ownership of a home culture I never knew and afforded me a certain level of Chineseness. I was fascinated to discover that despite its instant association with China, the erhu, and the entire *huqin* family of bowed fiddles, is descended from the nomadic Turkic speaking Xi people. "Hu" in fact means "barbarian" (Stock, 1993, pp. 91–92).

In the years to follow, I went from wanting to play "authentic" Chinese music to associating with active and willing participants of my home culture, who did not necessarily play music that could be considered traditional. From 2003 to 2008, I found myself engaged in an extension of an undergraduate ethnomusicological project that

I began with Dr Aline Scott-Maxwell, then at the University of Sydney Music Department. This was the doctoral study (conducted at the Australian National University School of Music) of two genres of Chinese sacred music performed by Chinese immigrants in Sydney. The interdisciplinary framework suggested by Dr Stephen Wild and supported by Emeritus Professor Larry Sitsky involved using the music I collected in the field as the inspiration and basis for various commissions.

The two sacred music cultures I studied were the Australian Catholic Chinese community and Buddha's Light International Association, Sydney. Both music-cultures were developed in East and Southeast Asia before their arrival in Sydney, where further developments took place. Beyond my doctoral work, I conducted periods of fieldwork with members of The Australian Chinese Teo Chew Association (henceforth TACTCA). These three ethno-specific organisations comprise Chinese immigrants and their descendants with diverse migration histories and settlement patterns. Countries of origin range from Mainland China, Taiwan, the Hong Kong SAR, Laos, Cambodia, Vietnam, Singapore, Malaysia and East Timor. Participating in an environment close to one's home culture continues to be an important activity for these Chinese migrants in contemporary Sydney since Chinese cultural and religious centres function as points of stability where community members may escape being an ethnic "Other."

Issues of race are very much embedded in our psyches. Caroline Knowles (2003) observes that:

> Race and ethnicity operate on the surface and in the deep structures of our world...Intricately woven into the social landscapes in which we live...[i]t is outside on our streets and inside ourselves...[i]t couldn't be closer to home or further away (p. 1).

Based on my observations in the field and personal experiences as a migrant child, the stigma of being different ethnically is felt on a day-to-day basis for many Chinese immigrants and their descendants. Carole Tan has written extensively on this issue with the position of Chinese Australians as "different" and "Other" because of their visible ancestry, a fact "pointed out to them in no uncertain terms" (2003, p. 101).

To assist migrants with the adjustment process in new areas of settlement, Chinese community centres across the globe are active in the provision of welfare, recreational, and where applicable, religious and ecumenical services. Community centres act as a refuge from racial ascription and help many Chinese migrants endure feelings of loss (Kuah-Pearce, 2006, p. 217). There is, for instance, financial loss due to an acute change in employment and environment (Mak & Chan, 1994). Further contestation of traditional values might follow with wives and teenage children finding employment to help support the family (ibid).[2] Diasporans across the age groups might experience an over-riding sense of cultural loss (Eng, 1999; Stein, 1981) with the possible consequence of home culture abandonment known as "passing" (Chan, 2005). The various efforts to cope with this and other complex issues of migration in ethno-specific cultural centres help locate and maintain the identity of diasporans in the process of assimilation and adaptation (Kuah-Pearce, 2006, p. 219; Lu, 2001; Scott, 1994; Wang, 1994; Warner & Wittner, 1998; Yang, 1999; Zhou

& Kim, c2006). During my time in the field, I found music to be a major component of the various ritual and recreational activities that make up the everyday life of community members.

Music that "sounds Chinese"

Recent research has found that group participation in the re-creation of familiar sounds in Chinese communities helps maintain a sense of home in the new country (for instance, see Johnson (2005), Lau (2005) Lum (1996), Ng (2010), Ng (2011)). This is certainly the case in the ACCC and BLIA SYD, where pre-recorded or acoustically performed sacred music — consisting mostly of chant items and hymns — instill members with a sense of belonging to a common, myth, narrative, history and future (Hall, 1993; Suárez-Orozco, 2000). In addition to repertoire imported from Hong Kong and Taiwan that "sounds Chinese" despite western harmonisation and compositional forms, members of both communities have created newer genres of devotional music performable within and outside ritual. From fieldwork conducted since 2000, I have collected many hours of sacred music, primarily vocal, that reinforces the theories of Ebaugh & Chafetz (2000) and Herberg (1960) that identity formation in migrants is intrinsically linked to religion and religious practices. This repertory is currently sung in English, Cantonese and Mandarin.

In the ACCC, traditional Roman Catholic music imported from Hong Kong is preserved in the singing of monophonic and harmonised plainchant responses and hymns translated into Cantonese and Mandarin. Nineteenth century Westminster and Wesleyan hymns are also sung in these languages. The Roman Catholic Church's Second Vatican Council (1962-1965) promotion of the use of the vernacular (or the "vulgar tongues") rather than Latin and wordwide "enculturation" of the liturgy^2 is reflected in the ACCC. Children are given the catechism in English, and often sing English hymns. The Cantonese hymn *Our Lady of China* is very often sung during the weekly Benediction service (Figure 1), but of great popular interest in recent years is Eddie Ho's bilingual hymn, *Jesus Forever Reigns*. At important functions, the Mass becomes a trilingual affair with Mass Ordinaries sung in English and a selection of readings, hymns and prayers in Mandarin, Cantonese and English to cater for non-Chinese dignitaries and visitors at important community events.

A similar situation of secularisation is found in BLIA SYD, an organisational arm of the Fo Guang Shang order of Chan Buddhism formed by members of the laity. Pop hymns and Buddhist hip hop are performed at festivals and recreational events. *Harmonise* and *Stars and Clouds* are popular, newly composed English "hymns" written in rock ballad style with matching hand gestures. Such pop hymns are occasionally heard as processional music as part of the traditional liturgy, which consists mostly of liturgical chant in unison with Buddhist percussion instruments. Hence, a certain Dharma Functions and other religious services while BLIA SYD is an organisation well known for its political aptitude. Public functions are always attended by local members of parliament, dignitaries from the police force, and other influential

FIGURE 1 — Our Lady of China

members of society. In 2004, the NSW Police Band played the well-known *Ode to the Triple Gem*, written and arranged by the Order's Grand Master, Hsing Yun (Figure 2). The community, and its sister communities throughout Australia, strives to present a harmonious, environmentally-concerned and Australian Chinese image. Ritual is accompanied by traditional music taken from the homeland in the native tongue, while official prayers have since the 1980s been recited in Mandarin and then English.

"Sounds Chinese": Musical meetings with China in contemporary Australia

In both communities, religion and music, in addition to language, helps define one's self from the multicultural milieu. Edith Lo has been a choir member in the Cantonese-speaking congregation of the ACCC since 1985. A former president of the Chinese Catholic Pastoral Centre Choir, Edith Lo believes it important to exhibit her community's Chineseness at large events that are open to the public eye (personal communication, 2000). Chinese New Year Mass is one example. Each New Year, Chinese hymns complement an ancient Chinese rite for the veneration of ancestors.[3] The observation below could be said to be true of the function of music in the two sub-communities:

> [M]usic can be used increasingly as a means by which we formulate and express our individual identities. We use it not only to regulate our own everyday moods and behaviours, but also to present ourselves to others in the way we prefer (Hargreaves, Miell & Macdonald, 2002, p. 1).

As observed in the quotation above, music has the ability to affect the identity of an individual externally and internally. The types of songs one sings, for instance, help determine one's very sense of self. Such use of music extends to the individual's social and political surroundings. Unlike the words of national anthems, which are often "remembered well enough to forget to understand" (Kelen, 2003, p. 162), community members connect deeply with the meanings of the text, particularly of hymns using vocabulary and phrases from daily speech. Singing, often said to be exaggerated speech, about ecclesiastical matters in a group binds the minds and hearts of participants in the sacred space of the church or temple, and in venues there ethnic events take place. ACCC members enjoy "backyard" produced CDs of newly composed hymns (Chinese Catholic Pastoral Centre, 2000), while BLIA SYD devotees listen to

FIGURE 2 — Lion dancing equipment. Photograph by Nicholas Ng.

FIGURE 2 — Chinese chess. Photograph by Nicholas Ng.

professionally distributed anthologies of Mahayana chant, harmonised with western sythesised chords and new age relaxation sounds (Voice of the Ganges, 2002).

Despite the many differences between the two subgroups, we may find in the ACCC and BLIA SYD, the preservation of culture on the one hand and on the other, the attempt to modernise due to the pressures of migration. There is also the conscious, or perhaps, not so conscious choice of maintaining both old and new in the hybrid combination of homeland traditions the modern practices as a means for adaptation without allowing the past to fade into obscurity. The catalyst for such culturally revitalising and what we might call a forward-moving, progressive attitude comes in part from the need to resolve the sense of displacement that is part of the migrant's diaspora experience (Hall, 1993).

Sandwiched between a large mansion and the Sacred Heart Catholic Church in the infamous suburb of Cabramatta, TACTCA is a meeting place for diasporic Chinese hailing from Laos, Cambodia, Vietnam, Mainland China and various South East Asian countries. Their common link is the Teo Chew dialect and culture, which originates in the locality of Shantou in Guangdong Province. Figures 4–7 suggest a thriving traditional community with a strong political presence in wider Australian society. The karaoke club, dancing group, and integrated kung fu and lion dancing school are attended by many, and youtube clips[4] reveal the online popularity of lion dancing, an cultural art form in great demand throughout the larger Chinese community with its popular appeal to both young and old. Since the 1990s, TACTCA's lion dance troupe has been a regular performance act booked by BLIA SYD for functions held at the mother temple of Wollongong and in Sydney.

Meanwhile, TACTCA hosts and produces the annual *Chaoju Dasi* (Teo Chew operatic production), which involves local performers and specially invited guests from Shantou.

"Sounds Chinese": Musical meetings with China in contemporary Australia

FIGURE 3 — *Chaoju Dasi* musical instruments. Photograph by Nicholas Ng.

Operatic arias from epic legends and heart-breaking romances are accompanied by an ensemble of live musicians. At first glance, this genre appears to be flourishing as a traditional artform and like the sacred vocal repertory of the ACCC and BLIA, participants engage in the highly efficacious "ethnic event", which involves the thickening of ethnic identity during which traditions are not simply repeated but selectively re-enacted (see Chan, 2005, p. 18; De Vos & Romanucci-Ross, 1982; Rosaldo, 1988).

On closer examination, the ethnic events such as the *Chaoju Dasi* only happens once a year, and although certain members of the community take vocal lessons and study their arias with great dedication, they are but a few such enthusiasts. The core ensemble of the instrumental music tradition consists of a small handful of elderly men who meet to play chess on Mondays with a general rehearsal on Wednesdays. These are old, tired and worn out musicians; it is not uncommon for ill health to prevent them from rehearsing. Although their passion for music remains, the natural tuning, antiquated folk instruments and nasal vocal timbres do not resonate at all with young Australian Teo Chew kids. The plethora of operatic stories, although archetypal in essence, are filled with musical imagery and metaphors from an irrelevant imperial past that are of little significance and interest to those who prefer singing karaoke and listening to popular Chinese or western music. The end of this particular tradition is almost certain.

"Happy hybridity"

Clearly, much of the music of the ACCC and BLIA SYD has assumed hybrid characteristics. Members take pride in a cultural identity advocated by locally composed compositions that have emerged out of the pulling together of elements from the "East and West." It is a kind of "happy hybridity", to borrow from Jacqueline Lo (2000, p. 153), generated as a stabilising function to settle cultural differences. In contrast to the imminent cultural stagnation of TACTCA, community members of the ACCC and BLIA SYD have generated new hybrid sounds of by which to identify themselves as settled migrants in contemporary Australia.

Sustainability through hybridity in their ongoing negotiation of culture and identity, however, comes at a price — in the creation of a hybrid species, only certain are elements taken from the parent sources while the rest are filtered out. But where things are discarded, there is always the creation of something new. Here, we approach a constantly negotiated balance between parent cultures in a kind of deliberate "happy hybridity", wherein ethnic actors choose which elements to infuse or develop, and which to discard (Ang, 2003; Lo, 2000). In Australia, this has led to many interesting cultural forms, particularly in food and popular culture — Australia is the only country in the world where one can buy unusually large and deep fried Chinese pork dumplings known as Dim Sims from suburban Lebanese-run milk bars.

As an Australian-Chinese artist battling with my own sense of cultural identity, I was inspired by the way community members have created a new artform in the negotiation of group and individual identities. Feeling a strong connection with them with the need to create a personalized sound world. I could claim as my own, I formulated my own processes of happy hybridity. This exercise involved drawing on certain musical elements from my field recordings in the creation of folio of mostly commissioned for a range of instruments and premiered in a variety of contexts.

FIGURE 7A — In Meditation, quotation 1.

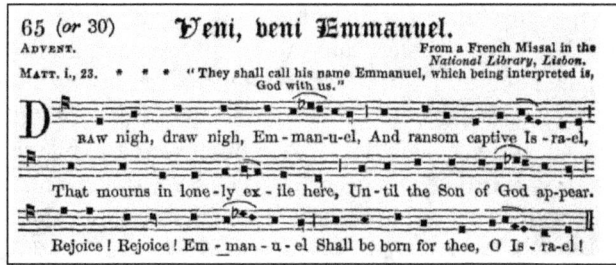

FIGURE 7A — Veni, veni Emmanuel. An extract in neumes, still used in Catholic church choirs (after Neale and Helmore, 1856, p. 131).

In Meditation

In 2004, I wrote an electro-acoustic work for the De Viana Music Liturgical Prize at St Christopher's Cathedral, Archdiocese of Canberra and Goulburn. *In Meditation* for erhu and electronics was premiered at the cathedral and awared an equal first prize. Written for the season of Advent or Lent, the erhu melody of *In Meditation* begins with a direct quotation of the Gregorian plainchant hymn *Veni, Veni Emanuel* ("O Come, O Come Emanuel") conjoined with the Paschal *Exultet* (literally "Rejoice"),[5] sung as part of the liturgy during the Easter Vigil of Holy Saturday.[6] The erhu part played to the pre-recorded and mastered soundscape is quasi-improvisatory and performed with great rubato. (It is my intention for this tune to be rendered in a slightly different way with each performance.) Hence the quotation is almost obscured at times but recognisable to those familiar with the plainchant. I have taken the following extract from *In Meditation*, illustrate its relationship with the original plainchants in Figures 7A-D.

This composition was based on sounds and timbres taken from the ACCC and BLIA SYD. Here, I integrated acoustic and electro-acoustic compositional methods through the sampling and manipulation of WAV files in the digital editing program Logic. Various sounds were chosen to form an accompanying palette in relation to the focus of the composition, which is a meditation on the second coming of Christ. This topic is quite prevalent in Roman Catholic teaching and consequently appears in much of the sacred text that is set to music in the ACCC. Prior to mastering, digital effects such as reverb, delay, distortion and transposition were inserted into the soundtrack. The texture comprises amongst other sounds a deep and earthy cello drone, electronically processed to create a mysterious resonance. This drone repre-

FIGURE 8 — Amen. A rendition often heard in Roman Catholic plainsong and hence regularly intoned in ACCC services.

sents God as eternity, just as the concept of eternity is symbolised by an underlying drone in the music of Middle Eastern and Indian cultures, and in the didgeridoo of Australian Aboriginal music. Other complementary sounds not necessarily from Christianity may be heard above the drone such as the Chinese Buddhist bell-gong (or temple bowl), which for me alludes to something sacred. While the bell-gong is one of the most prominent sounds heard at BLIA SYD rituals and services, I am aware that it might not be as readily available in orchestras and ensembles. Hence, I have specified for a Tibetan singing bowl to be used where a Buddhist bell-gong is unobtainable. The deep drum represents the beating of Christ's heart (and ours); and, at risk of gross intercultural hyperextension, the *muyu* or wooden fish symbolise the wood of his cross. Much reverb and delay was added for a damp, watery timbre suggesting early Christian worship in caves and during times of oppression.

The pain of such religious oppression is still a problem today and was brought to my immediate attention during ACCC prayers for what was often referred to as the "wounded Church in China." I chose to embody this pain in the distorted drone singing in the latter half of the piece. Here, I have altered my voice electronically as part of the digitally manipulated soundtrack with reverb and echo effects to suggest singing in the dry, barren lands of early Christendom (where it is rumoured that the erhu's origins lie), and the desert country through which the religion made its way to China. A non-standard and "avant-gardish" rising trill of a minor third may be heard towards the end of the piece, which ends with the standard melismatic plainchant response *Amen*, intoned on the erhu (Figure 8). This composition is in a sense written at the intersection of both my research areas into Chinese Catholicism and Buddhism.

The Great Invocation

In this composition, I used the melodic and textural essence of homophonic Buddhist chant that I encountered in the liturgical singing of BLIA SYD. In the parts of the chorus and small ensemble, I placed an indirect quotation of the original chorus of nuns with the bass part beginning the incantation with a slightly meter-less feel. This reflects the traditional way in which the lead singer or celebrant will intone the opening syllables. However, I have changed this entry somewhat through rhythmic diminution, while the sacred words chanted are taken from the Spiritualist prayer "The Great Invocation." The word "Om", which I borrowed from Buddhism (and Hinduism), is a featured syllable in this piece and may be heard in the beginning and at cathartic points in the composition. It is said that this sacred syllable summarises the *Boreboluomiduo Xinjing* ("Heart of Perfect Wisdom Sutra", otherwise known as the "Heart Sutra") and therefore the entire Mahayana Buddhist doctrine in fifty characters. Instead of directly copying the melodic contour of each homophonic chant line, I have used an approximated contour to recreate something of the essence of the chant (see Figures 9A-B). In *The Great Invocation*, I have also inserted a string effect with the violins bowed behind the bridge to evoke a mood of an ethereal or mystical nature.

FIGURE 9A — The Great Invocation. Indirect quotation from the Boreboluomiduo Xinjing ("Heart of Perfect Wisdom Sutra"). An extract from the score performed by the Sangita Choir and Instrumental Ensemble (with Susanne Peck, conductor).

FIGURE 9B — *Boreboluomiduo Xinjing ("Heart of Perfect Wisdom Sutra"). A partial transcription of the opening performed as part of a Buddhist*

I was compelled to write *The Great Invocation* to explore various instrumental textures and timbres, thereby developing and extending my orchestration technique. Moments of ambience (produced acoustically or electro-acoustically) for me represent the presence, or experience of the Divine. Apart from the ethereal sound mentioned earlier (produced by bowing the violin behind the bridge), there are moments of cello harmonic drones and a reversed cymbal on a timpani during a pitch bend. I have also prescribed a nasal vocal quality for in the solo soprano and alto line in imitation of Chan Buddhist singing as illustrated in Figure 10.

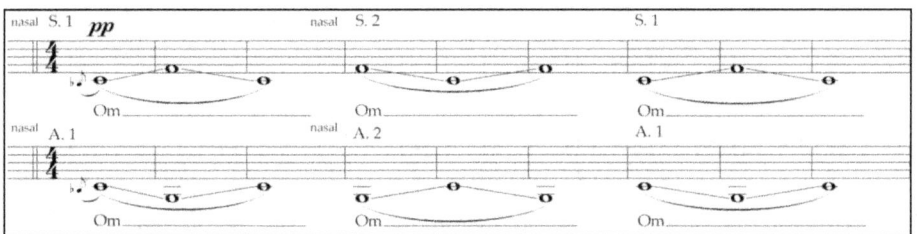

FIGURE 10 —*The Great Invocation*. Prescription of nasal timbres in imitation of the timbre of BLIA SYD liturgical singing

My fascination between vibrato and straight tones in Chinese and other genres of non-western music percolates my writing for voice and stringed instruments. Influenced by the unique vocal timbre of *fanbai*, the liturgical chant of BLIA SYD in contrast to the more western vibrato of church hymnody heard in ACCC, I employed different modes of vibrato in *The Great Invocation* for dramatic effect, one of which was the "pressed vibrato" as opposed to the regular rolled method. I have extended this technique to include a vibrato of increasing width, which may be found in the following excerpt from the full score (see Figure 11).

Slides and ornaments are a major focus point in my musical consciousness since both elements are characteristic of the erhu. They are also quite prevalent in Chan Buddhist singing. Consequently slides and ornaments may be found in my compositions. They involve a smooth transition from one pitch to the next as an instrumental portamento and rhetorical effect. Interesting, such effects are almost always questioned by performers at first reading. This is understandable as such effects, excluding the romantic expressive portamenti, until the time of Chou Wen-chung and Isang Yun, were not particularly a feature of western orchestral writing. In his unpublished book, *The Nature of Melody*, Henry Cowell (in Rao, 2004) discussed the slide in great detail:

> They [slides] are differentiated so as to express the finest shades of meaning in the cultivated Oriental systems of music. In our vocal music, they are a sort of skeleton in the closet. It is physically impossible for the human voice to proceed from one pitch to another, legato, without sliding. But singers, who often use sliding tones in wretched taste, are taught that to slide is lacking in musicality; and so they slide so rapidly that it is unnoticeable, after 'proper' cultivation...in all vocal music, and on all stringed and other instruments capable of sliding, they are used often according to certain conventions; but these conventions are a matter of feeling. They have not been formulated into works, and are not usually taught (pp. 136-141).

I agree with Cowell that the notation of slides is quite vague; it is useful for performers to know the duration for the length of the slide. Performers may find the notation of slide duration in contemporary music somewhat ambiguous, and often ask "when do we begin sliding?" and "for how long?" My usual response in rehearsal is for them to follow as marked while temporally interpreting and relating to the visual aspect of the slide. This is especially important in instances when the portamento begins after

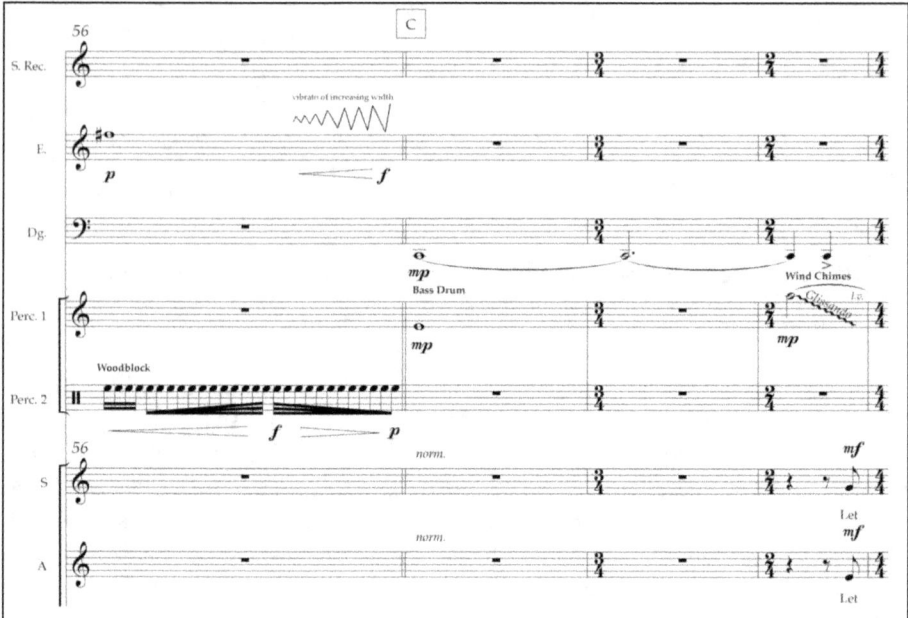

FIGURE 11 —*The Great Invocation*. An example of vibrato played on the erhu (bar 56).

the note is sounded. In some instances, the performer is given freedom to do as he or she pleases, however, in the case of The Great Invocation and the pieces contained in this folio, I have stipulated for slides to begin approximately halfway through the overall value of the note. Figure 12 is an excerpt from this section, in which tenor 1 and bass 1 are instructed to inflect upwards with a "slight pitch bend" (slightly sharp). This is inspired by the highly elastic Chan Buddhist singing with its unique pitch bends and inflections.

The techniques highlighted in the analysis above have enabled me to integrate aspects of my fieldwork with other musical and non-musical elements in the creation of my compositional voice to date. This music that may or may not "sound Chinese" was produced in the highly indeterminate third space of hybridity — much like the music of my research subjects. Based on the multi-layered and highly syncretic music of the ACCC and BLIA SYD, my compositions may be perceived as "a hybridity within a hybridity." That is, I have appropriated what is already hybrid into the genre of art music in response to the concept of Othering and positionality in my understanding of what is same, yet different regarding my cultural heritage. This approach was born out of my own sense of indeterminacy as a culture bearer. I have drawn on sonic devices in Chinese music that have long captivated me, as have the sacred songs of the Chan Buddhist (BLIA SYD) and Roman Catholic (ACCC) traditions. The exercise of translating non-western elements into various performance contexts has been vital in my current level of development and understanding of what may be

"Sounds Chinese": Musical meetings with China in contemporary Australia

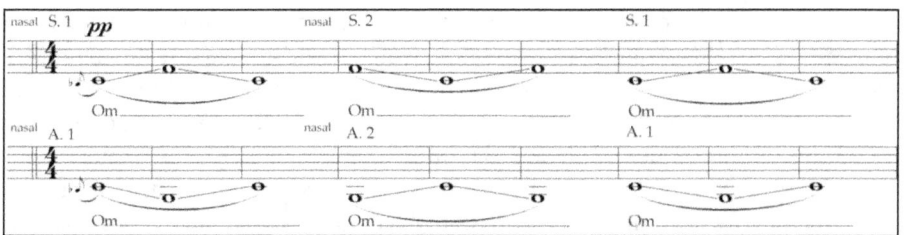

FIGURE 12 — *The Great Invocation. Slight pitch bends in the solo tenor and bass.*

written across a wide range of instruments. The fact that the various inflections and types of sliding tones I have borrowed are often new to performers suggests that writing in this way opens up new possibilities for the future; it certainly is a means of expanding both the performers' and my own musical knowledge and experience in the arena of contemporary art music.

Concluding thoughts

My search for cultural identity has led me on a journey into the world of Chinese music and beyond. As an Asian Australian artist and researcher, I have certainly benefited from having the "right sort of face" that functions as a kind of "cultural passport", a term coined by that scholar Dean Chan (2000). Today, I continue my observations of both the ACCC and BLIA SYD while tapping into the music of various ethno-specific community groups as a source of inspiration for my creative work. Clearly, ethnic communities serve to help mitigate feelings of loss and Othering in Australia. A potent method of cultural self-expression is through music. In the case of the ACCC and BLIA SYD, sacred chant and hymnody transports participants from the present to the home country through the re-enactment of familiar rituals and rites as part of an ethnic event. In recent years, both communities have exhibited signs of hybridity in their regular worship, a reflection on the negotiation between the two extremes of ethnic retention (resulting in cultural stagnation) and assimilation (resulting in cultural loss). English, and the composition of new hymnody based on western compositional structures are now in regular practice. One community intent on cultural preservation is TACTCA. In a similar way, popular cultural forms such as karaoke and the Lion Dance continue to flourish, while the traditional Teo Chew opera has been preserved as an antiquated art form that will survive only as long as its fast-aging practitioners.

Henry David Thoreau is credited with this saying: "[i]t is as hard to see one's self as to look backwards without turning around." My practice is as much about self-discovery as it is about music. Like so many other art forms, composition is a practice that requires much time, reflection and thought. While the path towards refinement of style is as yet winding, narrow and long, I am content to have found my current voice, my sound, my own particular noise. An ethnomusicological study combined with a musicological analysis of compositions, I hope for my practice-based project to be of significance in understanding one permutation of being a Chinese Australian and a member of the larger Chinese overseas community. The various issues that have arisen in this study may be further investigated, and it would be of scholarly interest for all concomitant issues in relation to immigration and identity to be brought onto a comparative plane. My study of the ACCC, BLIA SYD and TACTCA may well be the first ethnography with a musical emphasis in Asian Australian studies, and one of two or three existing contributions to the study of Chinese music in Australia. However, it is, after all merely a snapshot in time of the current state of just three sub-communities, which no doubt will continue to be affected by the impinging waves of global age developments and mass migration in the years to come.

Ethnicity is a growing issue in light of recent incidents concerning international race relations. In the end, it is not simply diasporans and ethnic actors alone who must attend to the question of "where they're at." Since the past, as succinctly put by Salman Rushdie "is a country from which we are emigrated" (1991, p. 12), finding "where you're at" in the present time with a functional sense of self is perhaps something that applies to us all in the search for who we are, and where we stand as we traverse into the future.

Notes

1. I attended a concert in Town Hall, Sydney. This concert featured erhu soloist Chen Xuebing with the East-West Philharmonic Orchestra in a composition based on Stalinist 'Red' orchestral techniques and harmonisation. I found the experience engaging, and Ms Chen's instrument extraordinary. She became my teacher. With great dedication, I progressed from raw scratching sounds to producing the pure singing tone for which the instrument is renowned.
2. Considerable study has been conducted on the viridity of loss experienced by female migrants (Halfacree and Boyle 1999; Silvey and Lawson 1999). As wives, sisters, aunties and housebound grandmothers, female migrants suffer from the loss of the support network of family and friends (Creese, Dyck and McLaren 1999; Man 1993), and a personal sense of financial security in employment (Bonney and Love 1991; Halfacree 1995).
3. For more on enculturation, particularly in Chinese Catholicism, see Ng (2009).
4. This ritual has been re-introduced into Chinese Catholic communities worldwide after several centuries of debate in the Vatican, which initially barred the practice.
5. See for instance, an upload from a performance at the Fo Guang Shan Order's annual Buddha's Birthday celebrations in Darling Harbour (Mysilentteardrops, 2010).
6. Also known as *Exsultet* or *Proemium Paschale*.
7. There are several versions of this hymn, which is traditionally sung by the deacon over the Paschal (Easter) candle after it has been lit during the first half of the liturgy on Easter Vigil, which takes place on Holy Saturday (the eve of Easter).

References

Ang, I. (2001). *On not speaking Chinese*. London & New York: Routledge.

Ang, I. (2003). Together-in-difference: Beyond diaspora, into hybridity. Asian Studies Review, 27(2), 141-154.

Canticum Novum. (2002). Exultet (Paschal announcement, Mass of the Easter Vigil). *Translation and scores for Lent - Easter*. Retrieved 12/09/2007, from http://interletras.com/canticum/Eng/Translation_Lent.html.

Chan, D. (2000). The Dim Sum vs the Meat Pie: On the rhetoric of becoming an in-between Asian-Australian Artist. In I. Ang, S. Chalmers, L. Law & M. Thomas (Eds.), *Alter/Asians: Asian-Australian identities in art, media, and popular culture*, pp. 141-151. Sydney: Pluto Press.

Chan, Kwok-Bun. (2005). *Chinese identities, ethnicity and cosmopolitanism*. London, Routledge.

Chinese Catholic Pastoral Centre. (2003). *Aì G Rén Sh ng Lù ('Music Lovers' Life Journey')*. [CD] No Label; available from Chinese Australian Catholic Pastoral Centre (http://www.chinese.sydney.catholic.org.au/E_Ccpc.htm).

De Vos, G. & Romanucci-Ross, L. (1982). Ethnicity: Vessel of meaning and emblem of contrast. In G. De Vos & L. Romanucci-Ross (Eds.), *Ethnic identity: Cultural continuities and change*, pp. 363-390. Chicago, IL: Chicago University Press.

Ebaugh, H. R. F., & Chafetz, J. S. (Eds.) (2000). *Religion and the new immigrants: continuities and adaptations in immigrant congregations*. Walnut Creek, CA: AltaMira Press.

Eng, D. L. (1999). Melancholia/postcoloniality: loss in The Floating Life (sic). *Qui Parle, 11*(2), 137-50; 161-64.

Hall, S. (1993). Cultural identity and diaspora. In P. Williams & L. Chrisman (Eds.), *Colonial discourse and post-colonial theory: a reader*, pp. 392-403. New York: Columbia University Press.

Hargreaves, D. J., Miell, D. & MacDonald, R. (2002). What are musical identities, and why are they important? In R. MacDonald, D. J. Hargreaves & D. Miell (Eds.), *Musical identities*, pp. 1-20. Oxford: Oxford University Press.

Herberg, Will. (1960). *Protestant-Catholic-Jew: an essay in American religious sociology*. Garden City, NY: Doubleday.

Johnson, H. (2005). Performing identity, past and present: Chinese cultural performance, New Year celebrations, and the heritage industry. In C. Ferrall, P. Millar & K. Smith (Eds.), *East by south: China in the Australasian imagination*, pp. 217-242. Wellington: Victoria University Press.

Knowles, C. (2003). *Race and social analysis*. London: Sage Publications.

Kuah-Pearce, K. E. (2006). Locating the Self in the Chinese Diaspora: introductory remarks. *Asian Studies Review, 30*, 217-221.

Lau, F. (2005). Entertaining "Chineseness": Chinese singing clubs in contemporary Bangkok. *Visual Anthropology, 18*, 143-166.

Lo, J. (2000). Beyond happy hybridity: Performing Asian Australian identities. In I. Ang, S. Chalmers, L. Law & Mandy Thomas (Eds.), *Alter/Asians: Asian- Australian identities in art, media and popular culture*, pp. 152-68. Sydney, NSW: Pluto Press.

Lu, X. (2001). Bicultural identity development and Chinese Community formation: an ethnographic study of Chinese schools in Chicago. *The Howard Journal of Communications, 12*, 203-220.

Lum, C. M. K. (1996). *In search of a voice: karaoke and the construction of identity in Chinese America*. Mahwah, New Jersey, Lawrence Erlbaum Associates.

Mak, A. S. & Chan, H. (1995). In R. Hartley (Ed.), Chinese family values in Australia. *Families and cultural diversity in Australia*, pp. 70-95. St. Leonards, NSW: Allen & Unwin in association with the Australian Institute of Family Studies.

Mysilentteardrops. (2010, May 9). Australian Chinese Teo Chew Association – Buddha's Bday 09.05.10 [video file]. Retrieved from www.youtube.com/watch?v=0dKsiraWvFc.

Neale, J. M. & Helmore, T. E. (1856). Veni, Veni Emmanuel #65. *Hymnal noted – Parts I and II*. London: Novello.

Ng, N. (2009). Domesticating the foreign: singing salvation through translation in the Australian Catholic Chinese community. In A. Chan and A. Nelson (Eds.), *Sounds in Translation*, pp. 111-144. Canberra, ACT: ANU E Press.

Rao, N. Y. (2004). Henry Cowell and his Chinese music heritage. In Y. U. Everett and F. Lau (Eds.), *Locating East Asia in Western art music*, pp. 119-145. Middletown, CT: Wesleyan University Press.

Rosaldo, R. (1988). Ethnic concentrations: the Ilongots in Upland Luzon. In A. T. Rambo, K. Gillogly & K. L. Hutterer (Eds.), *Ethnic diversity and the control of natural resources in Southeast Asia*, pp. 161-171. [Michigan Papers on South and Southeast Asia Center for South and Southeast Asian Studies, The University of Michigan, No. 32] Honolulu, Hawaii, Published in cooperation with the East-West Center, Environment and Policy Institute.

Rushdie, S. (1991). *Imaginary homelands: essays and criticism, 1981-1991*. New York: Viking and Granta.
Scott, A. (1994). *Chinese written language in Hawai'i: The linguistic, social, and cultural significance for immigrant families* (PhD Thesis, University of Hawai'i).
Stein, B. (1981). The refugee experience: defining the parameters of a field study. *International migration review, 15*(1-2), 320-330.
Stock, J. (1993). A historical account of the Chinese two-stringed fiddle erhu. *Galpin Society Journal*, 46, 83-113.
Suárez-Orozco, M. M. (2000). Everything you ever wanted to know about assimilation but were afraid to ask. *Daedalus 129*(4 Fall), 1-30.
Tan, C. (2003). Living with 'difference': growing up 'Chinese' in White Australia. *Journal of Australian Studies 77*, 101-108.
Voice of the Ganges. (2002). *Ode to the Triple Gem*. [CD] Taipei, Taiwan ROC: Voice of the Ganges Co. Ltd. BD 1042.
Wang, T. P. (1994). *The origins of Chinese kongsi*. Selangor, Malaysia, Pelanduk Publications.
Warner, R. S. & Wittner, J. G. (Eds.) (1998). *Gatherings in diaspora: religious communities and the new immigration*. Philadelphia, PA: Temple University Press.
Yang, F. (1999). *Chinese Christians in America: Conversion, assimilation, and adhesive identities*. University Park, PA, Pennsylvania State University Press.
Zhou, Min. & Kim, R. Y. (c2006). The paradox of ethnicization and assimilation: The development of ethnic organizations in the Chinese immigrant community in the United States. In K. E. Kuah-Pearce and E. Hu-Dehart (Eds.), *Voluntary organizations in the Chinese Diaspora*, pp. 231-252. Hong Kong: Hong Kong University Press.

三

PART THREE

Artistic Reflections

CHAPTER
8

Stylistic development and performance practice: From unpublished Chinese folksongs to new Australian compositions

Shan Deng

My exploration of traditional Chinese music began in 2008 when I was asked to present something "new and different" for the Sunday Live Program on ABC Classic FM. After consulting my father, Dr. Wei Deng, ethnomusicologist and performer on the pipa (Chinese four-stringed plucked lute), I decided on a program of contemporary solo piano pieces by Chinese composers, classical solo pipa pieces, a duet for piano and pipa, and some French pieces to highlight the similarities between Chinese and Impressionist composition techniques. As the concert was well received with many repeat broadcasts on ABC Classic FM, I decided to pursue this area of my cultural heritage further.

Together with Tasmanian composer Dr Maria Grenfell, I applied for the University of Tasmania's Institutional Research Grant Scheme. Our application was successful and we were awarded the grant. Our intention was to complete a unique Australian project, aiming to place the Conservatorium of Music, University of Tasmania at the forefront of collaborative research in composing and performing music for Chinese and western instruments.

Our research aim was inspired by the tradition among western composers to research and absorb aspects of folk music in the creation of new and innovative masterpieces, such as those by Hungarian composers Béla Bartók and Zoltán Kodály, and English composer Ralph Vaughan Williams. According to Kenneth Chalmers (1995), Bartók and Kodály collected more than 7,000 folk songs, which came to inspire many of their compositions through melodic quotation, rhythmic imitation, and other compositional methods. Integration of musical elements from folk and "Other" cultures has since become a significant composition technique in the development of Western art music.

A number of Australian composers have already incorporated ideas from Chinese culture in their music. These include Peter Sculthorpe, George Dreyfus, Richard Meale, Liza Lim, Larry Sitsky and Julian Yu. There are even a small number of Chinese music ensembles active in Australia, such as Wang Zhengting's Australian Chinese Music Ensemble in Melbourne, which perform traditional and contemporary repertoire by Chinese and Chinese Australian composers on traditional instruments.

Although there has been some contemporary exploration of the pipa with Western instruments in the writing of northern hemisphere composers (particularly in China), no works for pipa are listed in the Australian Music Centre (AMC) catalogue (http://www.australianmusiccentre.com.au). While this catalogue is by no means an exhaustive source, it is the primary repository for Australian composers, who must pass a peer review process to be represented by the AMC. The absence of pipa entries would suggest that has been little interest in composing for this instrument in the Australian art music scene.

With this in mind, our research project continues to further investigate and integrate Chinese music with western audiences in innovative ways. This is achievable by generating new Australian compositions for pipa and piano from unpublished source material, and developing new performance techniques. The documentation of the collaboration between composers and performers will hopefully act as a catalyst for further compositions and collaborations between traditional Chinese and Western musicians.

A major outcome of this research project is the transnotation of a selection of unpublished Chinese folk songs from the closed collection at the Institute of Chinese Musicology in Beijing from Jianpu to western notation. I travelled to China in early 2010 and was granted special permission to view an exclusive collection of folk songs at Chinese Institute of Musicology in Beijing. The institute was established under the direction of my grandfather, Professor Li Yuanqing in 1954. Several thousand unpublished folk songs were collected in various forms in the 1950s. The collection process was unfortunately abruptly interrupted by the Chinese Cultural Revolution (1966-1976), but work resumed after 1975 and the institute is now in the process of electronically cataloguing all their music holdings. These exist at the Institute as either tape recordings or transcriptions in Jianpu notation (numbered musical notation).

I have selected a set of folk songs and transnotated them from the original Jianpu notation to western notation. I found that transnotation process required the development of new ways of notating Chinese musical elements such as ornamentation, the frequency of vibrato, half a semitone, and timbral changes. The folk song selection I have made is currently being analysed for musical features such as ornamentation, subject material, text, rhythmic usage in original language, melodic shape, and harmony. These features will be deconstructed in the compositional process undertaken by Dr Grenfell, who is in the process of composing a set of five to six pieces for piano and pipa, a distinctive cross-cultural duo. She intends to focus on specific elements arising from the analysis in each composition. One of Dr. Grenfell's pieces was recently presented at the *Encounters Symposium* in May 2010 by myself and pipa master Dr Wei Deng. Dr Deng and I will continue to study the technique required to perform new Australian works with a Chinese folk influence. We will then document the collaborative process of the piano-pipa duo in a technical guide. We look forward to the development of this project as a significant contribution to the Australian art music scene in the months to come.

I wish to thank Professor Qian Jianzhong, Associate Professor Liu Dongsheng, Associate Professor Yu Qingxin and the staff at the library of the Chinese Institute of Musicology. Through their kind assistance, I was able to obtain valuable resources for this research project.

Bibliography
Chalmers, Kenneth. (1995). *Béla Bartók (20th-Century Composers)*. London: Phaidon Press.
Nicholson, M. (Presenter). (2008, July 6). Sunday Live. Hobart, TAS: ABC Classic FM.

Chapter

9

琴 Qin

Tony Wheeler

My encounters with Chinese music began at Queensland Conservatorium, Griffith University in 1981. At the time, I was in the third year of a Bachelor of Music course, studying clarinet and composition, and had the great good fortune to have Dr Dale Craig as my lecturer in music history. Dr Craig had previously lectured for some years at the Chinese University of Hong Kong, and had a deep passion for Chinese music. He ordered a selection of traditional instruments from Hong Kong and put the word out that he wanted to establish a "Chinese orchestra" at Queensland Conservatorium.

For some years, I had been reading books by Krishnamurti (1954), Alan Watts (1974) and Christmas Humphreys (1949), and was becoming increasingly interested in Eastern ideas, particularly Chinese philosophy and poetry, Daoism and Zen Buddhism. I jumped at the chance to learn some Chinese music, and immediately signed up for the orchestra. Because I already had some familiarity with the guitar, I chose the *zhongruan* (Chinese four-stringed lute) 中阮. Little did I know what would follow on from these early, innocent decisions.

With the help of two overseas students from Singapore, Dr Craig began teaching us how to read *jianpu* 简谱, the simplified number notation widely used in Chinese music, and to play arrangements of simple tunes. Before long we began to perform. Our activities included a concert for a visiting delegation of officials from China. Dale's unfailing enthusiasm led us to travel to Hong Kong in mid-1982 to take part in a music camp run by the Music Office, where we played in small and large ensembles, and mixed happily with local students our age who were much more proficient than we were on our instruments. I was befriended by Yi You Wu 易有伍, the man behind the Hugo record label, and it was in his company that I heard recordings of the *qin* (Chinese seven-stringed zither) for the very first time. It was at this time that I took the opportunity to buy my first zhongruan. This was a journey that left me without a doubt that, at some stage in the future, I would spend considerable time in Asia.

Shanghai

Three years later I found myself at the Shanghai Conservatory of Music on a two-year exchange scholarship, enrolled in zhongruan and composition lessons. This was by no means the first time I had travelled overseas, but the prospect of leaving friends and family in Sydney to live in a very foreign land, without much knowledge of what lay ahead, unsure of when I would be returning — all this was both exciting and scary. On the China Airlines flight from Hong Kong to Shanghai, I noticed a difference in the general atmosphere and in the demeanour of the staff and in the coarseness of the rice. Everything seemed less colourful, more reserved, yet surprising casual and by no means unfriendly.

By that time I had learned and practised enough Mandarin to be able to make appropriate meal choices on the plane, ask for a blanket and order tea. I was also able to find a taxi at Shanghai airport and to tell the driver where I wanted to go. The taxi was actually a minibus. It didn't seem to have a fixed route but set about dropping passengers off at the various locations, which they'd told the driver. The roads were chaotic: there were very few cars in those days but lots of bicycles, buses and trucks, and horns honking incessantly. Eventually, on this hot, late August afternoon, the minibus left me stranded in the middle of a large concrete courtyard at the Shanghai Conservatory, with my two very heavy suitcases, a pair of clarinets, one saxophone and a zhongruan. There were a few people walking around, but they ignored me. I was unable to carry even half of my stuff by myself, so I left most of it where it was and headed for the closest large building within sight. At the entrance I spotted a young guy and said to him,

"I'm a foreign student…"

"Ah," he said, as if that explained everything. He then miraculously picked up both my suitcases, leaving me to manage the rest, and led me to another building quite some distance away. This turned out to be the foreign students' dormitory, the place that would be home for the next two years.

The humourless clerk at the front desk seemed somewhat loathe to do anything at all, but he did check me in to a double room on the third floor. Unfortunately, this room already seemed to be occupied by two people. The second surprise was the taste of the water from one of the large thermos bottles: it tasted almost like pure chlorine. Just as I was wondering how on earth I was going to survive this, the clerk reappeared with an envelope addressed to me. A letter already? Yes indeed, a card in fact, posted weeks earlier from Australia by my sister, cleverly calculated to be here when I arrived.

At this point, I mustered up the courage to mention to the clerk that this room was already taken, to which he looked around the room suspiciously, sighed, and replied, "Oh, that's a nuisance, a real nuisance." He did, however, go and fetch another key and let me into a vacant room where I could sit in silence for a while, cry over the card and ponder my situation. Eventually, I ended up sharing a room with a man named Vindu, from Zaire. His English was even more limited than the occasional word of French that I could recall from high school, so we spoke to each other in our elementary Mandarin, which was good practice. There was only one other Australian student at the Conservatory when I arrived, and she was of Malaysian-Chinese background. The others were from Zaire, Japan, USA, Italy, Sweden and Singapore. In my second year another student came from Australia.

The first few weeks in Shanghai were very interesting for me. Of course, some of the time I was extremely home sick, but on the other hand, everything was so different that the even the simplest of tasks came with an element of adventure and surprise. The shops were open every day and at night as well. This may not sound unusual now, but in those days (even in Sydney), we were accustomed to most places being closed on Saturday afternoons and Sundays.

Wherever I went, I took two little dictionaries with me in the back pockets of my pants: English-Chinese on one side and Chinese-English on the other. Fortunately, there were other foreign students at the Conservatory who spoke both excellent Chinese and English and they helped me a great deal, but it soon became clear that administrative things happen very slowly in China. I had brought with me my meagre savings in the form of an international bank draft, but this little piece of paper had to travel to headquarters in Beijing to be processed, and then be sent back before I could access the funds. This process would take six weeks.

Choosing subjects, organising timetables and classes, meeting teachers, assigning practice rooms — all these things unfolded gradually over time. Although I had a solid foundation in basic conversational Mandarin, my vocabulary was limited, and I felt my best option was initially to choose subjects with one-to-one tuition. The school also (eventually) assigned me Chen Shang Ming 陈尚明 as a language teacher, a lady from the voice department with a beautiful northern accent, who was a great help.

I found operating on a daily basis in a foreign language to be a mixture of exhilaration, frustration and exhaustion. I worked hard at learning new words to boost my vocabulary. People could understand me very well, so well, in fact, that they would proceed to chatter to me at full speed, assuming I would understand everything. In addition, Shanghai-accented Mandarin took a while to become accustomed to, and at first I found people would be saying words I had already learned but did not recognise because of their pronunciation.

Zhong ruan lessons were with Zhu Xin Cheng 诸新诚 and I studied composition in the Chinese style with He Zhan Hao 何占豪. He is a very funny and animated individual, well known for his collaboration in the writing of the *Butterfly Lovers* Violin Concerto, and full of enthusiasm and hilarious anecdotes. One of the things he taught me was to study the scores of traditional Chinese folk song melodies from various regions, and to find motives in them, which could then be used as a basis for the composition of instrumental pieces. This can be a very useful technique and source of inspiration. In the Conservatory I was surrounded by other instrumentalists, and constantly exposed to the sounds of the traditional instruments. As an instrumentalist myself, I was also afforded the opportunity to play in small ensembles with others. Thus immersed in the traditional timbres and stylistic nuances, I was soon often hearing original sounds and melodies in my own head, "played" on Chinese instruments. This immersion has had an indelible effect on my work as a composer and performer.

Most of the pieces I wrote in Shanghai were in the traditional vein, but before too long I was experimenting with traditional elements and timbres in more contemporary musical contexts. In doing this, there is an inherent risk of the music sounding contrived, or simply patched together, but I think that being so thoroughly steeped in Chinese life and culture — not only in the music, but also the language, tea, scenery, food, way of life — has allowed some of the more essential elements and concepts to permeate deeply. This perhaps leads to a more intrinsic influence on subconscious as well as conscious levels of artistic conception.

During short holidays, mid-term breaks and the like, the Conservatory would sometimes organise a trip for we foreign students (there were eleven of us in my first year there, and eighteen in the second), or sometimes a few of us would just decide to go to some exquisitely picturesque place relatively close by, like Suzhou or Hangzhou, for a day or two. I often found the most potent of musical ideas would arise in my mind while travelling, perhaps inspired by some aspect of scenery, or situation. Some of these I notated, and later became the basis of viable compositions.

Incidentally, travelling, and reading maps in Chinese was a wonderful way to accelerate my language studies, and also brought some nice surprises. Once while in Suzhou with a couple of classmates, I spotted a place on the map called *Shuchang* (书场), literally "book gathering place", or "book stage," and suggested to the others we should go and look at the books. We promptly set of on our hired bicycles to find it, and came upon a large hall full of tables, with a raised stage at the front. Sitting at the tables were mostly older people, drinking tea and eating dried melon seeds, and there were no books in sight. After a while though, to our delight, there appeared on the stage a man with a *san xian* 三弦 (three-stringed banjo), and a woman with a *pipa* 琵琶 (pear-shaped lute), who then performed a local style of musical story telling known as *Suzhou pingtan* 苏州评弹. The vocal part was a mixture of lyrical speech and singing, with melodic but repetitive and slightly percussive accompaniment from the two plucked instruments. I was enchanted, and this is still one of my favourite genres of Chinese music.

Before leaving Shanghai, I was fortunate enough to have the opportunity to record some of the compositions I had written there, in the recording studio of the Conservatory. The performers were very talented local students, with some of whom I had had the privilege of playing traditional ensemble music in various situations.

The qin

An extremely important and influential focus in my study of music has been the qin. The qin has played such a significant role in my approach to performance and composition that it warrants some discussion here. Although I had heard a very small number of recordings in Australia and China, I had not actually seen a qin before I arrived in Shanghai. One recording was on an old vinyl record from the

Conservatorium music library, and the others I heard briefly at Yi You Wu's apartment in 1982.

In Shanghai, I noticed that some of my fellow students were learning the qin, and every so often their teacher would organise a qin gathering where they would all play a piece, drink tea, discuss the music, and sometimes entertain a visiting qin player who was passing through Shanghai. I went along, and after a while I was so drawn to the instrument that I approached the teacher, Lin You Ren 林友仁 to take lessons myself.

Mr Lin is a man of great humour, perception and directness. He retains a healthy reverence for some worthy values of antiquity, particularly pertaining to the qin. Richness of tone, simple elegance in expression, economy of movement in technique, intimate knowledge of the nuances in the written score, quality rather than quantity — these are some qualities that spring to mind. Very open to new ideas, he also believes in adapting one's technique and interpretation according to naturalness, with the resulting quality of sound being the main criteria for judging whether something works or not. After establishing basic techniques and understanding, much of his teaching is oriented towards encouraging his students to think for themselves, and towards fostering in them a capacity to continue learning and exploring independently.

Although the qin was used in ensembles and to accompany singing early in its almost 3000 year history, it has been primarily a solo instrument to be played alone, or in intimate circumstances. It has long been regarded as an instrument of self cultivation, very much in tune with other refined pursuits such as calligraphy, painting and poetry (Van Gulik, 1968, p. 17).

Despite the qin having been associated with the literati and with lofty ideals, (Van Gulik 1968, 43–44) its sounds bear no exclusivity. It has an immeasurably earthy presence, and a great capacity for direct emotional expression. While the overall volume of the qin is comparatively soft, there is a great deal of rich timbral variation, brought about by a wide variety of plucking techniques. This, along with the unhurried nature of much of the music, demands very attentive listening.

Throughout history, there has also been some association of the qin with Daoist philosophy and ideology (Liang, 1985, p. 208; Van Gulik, 1968, p. 48). Broadly speaking, the Daoist view is that human nature is inherently pure, and is simply a part of the all inclusive, all pervading energy or essence of which the cosmos consists. This essence is called the Dao 道 ("way"), and in Daoist terms, the highest ideal for a human is to become one with the Dao, in other words to return to the original purity of this basic nature (Van Gulik, 1968, p. 45). How does this happen? Some would say that all earthly desires must be transcended, left behind, as one enters into some other blissful, spiritual plane, free from the bondage of day-to-day concerns. Others would say that the way to the truth and to the ultimate freedom is not, paradoxically, to try to enter into some other plane of consciousness, but to fully enter into the experience of reality, as it is right here and now. The most effective forms of meditation tend to follow the latter path, with the practice of awareness rooted in the direct physical experience of being (Beck, 1995, pp. 182 -183).

A discussion of meditation per se is not my purpose here, but it is appropriate to draw some parallel with the qin. Since qin music has to be memorised to be played effectively, this paves the way for the experience of playing to be, at least potentially, primarily physical and auditory. We need only to consider how long the qin has been played more for its own sake, rather than in public concert settings to see how qin playing could be a very contemplative and meditative phenomenon. This appeals to me greatly and is one of the reasons why I was attracted to the instrument in the first place.

My teacher Mr. Lin says that the ultimate condition in which to play the qin is that of *wu wo* 无我 ("no self"). He means this in the sense that all thoughts of the self as a separate entity are absent, allowing the sound and touch of the qin to act as a magnet on awareness. In this way, player and listener alike become one with the music, with no thoughts of self, no cerebral dialectics. Blissful indeed.

Typically, a qin piece will begin slowly, the phrases unfolding in an unhurried manner, followed by sections with a more noticeable rhythm. The tempo may then increase towards something of a climactic peak, or several peaks depending on the length of the piece, perhaps followed in turn by a slow section to conclude. Often the music begins and ends with harmonics, though this is by no means a rule, and harmonics can appear in the middle as well.

The traditional notation used by qin players is elaborate, and very specific. It is a form of fingering tablature, consisting primarily of conglomerate characters assembled from bits and pieces of ordinary Chinese characters. Each conglomerate symbol, which can usually be said to represent a single note, displays all the information required to play that note: i.e. which string to strike; with which finger stroke; on an open string or stopped in a certain position etc. Ornaments and slides will appear between the conglomerate characters, which read vertically from top to bottom. The only information not included is the duration of each note. Perhaps the people who played, wrote and used the notation generally knew the rhythms of the tunes. Undoubtedly the rhythm would have been passed aurally from person to person, as it is today, but this form of notation definitely leads to a certain freedom of interpretation, and to differing interpretations of any given piece.

There is evidence from as far back as the Zhou Dynasty, during the Spring and Autumn Period (770–476 BC), of differences in the styles of qin playing from the north to the south of China. As time went on the regional differences became more pronounced, and this led to the arising of different schools of playing in various regions of China (Zhang, 2008, p. 129). Any qin piece may be rendered in an almost unrecognisably different fashion, according to the stylistic and interpretive tendencies of the school in question. Some schools pertain to family tradition, while others are broader in ambit. One thing, however, is for certain: the rhythm of the music can have a tremendous effect on the overall significance of the tune.

Aspects of qin music have certainly had some influence, both direct and indirect, on my composition and improvisation. These include: form; melodic and rhythmic style of some of the schools of playing; ornamentation; reiteration of a given note with subtle timbral variation. I don't, however, set out to consciously imitate qin music in my practice. Rather, it seems to have become an integral part of my life and musical language by a process resembling osmosis.

Hong Kong

After my studies in Shanghai, I went to Hong Kong to complete a Masters Degree in composition for Chinese instruments at the University of Hong Kong. There, I assembled a portfolio of a variety of works, ranging from duets to large ensemble pieces. My composition lessons were with Prof Anne Boyd, who had been invited from Australia to establish the Music Department. My plan was to begin using what I had learned in Shanghai in order to evolve a personal musical style, incorporating elements of Chinese traditional music in a more contemporary context. Because Anne herself had an interest in Balinese music and used its influences in some of her own compositions, she had a clear idea of what I was trying to achieve.

I found Hong Kong to be the ideal place in which to do this, mainly because multifarious musical and cultural opportunities were open to me: to continue playing ruan and qin, and to liaise and associate with colleagues involved in the Chinese music field; to play both solo, orchestral and chamber music on the clarinet; to attended concerts and musical festivals of a wide variety of styles and genres; to tutor and teach composition and orchestration at the University; to make regular trips to various places in Mainland China; and of course to teach myself how to touch type while working part-time in the library of the University's Music Department. All this, of course, in the midst of the excitement and energy of one of the most diverse and colourful cities in the world.

I was also able to continue having qin lessons, with Dr Liu Chu Hua 刘楚华, a student of the great Cai De Yun 蔡德允. She is a highly erudite and literate individual, completed a doctoral thesis in France on the subject of Hui Neng's *Platform Sutra* 惠能：坛经 and for many years has lectured in the Chinese Language and Literature Department at the Hong Kong Baptist University.

Dr Liu is one of a group of Hong Kong qin players, the main figures of which are also students of Cai De Yun, who have persisted in cultivating the art of playing on traditional silk strings. In the company of these players, one gains a strong sense of an ancient approach to the instrument, one of selfless cultivation and true dedication. Dr Liu will not take on new students without them first proving that their wish to study the instrument is in true earnest, and stems from a worthy motivation. In fact she once told me that a prospective student would have to ask her thirteen times before being accepted. I consider myself lucky to have only had to ask four times.

Concluding thoughts

Upon my return to Australia in 1991, I was first faced with re-adjusting to life in Australia after some six years in Asia. I've moved around a lot, and at that time, the longest I'd been in any one place was ten years in Brisbane during my high school and tertiary years. Consequently, my understanding of somewhere being "home" to me was rather tenuous. Even now I feel, increasingly comfortably, the same way. I began to seek out other players of Chinese instruments, continued to compose, and gradually found means of support as a teacher of clarinet and saxophone and freelance performer.

When I first began learning the zhongruan in Dr Craig's Chinese ensemble, I did not realise how far it would lead me, and what wonderful realms of experience and learning it would open up. The last time I contacted Dr Craig, he was in the USA, and very pleased to hear about what I had been doing since I left the QCGU.

I play lots of traditional repertoire on the qin, and have done some work in reconstructing pieces from the old manuscripts. I play the ruan in ensembles, mainly with other Chinese instruments but on occasions also with Western instruments and those from other cultures, e.g. *shakuhachi, tabla, mridangam, oud*. I have made extensive use of the *qin, ruan,* clarinet and saxophone in improvisation in various contexts, sometimes with echoes of the traditional Chinese tonalities, sometimes with more contemporary sounds.

My compositions now draw on influences from many directions. One could, I suppose, say that I use anything that appeals to me, depending upon the instrumentation and the overall aesthetic conception of the work in progress. These influences of course include Chinese musical elements, but also may encompass jazz, blues, serialism, Baroque style counterpoint, and other things too. The challenge is to allow any of these elements to exert their influence in ways which remain in keeping with the initial idea or artistic conception.

Qin players in Australia are few. Apart form my own qin students, numbering a small handful, I know of two others, but they are not in Sydney. A young professional qin player and teacher who is based in Beijing, Jin Wei 金蔚, visits Sydney two or three times a year and we meet whenever we have the opportunity. I have kept in regular contact with my qin teacher in Shanghai, Mr Lin. I call him frequently to chat and to discuss aspects of the qin and its music, and visit him whenever I am able to. I visit China every one or two years and am currently working on the reconstruction of an ancient qin score. I will present my work at a conference of Asian music scheduled for 2011.

While some people contest the unbroken transmission of the world's musical traditions, such as the that of the qin, the fact of the instrument's unbroken transmission over some two or three thousand years points to its ability to call forth a primordial resonance (albeit amongst a minority), a resonance that reflects something more enduring than the undulations in social and political contours throughout history. It speaks also of an integrity beyond words, one which we could perhaps refer to as the "Dao of the qin." Integrity, however, expresses itself in many ways: in music, in life, in nature, it is as much an essential aspect of composition as it is of any endeavour.

The Dao of qin is still as alive today, and indeed as rare, as it has been for many centuries. I would like to end this paper with an ancient Chinese verse that refers to the qin. This verse in very much encapsulates my fascination with Chinese culture and music:

In my rustic dwelling, I have qin and books.

Playing qin while chanting poems, hence comes joy.

Surely there is nothing to surpass this? The true happiness of a secluded life;

In the early morning I water the garden, at sunset I lay down in my thatched hut.

Tao Yuan Ming (365-427 AD)

衡门之下，有琴有书。

载弹载咏，爰得我娱。

岂无他好？乐是幽居；

朝为灌园，夕偃蓬庐。

陶渊明 (365-427 AD)

References

Addiss, S. (1999). *The Resonance of the Qin in East Asian Art*. New York: China Institute Gallery, China Institute.

Beck, C. (1995). Joko: Nothing Special – Living Zen Harper San Francisco. Humphreys, C. (1949). Zen Buddhism. New York: Macmillan.

Krishnamurti, J. (1954). The first and last freedom. Wheaton, USA: The Theosophical Publishing House.

Lai, T. C. and Mok, R. (1981). *Jade Flute*. Hong Kong: Hong Kong Book Centre.

Liang, Ming Yue. (1985). *Music of the Billion*. New York: Heinrichshofen Edition.

Van Gulik, R. H. (1968). *The Lore of the Chinese Lute*. Tokyo: Sophia University & The Charles E. Tuttle Company.

Watts, A. (1974). Cloud-hidden, whereabouts unknown: a mountain journal. New York: Vintage Books.

Zhang, Hua Ying – 章华英. (2008). *Gu Qin* – 古琴. Hangzhou – 杭州: Zhejiang Peoples' Publishing House - 浙江人民出版社.

Chapter
10

Musical encounters in The Wide Alley

Erik Griswold and Vanessa Tomlinson

In the inner suburban ring of Chengdu lies "The Wide Alley" — or *Kuan Xiangzi* — one of two historic laneways dating to the Qing Dynasty (AD 1644-1911). In the ten years since we first visited The Wide Alley, we've watched it undergo a vast transformation from neglected treasure to major tourist destination. Similarly, we've witnessed (and indeed, taken part in) a resurgence of interest in traditional Sichuan music. Issues of modernisation, authenticity, neglect and recovery of culture have coloured all of our experiences in China, and influenced the ongoing collaborations between Clocked Out and musicians and dancers from Sichuan Province. We conceived our latest project — titled "The Wide Alley" — in 2007 when the street was being disassembled brick by brick, in preparation for the makeover. After touring the work in Australia, New Zealand, and Canada, The Wide Alley will now return home for a series of street performances in February 2011.

The Wide Alley (TWA) is a musical and cultural meeting of five Australian and five Sichuan musicians. Commissioned by the Queensland Music Festival in 2007, and supported by the Asialink Foundation, it builds upon a series of collaborations and exchanges dating back to 1999. Earlier collaborations include "Chengdu Streetsongs" (1999), a quartet of Zou Xiangping, electronic musician Harry Castle, and the authors; and "Sichuan Fantasy" (2002), a vastly bigger project of seven musicians, four choreographers, fifteen dancers, elaborate costumes, lighting and backdrops at Chengdu Arts Centre. Each of the collaborations have involved research into a variety of Sichuan musical traditions, and creative recontextualisation into new hybrid works. Many of our first impressions of Chengdu have made it into TWA, evolving over several years of workshopping and collaborative performances in Chengdu and Australia.

The ten musicians in the ensemble all bring unique skills in a variety of traditions, including Sichuan Opera, Qin Yin, jazz, and free improvisation, and all have some previous experience with intercultural collaboration. Trumpet player Peter Knight and Trombonist Adrian Sheriff have both lead intercultural ensembles in their own right; bassist Robert Davidson, leader of contemporary music ensemble Topology, has been influenced Indian classical traditions in his own work. The Chinese musicians, vocalist Tian Linping, bamboo flautist Shi Lei, erhu (Chinese two-stringed fiddle) player Zhou Yu, and percussionist Zhong Kaizhi are all leading specialists in their own traditions, but also bring their experience with improvisation and western music to the project. Composer Zou Xiangping is well versed in both traditional Chinese and contemporary western music, and the authors have been engaged in the process of intercultural study and collaboration since their meeting.

Each partner in the cross-cultural collaboration acts as a mirror, reflecting aspects each other's culture. With the help of Zou Xiangping as our intrepid guide, we've been able to reflect our outsider impressions of Sichuan culture back to the local people, and at the same time play a small part in preserving and disseminating the local traditions to an international stage. While we created a link to contemporary western traditions of contemporary music, jazz, and free improvisation, Zou Xiangping guided us into the worlds of Sichuan Opera, Chengdu street music, and Jinqian Ban.

In TWA, aim to create a dialog between Western and Chinese music. The performance is a collage of elements: individual pieces sound like Chinese-inflected jazz, jazz-inflected Chinese music, or new, experimental hybrids. In some pieces there is a layering of textures: Chengdu street soundscapes blur into jazz improvisations; Chinese folk themes become enveloped by clouds of textured sound. While in other pieces, approaches from one form are used to structure the performance of another: Sichuan Opera conducting techniques guide free improvisations, or Chinese folk material is placed into jazz song forms.

If the juxtaposition of Chinese music and jazz seems odd, consider the close parallels between traditional Chinese and early blues styles: both focus on pentatonic scales, highly intricate ornamenation, and flexible metre which follow the text. Jazz' emphasis on improvisation and individual interpretation make it well suited to cross-genre and cross cultural collaboration. In a jazz performance, what is valued most is each instrumentalist's individual sound. Accompaniments, arrangements, and compositions are built around the individual strengths and capabilities of the performers. Though perhaps not yet established as a genre, nevertheless there are a number of innovative artists who have explored interconnections between Chinese and jazz forms, including Fred Ho, Liu Sola, Jon Jang and others.

With TWA, we wanted to create a work which would pay homage to the disappearing traditions of Sichuan music, reflect our personal take on the music, and also capture the feeling of bewilderment and wonder of our first encounters with Sichuan culture.

The urban soundscape of Chengdu was a revelation. On our first visit, in 1999, we were immediately struck by a variety of unfamiliar sounds: the gentle tapping of hammer on bricks as thousands of labourers dismantled buildings by hand; the myriad tonal inflections of night market vendors barking through cheap megaphones; and most of all a sea of bicycle bells and car horns washing through the city streets.

Zou Xiangping shared an interest in the street music of Chengdu, and he introduced us to traditional street songs and signature sounds of tradespeople, such as the metallic "di der ka" of the hard candy vendor, or intriguing twang of the ear cleaner. In the course of research undertaken with musicologist Emma Zevik, Zou also amassed a colourful collection of historic street songs used to sell all manner of wares — lard cakes, soy sauce. Even rat poison! Many of these sounds and street calls have been woven into the musical textures of TWA.

In *Bicycle Groove*, for instance, we create a shifting collage of soundscape, Chinese folk and original material. Seas of bicycles awash through the city streets has remained a vivid image from our first trip to Chengdu. That image evolved into the slow, loping rhythm underpinning "Bicycle Groove." Using a combination of found sounds from the urban environment (bicycle bells, horns, and brake drums), prepared piano and modified drum kit, we try to recapture the initial impression. To the gentle rhythm the Chinese performers add a chorus of street calls and songs, from mundane calls of

"*Shou feiping*/Rubbish collection!" or "*Huaxi dusee bao*/Newspapers!" to the poignant and a wistful morning song "*You gao*/Cakes!." From there urban and folk elements become entangled in a creative interplay of musical textures. a muted trumpet improvises over a Tibetan folk theme; a soaring bamboo flute completes a sweet jazz ballad.

Another recontextualisation of street music occurs in *Cotton Man*. This singular tradesman travels from neighbourhood to neighbourhood just prior to winter, to repair people's old doonahs before the cold season. This he accomplishes in an extremely unusual way, using a giant gut string bow to fluff up the doonahs, producing an absolutely amazing rhythmic twanging. In our homage, four live performers (trumpet, trombone, contrabass, and percussion) play in careful rhythmic unison with a video of the Cotton Man, underscoring the fascinating musicality of his work.

Sichuan Opera Percussion was another revelation that has influenced our work in China since 1999. In our first encounter, we attended a "tea house" opera (a small, unstaged version held in local neighbourhoods), where the director led the percussionists through a myriad of intricate cues — from gentle rolling rhythms to explosive cacophonies. We watched with amazement as he coordinated minute inflections of voice, stage action, and percussion using a highly detailed sequence of stick, hand and finger cues.It was a truly complex juggling act of rhythm, gesture, and smoking paraphernalia. If the music was fast paced, he puffed a cigarette in time; if it was slow enough, he lit up his pipe!

Sonically, Sichuan Opera Percussion features a sophisticated layering of metallic timbres (comprised of gongs and cymbals of varying size), along with skin drums and the piercing pulse of the conductor's wood drum. Sichuan Opera is known for its characteristic gao qiang style (one of five main percussion styles) of using percussion and voice with no other accompanying instruments. To our ears, trained in contemporary western music, gao qiang style sounded quite avant garde, reminding us of Luciano Berio or Stockhausen.

Needless to say, we were deeply infatuated with the Sichuan Opera Percussion's melodious resonance and wide range of colours from the beginning. At the same time we were intrigued by the tantalising possibility of adapting it's structures and elaborate cuing system to other musical materials. We envisioned a John Zorn–style structured improvisation making use of its modular, building block mechanisms.

To pursue this end, in our subsequent visits to Chengdu (2001–2, 2004, 2007), we took up studies with master Zhong Kaizhi, who patiently introduced us to the –quite unorthodox — playing techniques and lead us slowly through the list of cues which make up the language of Sichuan Opera (numbering in the hundreds). Though we have fallen well short of mastering the tradition, our studies have lead to three new works, using a range of collaborative approaches, and displaying a range of styles from traditional from avant garde.

In the "Sichuan Opera Overture", Zhong Kaizhi and Zou Xiangping have created a medley of opera themes which demonstrate the range of colours and moods expressed in Sichuan Opera Percussion. To the traditional gongs, cymbals, erhu, and bamboo flute, they've added the western instruments (trumpet, trombone, contrabass, piano), introducing fresh tone colours to the material. Similarly, in "The Way," an original jazz composition is given a fresh colour through the use of a traditional Sichuan Opera rhythmic pattern. In the most innovative cross-fertilisation of genres, "Brick by Brick," the cuing system of Sichuan Opera is used to "conduct" the ensemble through a wild free improvisation. Master Zhong performs the traditional cues, while the ensemble reacts to his cues in unexpected flurries of improvised sound.

FIGURE 1 — Erik Griswold & Vanessa Tomlinson, Clocked Out Duo with Zou Xiangping in Kuan Xiangzi.

The third revelation from our early visits to Chengdu was the *Jinqian Ban* ("Money Sticks") itinerant storytelling tradition. We were very fortunate to work directly with its last living master, Zou Zhongxin, whose amazing energy and vitality belied his then 78 years. At the time we met, Zou Zhongxin was living in relative obscurity, known only to a few music insiders, including our friend Zou Xiangping (no relation). The older Zou expressed his enthusiasm for our project of combining contemporary forms with traditional Sichuan music, encouraging us to incorporate *Jinqian Ban* in our work, instructing us and the younger Zou in the technique of the bamboo money sticks and collaborating with us on the 2002 piece Concerto for *Jinqian Ban*.

Jinqian Ban has continued to play a part in TWA, in our piece Di Da Kwa — the title an alliteration of the money sticks' three basic tones. In Di Da Kwa, we combine authentic folk material from *Jinqian Ban* with original material and improvisation. Beginning with a nostalgic piano solo, framing the piece as a fading memory, the bamboo money sticks establish a driving rhythm. The band picks up a fragment of the piano theme with the bass driving forward with a funky syncopation until the whole ensemble suddenly erupts into a vocal call and response" "*Di da kwa*! *Di da kwa!*"; "*Kwa! di da Kwa! di da.*" Echoing the youthful energy of master Zou Zhongxin, a childlike melodica solo takes off, propelling the piece into its climax: a rendition of the traditional song "12 Month Story" taught to us by master Zou, and sung by the younger Zou Xiangping. Our goal again is to pay homage to the tradition while at the same time re-contextualising and by placing it alongside our own musical impressions. Since our work with master Zou Zhongxin, we are happy to report that he has been named as a National Treasure, and his tradition is now being archived.

While TWA was strongly directed by Clocked Out with input from Zou Xianping, we now hope to develop new material with creative input from all of the musicians. As we have continued to tour TWA — it has now been presented at Queensland Music Festival, Sydney Opera House, Auckland Festival, Vancouver International Jazz Festival, Victoria Jazz Fest, and Ottawa International Jazz Festival — a strong group sound has developed. Pieces have evolved as individuals have taken chances on stage, moving the music into new directions. Although verbal communication is not always straightforward, the hybrid musical language we've created together will hopefully lead us to deeper cultural understanding.

Chapter

11

My performance pieces — a self-reflection

William Yang

Usually, my pieces have started with images. I would push the slides around on my light box and sequences of images would form. From this, I would tell a story. I used to write my stories down, but now I present them as a continuous narrative. I find the spoken word a more direct way of communication than writing. Whereas grammar gets in my way, and pushes me in the direction of sentence construction, I can get straight to the point by talking (shorter is better). However, I do enjoy writing and think my texts veer towards poetry rather than prose.

I began working with slide projection in the early eighties. Ian de Gruchy taught me how to project using a dissolve unit and music. This was known as the 'audiovisual' approach and I still use this art form. When showing slides, there is a natural tendency to talk about the images as one would in a living room slide show. Although this form has a terrible reputation associated with the sharing of unedited pictures to family and friends, I acknowledge it as the genesis of my present-day work. Projection was also a cheap way to show my colour photos, as colour prints were quite expensive. I worked intermittently for about seven years on a collection of projection pieces and in 1989, I presented *The Face of Buddha* at the Downstairs Belvoir Street Theatre. It was a collection of nine short stories or photographic essays, which combined image projection, spoken word and recorded music. Everyone liked this form and I could see its potential. The most popular piece from the collection was called *For My Mother*. It was a sketch of my family history.

For most of my early life up until the time I was in my mid thirties, I knew very little of my family history. I'd been brought up as an assimilated Australian. The reason was partly cultural when I was growing up on the fifties; everyone in Australia was expected to assimilate, to speak English. My mother thought being Chinese was a complete liability — she wanted me to be more Australian than the average Australian. So the Chinese side of me was unacknowledged. Simply put, I felt uncomfortable and ashamed of being Chinese. In my mid thirties I met a teacher who taught me Taoism and she connected me with that Chinese part of myself that had been denied. I researched the history of the Chinese in Australia, which included the history of my family. Both my paternal and maternal grandfathers came to Australia in the 1880s to the north of Australia to dig for gold, and both my parents were born in Australia.

Three of my performance pieces dealt with my Australian Chinese family. *The North* was about my childhood, growing up in North Queensland. Sadness dealt with family stories of my mother's generation. The main theme was the murder of my uncle, William Fang Yuen, who was shot at Mourilyan near Innisfail in 1922. *Blood Links* told the story of my contemporary family and the Chinese Diaspora, where my relatives have been scattered around Australia and the USA. I feel I have told all my family stories and I need to wait another ten year for a new one to emerge.

One of my more recent pieces, *China*, continued the search for Chinese identity. It dealt with my five trips to China since 1989. I thought of calling the piece *Claiming China* as it was something of that process. Certainly, I felt I had returned to the 'Motherland' on my first trip to China. The Chinese I met who always told me, "You've come back, you've come back home," reinforced this feeling. But I can't speak the language and thought that there was only a certain penetration I could make into China. Even my best experiences reinforced the fact I identify as Australian. I like China and at times I have tried to be Chinese, but my cultural conditioning, which formed me, was so strong it was almost impossible to break. Now I don't see the point in trying: I don't want to live in China and have accepted the fact I am Australian. That is my story.

For the performances of *China* I engaged a composer and erhu player, Nicholas (Nick) Ng, to play live with me on stage (I had conceived the piece with the sound of the erhu in the back of my mind). Much like my other productions, I wanted the music to provide an emotion to the pieces. When developing *China*, we found that for every emotional moment in the work there was a traditional piece that expressed the emotion: noble sentiment, great sorrow, the pleasure of travelling down the river, or the exuberance of galloping across the grasslands. There was even a traditional way of expressing water. In most cases, I went with the ready-made piece but found that we needed to use extracts, or speed up or slow down certain musical sections to suit the nature of the scene.

Finding an erhu player in Australia proved difficult. There are erhu players in Australia, some very good ones mostly trained in China, but they all find it hard to earn a living as musicians. I've read their CVs: a Chinese concert here, work on a film there — but nothing substantial to survive in their preferred occupation. So they teach, and have up to 40 students. This means that they don't have time to come to rehearsals or join me on tours. They wanted to play with me and a few tried. But in the end, I didn't have enough continuous work for them to match their teaching income. Eventually, I reconnected with Nick at The Australian National University, where he was completing a PhD. He was lecturing only half the week and spent the rest of his time studying and freelancing, so we were able to work together.

When we were touring *China* in Europe, Nick had to perform in a concert of one of his compositions in Australia. So for our season at Halle, we had to find an erhu player in Germany. There were a few candidates and we settled on Mr Lui, who had trained in China. Mr Lui had lived in Germany for 20 years and owned a restaurant. He spoke Mandarin and German but no English. I speak only English, so of course all the cues for the piece are in English, which meant that we had to devise a series of cues based on disguised nods and gestures so that he would know when to start. Mr Lui played extremely well, but was of the old school and used to the concert platform. "This piece," he would say through the interpreter, "is the most famous erhu piece in the entire repertoire, and I can't play it at the speed you want." In short, he found the bastardised form of theatre music a little uncouth. But he came around in the end and even found the experience enjoyable.

When I first started doing my performance pieces I used recorded music from CDs and cassette tapes. Minimal music worked best and Philip Glass was my favourite composer. I needed music that was amorphous, that didn't have an obvious structure so the images could form their own narrative without the music being too insistent on its own shape. Slow, flowing melodies worked too. I needed to induce an elevated, meditative state of mind for the audience.

When I started receiving grant money for the pieces, I commissioned composers to compose soundtracks. I employed film score composer Stephen Rae to write the recorded soundtrack for *Blood Links*. He also reworked *Sadness*. I engaged Simon Hunt, who also worked in film for *Friends of Dorothy*, a piece about the gay community in Sydney. The soundtrack was more of a soundscape, using sounds from dance parties. In several of the sex scenes, Simon used the grunts and moas from pornographic films.

I then started engaging live musicians in my pieces. Colin Offord, a consummate musician, worked with me on *The North* and later appeared in *Shadows* (Figure 1). Colin played mouth bow, an instrument he developed. It consisted of strings stretched over a tree trunk. The strings were bowed producing a raw sound that resembled a rough cello. With the mouthpiece, Colin changed the shape of his mouth and throat and this produced a series of harmonics (he did not blow into the mouthpiece). Amplified, it produced a wide range of sounds. I like to think of this music as "synthesised", although it was naturally produced. Certainly, people were intrigued by Colin's instrument wherever we travelled.

I've also worked with Paul Jarman who played wind instruments in *Objects for Meditation*. This piece was a meditation and I used video for the first time. The images themselves were trance inducing, and I encouraged Paul to play sustained, open notes on his *tárogató* (a Hungarian reed pipe). He's a good player and was able to produce a pure sound. I always gave him the instruction, "longer breaths, fewer notes."

These days, I always have a live musician accompany me in my productions. Their presence adds a dynamic to the performance and this helps me feel less lonely on stage. I'm always there as the talker, the monologist or the story teller — that never changes. The images are always there — that never changes either, but I can change the musician, so I try to find a new one for each piece.

When I first began this work, the form of talking, slide projection and music was considered a new format. Practitioners of this art form lamented on the difficulties of selling their productions to potential audiences. Once we get them along to experience the form, then they are converted, but it's hard to get them along in the first place. The combination of text, image and music works in unusual ways and is difficult to describe.

I like to think of my shows as raw films since there's a projected image and a voice, which suggests the cinematic format. The images, although still, are not ineffective because they give the audience a chance to take a good look at the image as one does in a gallery exhibition. The images have their own story. I never describe things — the images do that. Sometimes they do not match up completely with the text (I wish I had an image for every moment of my life), so sometimes the brain has to work a little to make sense of the image and the text. I think the brain likes this. There's nothing so stultifying for me than to watch formulaic, sitcom comedy on TV.

The music in my pieces supplies an emotion. The very best moments are operatic where the dissolving, meditative images and music carry sustained emotion. People have written up my work as new art, but actually it is an old form, the trio, used in an unusual way. The elements are from different mediums: voice, image and sound. Over the past twenty years, overseas presenters have requested my performance pieces and they have toured extensively. I think of these works as alternative histories of Australia.

FIGURE 1 — William Yang with Colin Offord in Shadows. Courtesy of William Yang.

四

PART FOUR

Conversations

As part of *Encounters: Musical Meetings Between Australia and China* (2010), Vincent Plush, curator of *Encounters: Meetings in Australian Music* (2005), participated in three public interviews with key figures in the Australian music scene who are connected to China through birth or professional affiliation. Following are their transcribed conversations, which took place in the Queensland Conservatorium Board room. This section concludes with a conversation between Ash Dargan and Nicholas Ng, which took place at the conclusion of *Encounters*.

Abbreviations

AB   Anne Boyd

AD   Ash Dargan

JC   John Curro

GP   GAO Ping

JH   John Huie

JY   Julian YU

LS   Larry Sitsky

NN   Nicholas Ng

VP   Vincent Plush

Chapter

12

Conversations with Gao Ping and John Huie

4 May 2010 — Queensland Conservatorium Boardroom
Transcribed by Michael Bakrnchev on 27 November 2010, Brisbane

---

VP: This is a very interesting week to be talking about China and Shanghai.

Those of us who travelled by Qantas today would have picked up this amazing publicity bulletin. It is of course the week of the opening of … The Shanghai World Expo, better city, better living, or the other way round. And Shanghai will feature very prominently in our thoughts and liberations throughout this week, particularly on Saturday, when we convert to an evening of Shanghai stuff: nonsense, revelation, music, and cuisine.

As it transpires, both of our guests tonight do have a strong association with various elements of the Shanghai — La Vie Shanghai.

Gao Ping, who has been here for several weeks at the Con already. Gao Ping is an eminent pianist and composer and many of you would have heard his piano recitals already, and you will be able to hear them later in the week as well.

And we're joined also by John Huie. John: Australian musician, composer, band director, guitarist. And also we reminisced this afternoon, a member of my Conservatorium High School orchestral workshop group in 1974 at the Sydney Con. So we haven't seen each other for a little while.

So … this is not the place for the grand speech between Australia, China

Except to say that many of us have been conscious of China as a factor in our life since about 1973, and the opening up of China occurred for us incredibly quickly with the ascension of the Whitlam government at that time.

Overnight, we virtually dispensed with Taiwan and its membership of the UN security council and went down the Chinese track, and of course Whitlam himself was the first prime minster to make the journey there.

And his first ambassador Stephen Fitzgerald is still with us these days and we've had very distinguished ambassadors and indeed cultural attaches.

So Australia has always placed great importance on the people that we place in Beijing as our representatives diplomatically and also culturally.

So our relationship with Chinese culturally goes back about 40 years now. So it's appropriate that we reflect on how we have moved through those 40 years.

This evening, we're going to talk to these two musicians about their particular journeys — how they arrived at where they are through their association with China. And we will have occasion for questions and answers at the end, so I want to keep it fairly relaxed and not too arduous.

VP: Gao Ping, if I might just start with you, your journey was a fairly personal one, because your father is one of the most eminent composers in China, and you both had first hand memories of the Cultural Revolution. The Cultural Revolution stands as this gigantic wall in a sense in Chinese culture, before and after. So, you've written about your memories of the cultural revolution, but could you share some in relation to how your father fared through it particularly.

GP: I was quite lucky, I was born in 1970, so by the time I understood anything, it was almost over. The worst part of it. 1976, when Mao died was pretty much the end of it. My father was in a lot of trouble during that time.

VP: Your father was very eminent, though, before that. Before the revolution.

GP: Not really, he had just started teaching at the Sichuan Conservatory of Music, and he didn't have big ideas about politic things at all. It was more of a mistake that he was picked as having counter-revolutionary thoughts. In fact, it was one of his best friends, back then, who reported him.

FIGURE 1 — Gao Ping performing an original composition assisted by composer Annie Hsieh (page turning). Photograph by Sharka Bosakova.

He (his friend) was labelled as right wing early on, so to redeem himself, he had to do this sort of thing — he had to report on other people, maybe make himself a little more favourable.

Of course, I didn't experience all that. But my father was actually locked up, in a sort of … we have a term this, which is … *nui bi se shen*, which means "the cow ghost." *Se shen* is "snake spirit." Nu bi se shen is for people like my father. So bad, bad people. And they are locked into what's called a *nui peng* which is a … stable … He was locked up with several other people like him. No contact, you know, just like a jail.

And the most interesting story about that period when he was locked up, was that he was actually ordered by one of the guards to write a song about themselves. To sing "we are … snake spirits … ", and my father did. He had to write a song. And the choir, you know, it was multiple lines … harmony and everything … so counterpoint. And he wrote this song. And the guard said "if you don't sing this, finish rehearsing this and perform for us, you don't get your dinner tonight."

He did, and they sang, and this guard got very mad. "This sounds too pretty! Not the right sound for you guys!" So they changed it. Finally they were really satisfied with the version they came up with.

VP: I read somewhere that a million intellectuals and artists who suicided rather than submitted themselves to the regime of the red guards, and those of us who have seen the film & read the book *Mao's Last Dancer*, will know the context of some of that because Li Cunxin's main teacher was subjected to disparagement and dismissal, and eradication from history too.

I wanted to ask more particularly in relation to your own upbringing, basically, the progress of western music, which goes back to the Jesuits in the 1720s, as a matter of fact.

JH: 1608.

VP: 1608 — thank you — goes back many centuries. But at this point, 1968 and onwards, is arrested. And indeed almost destroyed: pianos, music schools, instruments, sheet music, all that?

GP: Well, we did in the early 60s before we broke away from the Soviets, we still had … contact with … Soviet composers' music — "correct" sort of music — was still OK. But then after Mao labelled them "The Revisionists" of course, that was the end of that.

But the model opera, you know about Peking Opera, the great operas, were made into versions by a pianist…his name is Yin Chen Zhong, who won a big prize … early on, I think, in the 2nd Tchaikovsky Competition. He was a favourite of Madame Mao … actually she got him a beautiful piano … he could play the piano, but not so much the western repertoire. So he made arrangements of these operas — virtuosic, you know, piano versions. They were quite something actually.

VP: But in general throughout the country side, is it fair to say that there was a dismantling of the western musical tradition —

GP: Yeah.

VP: — for eight years?

GP: Yeah. Sometimes, this can be bent a little bit, for example, [it] depend[ed] on the composers background. For example, sometimes Beethoven [was] OK because he came from a lower class. So it depends, sort of depends, on … you're ok if … you're a poor peasant composer … you know … you didn't have … It's strange, it's not so uniform, actually.

VP: Gao Ping, thank you. We've heard a little bit of your prehistory. The sort of influences that inform you.

But, John: a Sydney boy, a guitarist, a jazz man, China — how do you … what's that journey?

JH: Well, it was a long one, Vincent. And it began in Hong Kong, because I felt safe in Hong Kong in 1991. I thought … like tourists, they'd go to Hong Kong, they wouldn't go to Shanghai because that's China, and we didn't know much about China then. So I began in Hong Kong doing arrangements for the traditional instruments.

VP: How did you fall into that?

JH: Fall into it … well, I began by attacking the movie industry when I first arrived, and then gradually I [had] associations with the string quartet, the Hong Kong philharmonic … [got] to know the people, and then writing, and doing festivals, a lot of artistic stuff, because I mean, the first three years I was really a musical prostitute, I have to say, and people would bag me about it and would say "why don't you do something properly", you know, instead of writing commercial music or film music for Stephen Chow … *Kung Fu Soccer*.

You know, these sort of things.

Gradually, I got a little bit sick of the whole western culture in Hong Kong, and I thought, "no I gotta move outta here, I gotta leave." It's much the same as it is in Sydney.

VP: Anne Boyd who was at the University of Hong Kong for ten years used to say, there was never a more British institution than the University of Hong Kong. The cathedral culture, for instance, the whole festival culture, publishing, radio, was incredibly BBC.

JH: Oh yeah, it really was

VP: That was in your experience too?

JH: Oh totally, the main radio presenter on … RTHK, Phil Whelan, had a *beautiful* British accent. He was an excellent clarinet player also, from the Hong Kong Philharmonic … It was *so* British. Everything about Hong Kong.

But anyway, I decided, right … I only needed a push; I only needed somebody to say, "have you been to China?" And it was actually … mum rang up one day and said, "you haven't been to China. What about Shanghai?" [clicks fingers] That was it enough. 'Cos I'd heard so much. Yeah, mum, mum rang up: "[w]hy don't you go to Shanghai?"

VP: The power of mum.

JH: The power of mum. That's what hit me. Of course, you know it all hit me, all the stuff that we've been reading in the 90s about this place, Shanghai up north. And Beijing too. Not to mention Wuhan, Shenzen. I mean those cities are *huge* Shenzen is so big, nobody's ever heard of it.

GP: The Las Vegas of China.

JH: The Las Vegas of China: Shenzhen! That's right.

Anyway, I took the step ... got there and [on] the first day I was walking through the park, Fuxing Park, with a briefcase and a mobile phone. And I was wearing a jacket much like that and I saw some westerners and Chinese people in the rotunda. One of them had a saxophone, one of them had an *erhu*,[1] and there was another guy with a cello, and I basically dropped everything I had and said, right, "this is culture, this is it, this is *real* culture; it's not propped up by anyone. It's not propped up by a government ... this is just happening in the park, and I want to be part of that."

VP: Were you ever associated with the Conservatory culture of Shanghai? I mean we in the west know the Shanghai Conservatory as being the factory that produces the singers, and the pianists in particular, who play the loudest and the fastest than anywhere else in the planet — did that world impact on you?

JH: Totally! I went after the fastest and greatest *guzheng*[2] player in Shanghai and she turned out to be an absolute goddess, and so wonderful. I mean there are many *guzheng* players, you know, many, and ... the *new* Shanghai String Quartet — you've heard of the Shanghai String Quartet, well, this is the one that doesn't live New Jersey, this is the one in Shanghai, the *real* Shanghai Quartet — and we did a lot of work with them.

VP: Shanghai has had vigorous cultural connections with the west since at least the 20s. Shanghai had a Hollywood type film industry in the 20s. The star system that could today eclipse ... and a lot of that musical accompaniment for those films were western jazz orchestras. Do you want to deposit a notion of how the Shanghai film industry connected with western jazz and how you came into the same scene?

JH: Well, sure, the pop stars you could call them, the Zhou Xuans[3] ... I can't — you know the names of the singers that were famous — were really from one tiny little school, headed by a fellow named Li Jinhui, who was doing a lot of work in jazz, and jazz arrangements. He was obviously persecuted later on (they made sure of that), but he did a lot of work and in fact he really trained and brought all those girls through his school. There were all sorts of little ensembles and theatres that his groups were ... he had a monopoly on the place really.

VP: But there must have been American jazzmen who made their ... prior to him even ... in the 20s.

JH: No he was the first, and then because of the interest, because he brought the interest out in the open, then they did come in, and as I mentioned to you, Buck Clayton was probably the most famous of all of them. A Black American trumpet player who came out in 1934, and … stayed … well, he had one gig and stayed for two years because he love it. There was no racism there. He was teaching and arranging. He would have met Li Jinhui — I'm sure they would have worked together.

And my personal involvement I guess was when I first heard all this music that the pop songs, the Chinese pop songs, which I thought were just beautiful. Not just musically, but lyrically. They were so different to anything you would read these days. I don't have an example here. I might have an example actually, but just lovely, lovely songs about love. Not like pop songs today that are about love. But they're really beautiful poetry. Even in the translation of just words. So I fell in love with that stuff, and I fell in love with Shanghai.

VP: Gao Ping, you've written about the influence of storytelling in your life and the fact that stories are told to you by grandparents and then passed through generations etc, and that this process continued through the radio: I'm wondering also whether you might have had the same experience as John did of experiencing American popular music on the radio *before* the revolution?

GP: Me personally? Well, I wasn't quite …

VP: You weren't born yet, but *was* American pop music prevalent on Chinese radio *before* the revolution?

JH: Oh, yeah.

GP: Probably.

JH: Yeah.

GP: It's probably true.

JH: Of course. My friend, I think his name was Gao as well, actually, a 92 year old jazz guitarist in Shanghai, and —

GP: — the grandpa I didn't know.

[laughter]

JH: You probably might have known [him]. He was … very influenced — he told me — by the greats: Benny Goodman and Louis Armstrong. All the greats: American jazz people. And … 1951 he was actually put away for playing a Latin jazz song, for a year.

VP: And of course there's that wonderful scene in John Adam's opera *Nixon in China* where Madam Mao puts a fox trot on the record player and she and Mao dance into the night. So, you know, American popular dance music percolated … as far as the top.

GP: She was a movie star …

VP: Yes … but getting back to this idea of story telling, and there seems to *again* —

another interruption with the cultural revolution — but the notion of storytelling, then becomes an important part of your own composition doesn't it.

GP: It does, well … in Sichuan because I mean China is a big country so there are all kinds of different cultures around the place, in around Shanghai was the sort of storytelling, which was popular was *pingtan*, which is a really beautiful *umm*, usually two, a couple of musicians, not musicians but story tellers, but also accompanied by *ipa* and it's a very beautiful form. My father was from Shanghai, but grew up in Shanghai so that's the sort of…

JH: But that was really Suzhou, but of course …

GP: Suzhou. Exactly.

JH: Shanghai was the closest big city so —

GP: — popular in Shanghai as well.

JH: Yes, sure sure.

GP: And this would go on for weeks sometimes, epic stories, long stories, and told in this manner. Very delicate, extremely delicate.

But the story telling I was used to is from Sichuan tea house, which is called *Chaguan* … where the artists would perform. And very stylised. And this sort of vocalising, which came into my world later on, maybe came from that sort of influence, I would say.

So it's … acting out different sort of characters. Also quite stylised structure, of the storytelling. You know there's always that sort of, the same sort of ending, and the beginning. The forms … very formal sort of thing.

VP: And do the audience actually expect what happens in the context of that form as in Japanese melodrama, the audience actually sits on the edge of their seats, and they know the form, they know how the story is going to evolve?

GP: This is much more, more much casual, I think. It's really sometimes happens in the tea houses where people drink tea. If you know the story, it's not as formalised as the *Noh*, and people follow the same story, but each story teller is … has his own version. Sometimes it's even improvisation.

JH: It's like the newspapers.

GP: In a way, commenting on … yeah. And that's where the Chinese novel come from, by the way … the Chinese novel, the two words for Chinese novel is *xiao shuo*, which means 'little speaking', actually … literally … Novels were the basic framework written down for this, storytelling, and it's very basic — they just sort of made up, all kinds of things —

JH: — [it] changes.

GP: Yeah, to fill up something.

VP: And your music too?

JH: Yeah.

VP: Same sorts of notions of storytelling, characterisation, and vocalising it.

JH: Yeah, but not so much as Gao, of course, because … in the music I've done is … I've done very little vocal music out of Shanghai Jazz, and it's all instrumental stuff and...

VP: But there are vocal inflections.

JH: Of course, and in fact on that subject … well, the *erhu*, which we both deal with a lot: it *is* the closest instrument to the human voice. There is no other. [To GP] What do you think?

GP: Yeah … [nods]

VP: The categoric statement has been made

[laughter]

JH: Vincent — what do you think? The erhu, think you about, you know …

VP: [pause] We'll have to get Nicholas[4] in to …

[laughter]

VP: … do a demonstration. See whether we have are any contenders.

You still maintain a classic association with Shanghai, John, even though you are based back to Sydney. I should ask you now, what are you doing in Sydney, in particular, but then I want to go back to Shanghai. So what are you doing in Sydney?

JH: Well, I'm maintaining the Chinese Garden Chamber Music Festival once a year, which is —

VP: — Darling Harbour.

JH: Darling Harbour Chinese Garden, and that's a three day event. And it's … we have musicians from China and...it's basically Chinese music, and contemporary Chinese music with Australian musicians, Chinese musicians, and so far it's been a success. We make a CD from each festival and that goes out for promotion for the next festival.

VP: Do those festivals have themes, or particular focuses in location or instrumental —

JH: — they —

VP: — or vocal styles?

JH: They do, the theme really is without getting in too heavy and stuff, it's just commonality. It's commonality … I mean we're all the same. I've chosen China because I know China, the music of China, but the similarities between Western & Chinese music: there are so many, and I don't like the way that we try to segregate even the music, 'cos we've already segregated the people, so I try and make them blend as much as possible.

VP: You've picked up most of this though, almost by osmosis, I mean when you left Australia, would there have been *any* place you could have studied traditional Chinese music? Dale Craig here at the QLD Conservatorium in the 70s and early 80s was I *think* maybe the only proponent of Chinese music and there *was* indeed a Chinese orchestra here at that time, so ... But I can't think of another location in Australia where you could actually study —

JH: — not, what ... you mean then?

VP: Traditional.

JH: Now?

VP: Back then.

JH: Back then.

VP: When you left Australia. At the time that you left Australia.

JH: No there was, look, when I went to the Conservatorium. I was the first guitarist! Philip Moran, myself, Pickler ... was the teacher, Greg ... 1974 was the first time they've got a guitar at the Conservatorium. My point is that they still haven't got one Chinese instrument, you know, at the Sydney Conservatorium. That is interesting.

VP: It was also 1974, if we're being reminiscent ... was the first time the jazz course actually found its way into the Australian teaching institution. The director of the course was to be Garry Burton, but Burton was too busy, and he recommended a

FIGURE 2 — Gao Ping converses with Vincent Plush after a performance. Photograph by Sharka Bosakova.

mate of his, a saxophonist, Howlie Smith. So the incursion of Jazz in to our conservatory life is still very young, within living memory.

So maybe you really hadn't studied much, or knew much Chinese music until you landed there?

JH: Well, perfectly honest I hadn't studied. I went to the east to get money — and then after three, four years of just being a musical prostitute, I thought, well, there must be more, and as I say, that was when I dropped my phone and my briefcase and that was it. Um, it was a …

VP: And now, you, although you live in Sydney, you still have a residency in Shanghai. Tell us about your residency.

JH: Well, I bought a place in Shanghai only because … I thought, well, I was correct in speculation …

VP: Real estate you mean.

JH: Yeah … so it's a nice place to go back to …

VP: You were telling me about it today that it was incredibly quiet. Can I believe that?

JH: Oh, yeah, look I could go on, but it is actually comfortable in some cities in China to live, it is actually comfortable. Where I was living … in

VP: French.

JH: Fu Shi Lu, in what's called the French concession … it's absolutely gorgeous.

FIGURE 3 — John Huie & Shanghai Jazz diva, Jasmine Chen. Photograph by Sharka Bosakova.

Admittedly, the place was set up a hundred years ago for banking companies and important elite, but now it's just a beautiful area, and ... of course there are noisy parts of Shanghai — you can imagine. there are dirty parts and noisy parts. That's the noisy part here [indicating on brochure].

VP: It got a whole lot noisier too this week, too I must think.

JH: Yes ... anyway ... it's a great place to live, I gotta tell you.

VP: So Gao Ping, your journey, then, from China to Cincinnati, to a community that is principally a German community. The original name of Cincinnati was 'zinzinnati' ... with lots of Jewish families etc. You went there — why? To the Conservatory.

GP: I wonder that too...

[laughter]

GP: I was in contact with ... at that time I was in contact with a piano teacher. You might know James Tocco.

VP: Oh, James Tocco. Yes.

GP: The pianist. Yeah. And ... that was the reason really. I went to play for him, and he said "you should come to study," and I was looking for a graduate school so ... I went there.

VP: And you discovered there, a very vigorous composition school.

GP: Well [slight pause] yeah, sort of. Well, I was composing anyway, but I sort of [slight pause] I don't know, it was more practical thing, I thought well, I already had a piano master degree, and maybe I should have a composition doctorate degree, you know? And ... I had a very good teacher, Joe Hoffman you know, and ... there were a lot of great people coming through there. Like Fred Rzewski, I met in Cincinnati. So Cincinnati was very important to me, even though I really didn't like the city itself ... and the school was —

VP: Interesting connection: Larry Sitsky also spent a year in Cincinnati —

GP: He did?

VP: — during the Australian bicentennial exchange program in 1988. And ... Jonathon Kramer, came down to Canberra ... so there was already a musical connection between Australia, China and Cincinnati.

But you would have come into a town with six Chinese restaurants, and would be about the end of the Chinese presence.

GP: Well actually, no. Cincinnati was —

VP: Not true?

GP: ... Well ... there was quite a big Chinese ... community. There is even —

VP: In music?

GP: — that Chinese ... musicians association in Cincinnati —

VP: Oh!

GP: — which actually commissioned me a couple of pieces. So there was ... no, there were a lot of restaurants; they were not very good.

[laughter]

But there were a lot of Chinese restaurants.

VP: I imagine in that context that one of the connections you would have made, you've already mentioned Fred Rzewski and other people, is there notion of a political music that can embody ideas about politics or things outside itself, some of them controversial, etc etc as impetus for creativity.

GP: That is probably more through my contact with my friendship with Frederic, but already before that there was interested in that sort of thing, I think as a Chinese person, you're naturally sort of sensitive to it. Either you try to stay away from it, or you try to be outspoken. But we are political people you know, we went through a lot of movements. But through the music of Frederic Rzewski —

VP: For those of us who don't know this name, and his name is not really well known in Australia,

Rzewski, R-Z-E-W-S-K-I ... and a very prominent pianist-composer too, whose music is very, very political in many respects.

GP: Extremely.

JH: Well, on that subject, what I was going to say, the composer — you might be able to help me here — now I read his name is "ni o er."

GP: Ni Er, oh yes, yes.

JH: Ni er, OK.

GP: Chinese composer.

JH: OK. Well, now he's the writer of the current.

GP: Of the anthem.

JH: The National Anthem [hums opening tune]

VP: Stands.

[some laughter]

JH: Anyway, back in the 30s he had a teacher ... for a very long time, by the name of Lee Jin Huai.

GP: Oh, really.

JH: So, what, in fact happened was, the National Anthem of China is written by the student of a big band arranger. So there you go...one for the books.

GP: Yeah.

VP: Thank you for that, John. Good to know there's another trivia buff in the room.

JH: I'm full of trivia.

VP: Look Gao Ping, I think one of the most striking things about your music is the ... presence of Chinese folk song as a metaphor ... in an almost rzewski-ist fashion. Can you play those pieces in China?

GP: Folk songs?

VP: Your piano pieces.

GP: Oh, I've played all of them —

VP: You have.

GP: — in China, yes.

VP: But without the irony.

GP: Um...with irony.

VP: Do people get the irony?

GP: Some do. You can ... always think differently about it. But no, my Chinese folk song pieces were not political, in that way.

VP: They weren't viewed as proletarian music in the way the Russian ...

GP: [slight pause] No ... they are not meant to be, but there are pieces which have messages, but I've made them — I was very careful about not making them very obvious so that's ... a number of composers.

JH: But that's it. Yeah, of course.

GP: But I'm not stupid you know, I'm not going to put myself in trouble by standing on the street, shouting something, singing some slogan, like the Falung Gong. But I have my view on things.

VP: Some composers have sort of secret agendas, in their music I mean, secret messages, codes...whatever whatever. Are there similar approaches in yours?

GP: Yeah.

VP: Ah ...

JH: Ah, code.

GP: Yes, code.

VP: Would you have studied with George Crumb at all?

GP: No, but I knew him.

VP: He's very popular as an influence in China.

GP: Huge.

VP: George Crumb's brother was a cryptographer, during World War II, and George's study is lined with books of … "decoding codes" and all that sort of stuff, and he maintains that every note is a code for something that is sent out into the ether(net). That would appeal to some Chinese, I'm sure.

GP: You know like IChing … Book of Change.

VP: Similar messages in your music, John?

JH: Oh …

VP: Messages.

JH: Yes … yes, there was. Yes. [pause]

VP: Insufficient answer.

JH: OK, OK, I'll give you one of the age-old conspiracies…the one about China discovering America, and … it's a possibility.

GP: There was this book by um —

JH: Well, there were a few books … I did a whole suite, 4 movements … with … there was … let's see who was involved? Guqin, cello, piano, double bass … yang qin, erhu, and lots of big red drums. Lots of big red drums. [demonstrates]

Anyway, this was called *The 1421 Suite*, based on Gavin Menzies' research as a navigator, which he was. Unfortunately —

VP: Discredited by historians, yes.

JH: Well totally discredited by historians because of his publisher who I've met, and is a complete idiot (I'll say that on the record).

GP: [laughs]

JH: And in fact *he* was the reason that a lot of the lies, and the extra stuff, that was put in that book, because it sold copies. So you could say that some of that is truth in that book. I strongly believe that, but then a lot of it is just made up stuff that may be true [that] this Hong Kong publisher pushed him into doing. Anyway, *The 1421 Suite*, I've got it here.

VP: We should be hearing it.

JH: We should be hearing it.

VP: Any prospect of a Chinese discovering Australia in your music? There is one other theory.

JH: [slight pause] Oh ... [pause and points at GP]

VP: We'll talk about that [later]

JH: [laughs]

VP: Gao Ping, the other striking element of your music for those and many of us who have seen you perform ... is the business of gesture. Not just the vocalising — and as you point out somewhere, can you imagine asking Glen Gould not to make a noise while he's playing — but ... deliberate singing, vocalising, shouting slogans, turning the piano into a sort of music box or what have you. Is that Chinese opera?

GP: I'm sure there was ... some of it came from that. Because if you go to China you'll see these musicians, folk musicians that when they play ... well, some of Chinese classroom music is very quiet, you're not supposed to move much, but folk musicians. You know like some of this, particularly these minority groups (like the Liao people, Dong people) —

VP: — we won't mention them.

GP: They [laughs] when they play this, you know the Chinese Sheng? The big

VP: Yes

GP: Um, mouth organ. They dance also. I mean it's enormous physical ... um, and I think I love that, you know that feel. I don't want to make myself just do this, but the actual involvement with your person, um, and it's very attractive to me. So it's maybe not a conscious thing but unconscious one.

VP: You two, are almost mirror images in reverse, in some respect: an Australian who finds himself in China, and a Chinese who's come to the west, and whose career and identity is formed, by your transference. So really, here are, two journeys that have almost bisected and transferred each other —

JH: — In Chinese terminology, I'm an egg and he's a banana.

GP: [laughs] Yes, yes.

JH: That's how it works. You understand that? I'm Chinese on the inside and western on the outside.

VP: And a banana is.

JH: Gao is...

GP: White inside you mean? Not quite. No I'm still an egg.

[laughter]

GP: I'm a banana egg.

JH: Banana egg.

VP: Well, on that really interesting metaphor I think we should maybe wrap up our part of the conversation. There are many other things that we could do, but I mean this has touched commanalities that we're going to see throughout the week through … Anne Boyd in Hong Kong, through Larry Sitsky's own history as a Russian émigré to China, and coming to Australia. The whole Shanghai experience on the weekend and so on, so these resonances will now flow on throughout the week.

Endnotes

1 Chinese two-stringed fiddle.
2 Chinese twenty-one string zither.
3 Zhou Xuan (1920-1957) was a popular actress and singer known as the "Golden Voice" and one of the "Seven Singing Stars" of China.
4 Nicholas Ng, who plays the erhu.

CHAPTER
13

Conversations with Anne Boyd and Julian Yu

5 May 2010
Queensland Conservatorium Board Room
Transcribed by Jaret Choolun on 20 October 2010, Brisbane

VP: I'd like to welcome Anne Boyd from Sydney, and Julian Yu from Melbourne. Anne comes to us from the University of Sydney where she is Pro Dean of Academic Studies, and Julian from Melbourne where he is a freelance composer — he is one of the rare examples of people who can live mainly through their compositions.

I'd like to start with Julian, because his life story is really very interesting. We were reminiscing: the first, and indeed it may have been the last time we met, was soon after you arrived in Australia in 1986. I was preparing a series of radio programs about Australian music to be sent to America for 1988, the Australian Bicentenary. Back then, I remember trying to get a radio interview out of you was extremely difficult. And in fact at one stage in the interview I had to write out a sentence for you.

JY: My English was so bad.

VP: Well, that just proves something because you had arrived in Australia not too long before that time. You have to tell us, firstly, why you came; and what you found when you first arrived.

JY: I graduated from Beijing Conservatory, and then I went to Tokyo to study modern music with Joji Yuasa.

VP: Yes, Joji Yuasa, which is a name not unknown to Australians because he was based at the Sydney Con for several months in the late '70s, and also a colleague of mine at the University of California San Diego too, so we have a connection with Joji, yes.

JY: And then when I returned to China and met an Australian student. We decided to get married. She wanted to come to Australia; she didn't want to live in China. I had to make a decision: either not to get married, or get married in Australia. It was a big decision to make. At that time I had one commission from Tokyo to write a ballet in collaboration with my teacher and a Chinese ballet company. But if I went ahead with my marriage plans I would have to give this up. So in the end I said, OK, I'll migrate to Australia and have a free life, and a fresh start. When I came here I realised nobody knew me — nobody knew I could compose.

VP: But I knew you through a recording of a percussion piece, so people had already started to play your music: Synergy, I think, had recorded that percussion piece, which I put into that radio series. So your music was a little bit known even before you came, I would suggest.

JY: 1988, yes. After I migrated to Australia I wrote three pieces, and that was one of them.

VP: So this is soon after you arrived. You came to Melbourne — fresh start, clean slate — knowing no one in music?

JY: No. I said to myself, "If I want to be involved at a professional level, I have to be involved with institutions." I had to get my degree, or start it. So I enrolled in La Trobe University to do my Masters. So at La Trobe I met Keith Humble. Joji is his friend.

VP: Yes, he was around the same faculty. This is in the twilight years of La Trobe University, because their music department then closed. Was La Trobe a good place to go for you? You're not a technological person.

JY: No, I'm not. But they had good composers there. Lawrence Whiffin, Keith Humble. A two-year scholarship provided me free time to write music so I could

FIGURE 1 — Julian Yu. Photograph by William Yang.

submit it to competitions and orchestras. I sent many pieces. I realised that if you're over thirty-five you don't have the chance. A lot of competitions have a limit of thirty-five or forty years old. Out of fifteen pieces I'd normally have one or two get back to me either recommended or with an award.

VP: But you won the first two Paul Lowin awards in 1991 and 1994. These were Australia's most prestigious and indeed most beneficial awards in terms of money, and you won the first two of them. That was extraordinary.

JY: Because at that time I had an unperformed and uncommissioned piece, which fit the regulations of the first Paul Lowin Prize. I think many composers had pieces that had already been performed. The second time I submitted and won again.

VP: Julian, that's remarkable in itself, but even a few years earlier you won the Koussevitzky prize from Tanglewood in 1988. And then every year there's an award from the Vienna Modern Music School. You were very good at entering competitions. This is the springboard for you career.

JY: I met X in Melbourne. He looked at my music and gave me an application form for Tanglewood. This gave me a chance to present my score to masters like Lenard Bernstein. He looked at my score and said something, which I can't quite here ...

There were fifteen composers who spent the afternoon with Lenard Bernstein. He looked at my piece and said "You're a fucking genius." [Laughs] After this session, a friend of mine said, "Julian it's a pity you can't put that in your CV."

VP: Well, from here on you can use it. We'll give you permission for that. Now, Tanglewood's a very heavy environment. I also went there for several years, and actually had conducting lessons with Bernstein. We won't go there. The world is at Tanglewood. How did Melbourne look after Tanglewood?

JY: Well, for a period ten to fifteen years, my performances mostly happened in Sydney and Brisbane, not in Melbourne. It seems like if you live in a city you are not important to them anymore, because you are a real person walking down the street or taking the bus; if you live in another city people think you are an imaginary object: you're special to them.

VP: I would disagree in your case to some extent. You've been adopted almost as an emblem by the Melbourne Symphony Orchestra. When they go to China they take Yu as an emblem of Australian multiculturalism. This is what you've become in the MSO's[1] eyes. Going back to China as a composer accompanying a major orchestra on a major tour, performing in the major performing arts centres of China, how did that feel?

JY: Terrific. A once in a lifetime experience. Twenty of my relatives' friends' circles bought tickets to my concert. I had to give a talk before my piece; I was so nervous because there were so familiar faces in the audience. It was a terrific opportunity, I felt very proud to be part of it.

VP: Thank you for sharing all that with us. I haven't read much of that in print and it was very good to hear what Australia did to you in the last twenty years.

Anne and I have known each other for a really long time. We recently had a wonderful experience in Canberra where she was based at my institution, the National Film and Sound Archive, for a month, preparing materials for a new opera. We had occasion during that time to revisit a film that was made about you in 2001: a film called Facing The Music, which, basically, was one of those *cinéma vérité* numbers where a film crew chased you around for several months as your department, the University of Sydney music department, was basically being closed in front of your very eyes. It was a very moving occasion, and I think both of us revisiting this a decade later, caused us to pause on where we've come from and where we've gone. Anne's had a remarkable journey, firstly at Sydney University in the 1960s, and going from Sydney to the University of York, working with Wilfred Mellows. York was this sort of Australian colony, wasn't it?

AB: It became this Australian colony. I'm the first of the baby boomers, I say. I have this thing of where I've *been*. Quite often other composers have *come*; there's been this little coalescence. So in York I was the first of the Australians to arrive as a graduate student to do a PhD in composition. And the next year Alison Bauld came, and then Martin Wesley-Smith came. Then Ross Edwards came to live in the same area; he wasn't actually enrolled in the department. So we had this lovely little enclave of Australian composers, it was lovely. Roger Woodward used to come often and visit. Similarly at Pearl Beach.

When I came back to Australia after being abroad I had absolutely no money, and I had to live somewhere that was pretty cheap. I found a beach place I could rent, a lovely place called Pearl Beach just north of Sydney, and lived pretty cheaply there. It was a bit lonely at first, but before long there were other composers like Vincent Plush, and Ross Edwards, and Tony Gilbert and his wife Allison Gilbert: all composers came to Pearl Beach. Then there was Don Oh Kim, a Korean-born Australian writer, who was very important for my development as a composer. He was the first librettist I worked with for a number of years — that helped frame my aesthetic. He brought an Eastern aesthetic to a Western context, and that was very important to me; I brought a Western orientation to an Eastern context.

VP: Every ten years you uproot and go somewhere else just to continue that process. I got so sick of Pearl Beach because there were too many visitors. You go away from places like Sydney to remove yourself from people, but when the people come to you — I had to go back to Sydney myself. The 1980s was your Hong Kong period, and after Hong Kong is the Sydney University period, which continues to this day. So, Anne has had this extraordinary career of moving every decade or so, and making substantial contributions in each place. The place we want to talk about today is Hong Kong. Last night with John, and with Gao Ping, we talked a lot about Hong Kong being a very British place; the garrison almost of the empire. Did you feel that?

AB: I came into the tale end of that. I arrived in Hong Kong in 1981, and by then my Chinese friends were refusing to call Hong Kong a colony; they insisted on calling it a territory. But of course Hong Kong had originally been a colony.

VP: So how did you actually come by the job in Hong Kong?

AB: My early life was here, but then I went to England, and I was at the University of York, and then I found myself employed by the University of Sussex after I'd graduated from York. I spent eight years all up in the UK, turned thirty, and had to decide whether to stay on in England and adopt it as my home, or whether to come back to Australia. There was something telling me to come back to Australia, or I wouldn't be able to write the sort of music that I thought was in me to write. And I came back to Pearl Beach. I found subsistence very, very hard. Unlike Julian I've never been very good at winning prizes; I've always been very individual, too individualistic as a composer in some ways for my own good, I suspect. But I'm probably not as brilliant as Julian either. Lenny Bernstein would have never called a score I wrote genius. Although Morton Feldman did once, which was lovely. He said, "You're more talented than Stockhausen, kid!"

VP: Which might not be a compliment.

AB: No, it might not. But it was very hard to subsist in Australia. Also, much to my surprise, I found that I missed an academic environment. I love working with other academics; I love operating in a milieu of ideas. Universities, at their best, are great hubs of ideas and challenges. I love being contest to having ideas contested, and people disagreeing, I really get a buzz out of that. So I was looking for another university job. There was nothing becoming available for about ten years. So I had to go back to the UK and look around to see if there were any jobs in British universities; there weren't.

But while I was there I heard through the Association of Commonwealth Universities that the University of Hong Kong was looking for someone to start a music department. They'd already interviewed three candidates and weren't happy with any of them. There was just an offside chance, because I was travelling back to Australia, and could travel via Hong Kong, that they might see me — especially because I had a lot of Asianist influences and interests: I'd been an Asianist pretty much since the mid 1960s. So, the secretary wrote to the University of Hong Kong, telling them about this young unemployed academic who thinks she might be the person to set up your music department for you. So I got off the plane in Hong Kong and looked around at the lovely mountains and thought, "Oh, I'm going to live here. This is the place I belong." I don't know why I thought that, it was one of those wonderfully intuitive things. Probably because I was an Australian and not British, helped me get that job; but mostly because I adored Asia and already knew quite a lot in a broad sense about Asian cultures and musical traditions, particularly of Japan and Indonesia, but also a little of China and Korea and Thailand. They were really interested in that.

I'd been the first appointee at the University of Sussex, so I'd been in on the birth of another music department, so I had a bit of relative experience. So they took a risk and said, "Alright, we'll appoint this young, inexperienced woman to this job." It was wonderful, and I didn't look back.

VP: So in a sense the two of you had clean slates: in Hong Kong, and in Melbourne. Julian, you've been able to live as a freelance musician with a little bit of teaching.

Also, you've had some degree of commercial success as an arranger of Chinese folk song, with the ABC recordings, which are played a lot on ABC radio.

JY: Yes. There's a Chinese singer who used to be very popular in China. When she came to Australia she asked me to orchestrate some Chinese songs for her, which was very easy, so I did that for her. ABC put them on two discs: one called *Lotus Moods* and another called *Willow Spirit Songs*. These are the old proper Chinese melodies, art songs, folk songs. I had written so many serious works — concert works, but it seemed nobody knew me; but after these two discs, everyone knew I could write for orchestra.

VP: And that wonderful review in *24 Hours*, which said you were the Canteloube of Australia; your *Songs of the Auvergne*: this gave you a public profile. People know you now through those two recordings I suspect.

JY: The problem is many people ask me to arrange music rather than to write a new work.

VP: Did you arrange *Waltzing Matilda* for the MSO?

JY: I arranged *Waltzing Matilda* for Chinese orchestra, which is on CD now. I also arranged the *Advance Australia Fair* for Chinese orchestra. It will be used for Chinese citizenship ceremonies. I also applied to have my arrangement played at the 2008 Beijing Olympic Games at medal ceremonies when Australia won, but the application was not successful.

VP: Bureaucracy, bureaucracy. I've always wanted to ask you, have you ever approached film music? Have you ever been approached by film makers?

JY: I did several film scores when I was in China after I graduated from the conservatory. But that was as a toast composer. They would only give me some simple melodic lines using numerical notation: 1, 2, 3, 4, not using staves. So I did some of that. It's a good opportunity to practice orchestration because you can write anything — test effects — using someone else's name.

VP: So it can be someone else's failure.

JY: Yes, somebody else's failure.

VP: But — and I think this is what we all think about your music — it does give you an enormous command of orchestral technique. You probably have the finest ears, I think.

JY: … Having had the opportunity to practice the sound.

VP: Other composers — everyone things of Brett Dean, for instance — who know the orchestra from inside out (Brett is a viola player from this institution, too) know the orchestra either as a conductor or a player, but you don't play.

JY: No, I only play the piano and the Chinese erhu, a two stringed fiddle. But I listen to the sound of instruments. At VCA in Melbourne, if I hear someone playing the harp, I will knock on the door and say, "Can you play this for me? Can you play that for me?" After a few minutes, I'm knocking on another door.

VP: That's why the sign at the keyboard department reads "Julian Yu not welcome."

JY: [laughs] It's terrific writing for orchestras.

VP: Anne, you came to music as a flute player. The flute is almost a spiritual emblem in your music. The single wind line that appears in all your phoenix pieces and Asian pieces, with its Asian inflections, is another dimension of the Asian influence.

AB: Absolutely. I was thinking, when I was preparing to come up here today, "When did I first hear Chinese music?" And I remembered, as a tiny little girl, living on this huge sheep station, Manaru, outside Longreach in Central Queensland, hearing on shortwave radio the broadcasts of Chinese orchestra coming from Singapore. That was the first time: I can still remember the static, I can remember the sounds of the urhus and the bauhus and so on in the orchestra, making these wailing sounds and being totally fascinated by it. It was like a dream world for this little girl way up in the outback here.

VP: Was it an escape world? Out of the realm of sheep stations?

AB: I don't know, it was too young. It was just something that happened at night. We could only pick up these frequencies when the air was quiet. There was a huge chestnut wood radio right outside the door of our room, and I'd hear it when I was partly asleep, and yes it really was like a dream world. My next contact with China was also as a tiny child, living in that same place, on the Dire River, which is a tributee to the Thompson River, which flows through Longreach. Out on the Dire there were remnants of an old Chinese market garden. It was wild and overgrown; the man who had owned it didn't live there anymore but there were wild vegetables that would

FIGURE 2 — Julian Yu, Gao Ping & John Huie. Photograph by Sharka Bosakova.

come up after the wet season. That was my other earliest contact with Chinese culture. Again, it fascinated me as a little girl. Out there we didn't go to school; we were very isolated so anything that, as a child, your imagination could play on, became very important in life.

VP: Two other important composers have almost identical stories: Lou Harrison's early experience of Asian music was through Chinese markets in San Francisco; Percy Grainger's earliest experience of all oriental music was through the Chinatown in Melbourne. Those are the experiences that remain with you, and you continue to develop them.

AB: And, interestingly, another experience then, which is not specifically Asian, but sort of got mixed up with it, was that we used to have itinerant Aboriginal workers who would come through the property and do stock work. I can remember, again as a tiny child, hearing the distant sounds of Aboriginal ceremonial music being performed: I don't remember the sound of didgeridoo, but singing and clapsticks being heard, again, at night. That got mixed up with the Singapore stuff: the Chinese orchestra and, of course, the landscape itself.

Those of you who have been out to Longreach would know that it's very flat, very red soil. It's very beautiful, actually. Nature is vast; you seem very small and nature seems very big. All that got mixed up with the Australian landscape for me. The last thing — which is really important — is that being isolated I was sent a plastic descant recorder when I was five or six years old. I could read by then, and I taught myself to play on that instrument. My very first instinct learning music was to write some down. So, that single wind sound, mixed into this strange whole lot of influences, was where my own musical sound was from.

VP: Leaping ahead, you became a flute student of Victor McMahon at the Sydney Con, and then you both decided that you were not going to be a flute player, and that you would enrol in a music degree at Sydney University. You enrolled at precisely the time that a young music lecturer had come up from Launceston, whose name was Peter Sculthorpe. I think Peter gave the first courses in what was known as Ethnomusicology. Peter set off a whole new direction for Australain music through those classes: yourself, Barry, Ross ...

AB: Yes. I remember Peter putting on Gagaku, the traditional court music of Japan. His first playing of *Etenraku*, and I instantly heard the outback of Australia in that music. I had never known why, but of course it's because it sounded a little bit like that music from Singapore I was describing, on the shortwave radio, which is linked in to this sense of landscape. That became for me the starting place of a musical language.

VP: Julian, have you ever tried to teach Chinese music in Australia, or in an Australian environment?

JY: From time to time, I've been asked to talk about Chinese music. Basically, just showing some traditional forms of music, playing some recordings.

VP: Are you in touch with current developments in Chinese new music, so to speak?

JY: I have a lot of friends in China. I sometimes hear the music they write. In terms of incorporating traditional Chinese music there are probably two types: one is direct importation of raw material, like timbre, scales, melody and instruments into a piece. That's very commonly done. It's good- I'm not criticising it. And I sometimes do it. The other type is how to inherit traditional music into contemporary composition by way of thinking, or method. When you listen to Chinese music, why does it sound like this? Why is it different to Western music? Put this reason, or method, into the music.

Chinese musicians never play the same as what is written on paper. It may say "mi" [sings, quavers: *mi mi la re ti*), and the erhu player [sings, semiquavers: *mi re mi fa la re do re ti*], or even some more into it, and this version then becomes another standard of the song. And then somebody will do: [sings with more ornamentation] with a lot of decorations. You then have a lot of pieces, all with different titles, and from different geographic areas. But if you line up all the skeletons, it's the same piece. I think it's a very unique way of producing music.

I watched a program on SBS about Christian music in Chinese rural areas. An interviewer asked a Chinese woman, "Can you sing this Christmas song for us?" [sings "Deck The Halls"]. The way she sings it is ornamented [sings]. So that's a very Chinese way of producing versions of traditional themes. Composers often use this method rather than the material. A lot of my pieces are produced in this way, so you can pick up my score and I can say that this music belongs to the skeleton of one particular piece. Almost every one of my pieces has a reference to original Western European pieces.

FIGURE 3 — Anne Boyd. Photograph courtesy of Anne Boyd.

VP: The secrets that do emerge. I wonder if we're going to see both approaches in the music of the Purple City Forbidden Orchestra this week. They are a group of contemporary musicians who play Chinese traditional instruments, and have this mix of the two paths: the traditionalist and the absorbed, contemporary strains. So we may indeed hear some of that this week. Anne, you were nodding your head with, I suspect, some degree of not very pleasant memories of trying to get Chinese musicians to play a notated piece.

AB: Oh, no, on the contrary. I was just thinking about it as a method of composition, and how close it is to the way I work myself, which is this elaboration, making flowers: taking a single idea and then making ornaments, and flowering around a single melodic line is often how I construct music myself, both in a horizontal and a vertical sense.

VP: How did the experience of living in Hong Kong … you lived in a high-rise building as a single mother, with your daughter Louise; you imported a number of Australians; you had Nicholas Routley live there for a while, and various others. At the English-speaking University, you had Peter Wesley-Smith, Martin's brother who, when he left, had been there for thirty years as an expert in Chinese legal history, and Martin would come in from time to time. Was it an Australian enclave?

AB: It was very mixed. Peter was already established in the university when I got there, so Martin did visit. We had an American, we had an Englishman: Nicholas Cook … my other main colleague, who is now a Professor of Music at Cambridge — a scholar and wonderful musician. It was a real mixture.

FIGURE 4 — Julian Yu & Gao Ping. Photograph courtesy of Julian Yu.

VP: What I'm saying is on the one hand, while you buttressed your Australianness by bringing these people around you, you were still very much impacted by that environment of the teeming city: of the noise, the clutter, the congestion, the wonderful character of possibilities it presented for you, as you were saying to me the other day.

AB: The thing that struck me about China most was energy. It has enormous energy and vibrancy. Anything is possible in Hong Kong — anything at all — it's a jumping-off place, where you can build mountains. Your future is limited only by your imagination and your capacity to work really, really hard- those two things together. That was an ethos that I found fantastic to work in and amongst in Hong Kong.

In fact, I didn't compose a lot of music in Hong Kong; I composed some, but not masses, not nearly as much as I composed in Pearl Beach. I was very busy. I became a mother when I'd been there for a couple of years, and that absorbed a lot of my time. I was very busy setting up the department. My other baby was of course the Music Department. They were very fulfilling. I didn't feel the need to write a lot, but I did write some music for Chinese instruments, including for our Vice Chancellor, who was an amateur violinist with a wonderful *enthusiasm* — is the best way of putting it. I wrote a piece for him when he retired for Yuanda violin with a big choir.

VP: And of course *Black Sun*, which I want to hold for a minute, to go to Julian. Anne is talking about finding a charged energy — an electrical atmosphere in Hong Kong. What was the sort of energy you found in Melbourne — or in Australia, which has sustained you all this time? It's different, isn't it? Not necessarily less, but different.

JY: It's very different. Everybody talks about Australia as the relaxed atmosphere, with no pressure and worry-free. I tried to compose when I was in China, when I visited my family for three weeks. I just couldn't write one note because there is always something happening, a lot of competition. People look at you, "What are you writing?" I have this opportunity, you have that opportunity, they're all trying to compete with each other. That's very disturbing for me. When you meet composers they all talk about how successful they are: "I got this position, I got that prize, I got this performance." When I came back to Melbourne, I thought "that's not my space," so I'm not interested in that outside world. That's what I find about Australia: it's far away from those people who disturb my composing.

VP: So it's your space: you've created your space. Most composers — whether they want to or not — establish a group of friends who are other composers or instrumentalists.

JY: I know that's very important. I recall, looking back on my performances of recent years: every performance has depended on one of my friends, or a person I know. It's very important if you want to be a successful composer, to have this skill. I don't have this skill, but I've accumulated it naturally for the last twenty years. I'm very bad with networking at functions, getting close to somebody. I tell this story: a very famous Chinese composer is networking at a function. He gives his CD to a person. Then he talks to another person who would be more useful. He goes back to the first person and asks for his CD back, gives it to the second person and asks him to promote his music. I think it's very rude for the first person. Successful composers have skills like this; I don't, so I'm not very successful.

VP: People would argue otherwise Julian, but that's alright. Anne, you were in Hong Kong until 1990. You left the year after the fateful year of 1989, which we associate as the year of Tiananmen. You had quite a vivid response to that due to personal associations. Would you share that with us?

AB: Yes. That was a big turning point for me. I was really very happy in Hong Kong, and at that stage I imagined I would stay on at the University of Hong Kong until retirement, which would have been in 2011. After the Tiananmen Square massacre it became very difficult. Some of our students were in the square, and I knew that Hong Kong was going back to China in 1997 — the basic agreement was already being negotiated in 1989 — and there was no escape, there was no way Hong Kong was not going back to China; unification being a very important part of China's strategy. I felt after that time that probably I wouldn't be comfortable living there under a communist regime. That was part of it.

The other thing was that the Chair at the University of Sydney came up. I'd always promised the first Professor of Music at the University of Sydney[2] that at Peter Platt's retirement, who was the second Professor, if the chair became vacant again, I would apply. At first I thought, "No, I don't want to come back to Sydney." I was very comfortable in Hong Kong — I loved Hong Kong. I was learning Chinese quite well, learning to write characters and so on, and it was becoming a very culturally fulfilling place to be for all sorts of reasons. But, somehow, the 1989 massacre, and the coincidence of that with the chair falling vacant at the University of Sydney … I put in a late application to Sydney and, when I was appointed, felt I had to take it for those reasons.

VP: But the events of June third '89 at Tiananmen Square elicited this extraordinary piece, *Black Sun*. How did that piece define the moment for you, in terms of your own composition afterwards? You'd been in Hong Kong for nearly ten years, now you produce a work that — even only ten minutes long — packs a punch.

AB: I don't know. It was an outpouring of grief. I just didn't know how to respond to the dreadful business that it was; the dreadful incident in human history that that massacre was. I didn't know how to respond in any other way. I wrote a piece of music — it was the only way. It was in fact a commissioned work for the San Francisco Bay area Women's Orchestra, so I knew I had to write an orchestral piece, and that was the piece that came out. Other than it being a very personal response, a response that I hoped would enshrine the memory of the students who died, in some small, humble way, I don't know that it had any significance beyond that. It was great that it was played for a number of years, by different Australian orchestras, nearly always, coincidentally, on June third or fourth, which commemorated the anniversary of the students who died.

VP: Do you ever envisage a performance in China?

AB: I don't think it will happen in my lifetime, and I'm not sure that it should. I think there are two sides to the China question. My then Vice Chancellor at the University of Hong Kong knew Xiaoping[3] quite well (then the leader of China) … would go over to China and speak with him. You have to remember that the idea of the iron rice bowl is that communism was introduced as a way of feeding people. So many people were literally dying of starvation; and yes, many people died as a consequence, and it was fairly terrible, but a lot more lived because of the iron rice bowl. Communism fed the people who were starving.

He also spoke with me about how too sudden change in China could create a situation of chaos, which would mean that many more people would die, and many more people would suffer, so change could only come gradually. So when I say I hope that in a way it doesn't happen in my life time, because I love China and I love the people of China, I want it to happen in a way that is right. The economic progress in China is astonishing; the progress towards democracy and human rights is happening, but it's happening in its own time.

VP: Julian, in the way that Anne produced *Black* Sun, is there a piece of yours that was a response to that?

JY: Not particular to this event. I'm writing a new commissioned work for Tokyo Philharmonic next year that is based on another political event. In 1958 the Chinese government started a campaign to wipe out all the sparrows because they'd been eating the crops. So everybody went out into the street, beating pots, pans, drums — anything they could find — making such a noise in the city for several hours, so that the birds couldn't land anywhere. All the trees and the roofs had people beating, keeping the birds flying. The birds eventually died of exhaustion. I called my piece *Descent from the Sky*. I think that was a very sad moment in human history: such a thing for nature, the birds dropping to the ground.

VP: You've just suggested a solution for Southbank Corporation's problem with the ibis.

JY: In this piece, I quoted a very famous tune *The East is Red* to represent the political policy. People know the tune and they know my political intention.

Endnotes

1   Melbourne Symphony Orchestra.
2   Donald Peart was Professor of Music at Sydney University from 1948-1974.
3   Deng Xiaoping (1904–1997).

CHAPTER
14

Conversations with Larry Sitsky and John Curro

6 May 2010 — Queensland Conservatorium Board Room
Transcribed by Jaret Choolun on 18 November 2010, Brisbane

VP: Good afternoon, and welcome to the third of our conversations in this week of conversations about China and Australia. The previous two conversations have been very interesting in the way we have been able to trace and move various cross-currents over lives from China and Australia. Today is going to be at least an entertaining session, with two of the elders of the musical tribe of Queensland, and Australia: Larry Sitsky from Canberra, and John Curro, conductor and viola player from Brisbane. They have a long history of association with this institution, and with each other; (to John Curro) you two go back fifty-something years I would suggest — perhaps you can reminisce as to when?

JC: Late 60s ... middle 60s, something like that.

VP: Larry, let's begin briefly with you – and we don't want to get too bogged down in the early history – you came to Queensland in particular to take up a piano position at this institution.

LS: Yes. I came here straight from San Francisco.

VP: We should go back. Larry was born in Tianjin, China in 1934 to white Russian émigré Jewish parents. You lived in China until you came to Australia in 1951 with your parents, so you were actually well into your teens. Larry and I have discussed over the past several months the vivid memories that Larry has of China of the late 1940s, and so on.

You came to Australia, studied at the Sydney Con, and then got a scholarship and went to San Francisco and studied with Egon Petri, the extraordinary composer-pianist-theorist, who was himself a student of Busoni. Busoni was, of course, a student of Liszt, so what we have in Larry is a direct extraordinary line from the romantic idealism of Franz Liszt, through to Busoni, to Petri, to Larry. I was present at a ceremony at the National Library a few months ago, for your 75th birthday, at which many of us felt that you'd passed the torch on further to Michael Keiran Harvey. One of the most important dimensions of Larry's life as a composer, musician, teacher, writer and everything is this notion of the transferrance and moving on of tradition, and a direct connection with tradition. Coming to a country like Australia, which has struggled to establish its own traditions, would have been a little bit odd for you. Coming back from San Francisco to a piano lectureship here at the Queensland Con in 1966 — how odd was it?

LS: It was very strange. I think I got the job because Egon Petri, in his reference, had said something about my extraordinary "double-octaves." So I think that's what landed me the job. When I got off the train in South Brisbane, to be met by Basil Jones, he quoted that. So I said, "Ah! I should let Egon know that that's what did it." But the transfer was extraordinary, simply because growing up in Tianjing, I was subject to a massive number of international communities. You might remember from your history that all the large cities in China had been carved up by the Western and Japanese forces. They called them Concessions. It was at the point of a gun of course: they split all the cities up, and Tianjing was just like Shanghai, Beijing, and what was then known as Canton. And so after a fairly short time in Sydney, where I

FIGURE 1 — Larry Sitksy performs a Chinese-inspired composition. Photograph by William Yang.

studied with Winnifred Burston, who was herself a pupil of Petri and Busoni, she arranged for me to go to Egon Petri. He very nicely and very kindly arranged a scholarship for me. I went in '58 and studied with him, coming back to my first job in Australia in 1961. I came here close to the beginnings of the Con, and in fact arrived at about the same time as Jan Sedivka. Not only did that cement a friendship, but I met this madman [Curro] at about the same time, and we gave quite a number of concerts together.

VP: And that madman: at the time, John, were you with the Queensland Symphony?

JC: No, I was an architect at the time. I then played the violin in the QSO for a couple of years, and then I was asked to come and teach here because the teacher at the time packed up and left two months before the final exams. There weren't too many students, but they were stuck without a teacher. So they said, "Will you come and teach for the rest of the time?" and I said, "Yes, but I've got a job. I need assurance that I will have full-time conditions even though the job will only be temporary." They said, "Of course, yes." So I taught for two months. It came to the Christmas holidays and I hadn't seen a pay check. So the minister sent me back a pro-rata cheque based on the percentage of the three months annual Christmas leave that the two months represented. So I tore it up! Isn't that silly? I've always been irresponsible with money. So that's how I came to the staff.

VP: This was mid '60s?

JC: No, that was later than that. I was just having lessons from Jan. I had almost given up the idea of doing music professionally when I heard that the new violin teacher was very good, so I thought I'd give him a try. He wasn't only very good; he was something of a genius with getting impossible cases like me to get a grasp of things, to get going. And so he more or less caused my removal from the architecture profession into the music profession, with considerable loss of money again. It's always been like that — it's a shame, isn't it?

VP: John, your growing association with the institution led you to form the Queensland Youth Symphony movement back in 1966.

JC: 1966 we started, and as usual, everything in my life is an accident, and starting the youth orchestra was also an accident. A very good friend of mine, John Stinson, who was a Franciscan priest at the time … he ran a nice music program at Padua College, and was on the staff at the Secondary School Music Teachers Association. He rang me and said, "We're going to put on a festival of secondary schools' music to convince the state government that they should do a structured music program in schools. We're going to invite the minister to come and hear this. I have this idea to put together a combined schools' orchestra. Would you do that?" I said, "Sure, I'll do that." I didn't know anything about conducting, but I said, "Yeah, I'll do that." So this came together, but the concert was pretty terrible. I've still got a recording of it if you're interested. Every time I think I'm getting clever I put that recording on and think, "Oh yeah, just don't forget about that."

VP: Well, from humble beginnings. I'm going to take you to China now. '73, of course, was the year in which we Australians woke up to the realisation that there was this giant, megalithic country on our doorstep called China. We were recognising it, and we turfed Taiwan out with the UN Security Council and so on. All of a sudden we were a neighbour of this mysterious beast called "China." One way of establishing relationships between countries is of course cultural coutures, education connections and so on. It wasn't very long after the Whitlam ascension that the first of the cultural tours of China actually happened.

JC: And the first of them was the Rosny Children's Choir from Hobart. I think they must have spent a long time at Foreign Affairs, trying to think, "What can we send to China that's not going to tread on anybody's toes?" because it was a really, really awkward time. Gough Whitlam had an instinctive genius at the time to re-establish these diplomatic ties in December of 1974. So they thought, "A children's choir: that can't upset anybody, surely!" Nice, lovely, politically neutral children singing. The only thing about it is the conductor was a Christian religious fanatic, and tried to make the all the Chinese officials, who were looking after them, say their prayers every day with them! They took it very well, the Chinese, and it was fine. The second program they sent over was me. I understand that all the big-shots around the place who were asked to do it were terrified, and poor little me was the only one left who was going to go. Nobody wanted to go without taking their orchestra with them or something like this. So I said, "Sure," and went.

VP: You and Jan went together?

JC: No, I went on my own in 1975, to conduct the Shanghai Philharmonic Orchestra for a couple of weeks, and then to have a look at the conservatoria all through China. The preamble to this is very interesting in the context of relations between China and the West, because in those days Western music was out of favour with Mao's wife and the Gang of Four; the cultural revolution was in full flight. There were God knows how many communications between Foreign Affairs and China and me, saying, "Yes, you can do Beethoven," then the next week "No, Beethoven — you can't." "Debussy's fine ... No, it's Ravel." Eventually we did nothing. I just went over there with the *Yellow River Piano Concerto*[1] and a couple of Chinese revolutionary skills. That's what I did for two weeks.

VP: That began a long association with Shanghai, did it not?

JC: Indeed it did. I did a lot of good early work at the Shanghai Conservatorium. I wasn't there for long, but one of the things I noticed, for example: I said, "Where are the viola players?" "The viola players? You don't want to see the viola players." Talk about viola jokes! This is a fact. "Who cares where the viola players are?" Anyway, eventually I found three or four viola students skulking, hidden somewhere; you weren't even to know they played the viola, practically. And so I thought, "This isn't very good." I said "Let me have a look at your library." So I went to the library: there were the Bach cello suites for viola; there was a Saint-Säens cello concerto, reprinted for viola; and there were a few Kreutzer studies. That was the library for the viola students.

VP: John, you established, at that stage, the beginnings of a formal connection between the Shanghai Conservatorium and the Queensland Conservatorium.

JC: I did go into that possibility, and I think we might have cemented that on the second trip. But I'm not so sure how well that was followed up; I think you'd have to look into the Conservatorium archives. I know that Anthony Camden, the director, went once as a visitor there, and I don't know any more about it. Tell us, Peter [Roennfeldt].

Peter Roennfeldt: We did have a memory of understanding sides, and there have been a few visits from cello teachers on exchange.

JC: But this is in recent years. Around the time that we did this, which was in 1979, I got four students to come here on my personal financial guarantee. They stayed for a year, and after that I think the whole thing went fuhtz, for I don't know how many years, which was a shame really because they were classy students who we could have done with at the time, really.

VP: John, there's a lovely reminiscence on the Sydney Symphony's website of a violinist named Shuti Huang, who's the acting assisting principal second violin. Of course, last October I think it was, the SSO went to China with Ashkenazy, and to Shanghai in particular. He said, "My move to Australia began in '79 when I was studying at the Shanghai Conservatorium. The Australian violist and conductor John Curro and violinist Jan Sedivka came to Shanghai on a cultural exchange program between Australia and China, and I was chosen to play for them at the masterclass. I spent almost two weeks with them, and forged a long-lasting friendship with them both."

And you arranged for him to be offered scholarship for him at the Con, so in 1980 he came to Queensland, and he says "What a change from Shanghai!" He goes on a little bit: "In my view, Shanghai changes every month. Twenty-nine years ago the site of the venue for our Shanghai performance (talking about the SSO in the Shanghai Concert Hall, the Oriental Arts Centre) was a rice field. People came here for picnics and fishing, and a few villages were scattered around. It was very rural. All of a sudden, in the last twenty years, it changed. Shanghai is like Manhattan now: the New York of the Orient. The construction and development of the city just continues. When I left China I could not imagine the amount of development that has occurred over the past twenty years; in fact, a lot of my colleagues wonder if I will move back here, because they like it so much. Larry: you were, I think, the earliest diplomatic visitor on a cultural exchange.

LS: I was, yes. I went on an official passport, on a cultural exchange program. They thought I was the right person because of my background, and that I would understand something of Chinese culture and, in fact, relate to it. I must say, coming back, I did feel a certain amount of homecoming, because it's where one is born. Even though I'm not ethnically Chinese, parts of me, culturally, are very much inclined that way. So, I was very happy to go, and we did a little pub-crawl through all the conservatoria along the coast, including Tianjing. When I was living in Tianjing the central conservatory was there; it was only moved to Beijing in later years, I'm don't know exactly when. So in the early years, growing up, I played with the orchestra from the Con there in Tianjing. It was really interesting: foreign players — Russians, but others as well, Spaniards, Portuguese, whoever, émigrés coming to China — they were all part of this orchestra. And so at that time I thought that's how the world was put together; I didn't realise that it was unique, in fact. So coming back had very strong elements of nostalgia. It was interesting: the Chinese didn't see Australians as ex-colonisers; they in fact saw us as a country that had been colonised by another power which — I hadn't thought of it that way — strictly speaking it's true. So we weren't on any kind of imperialist, capitalist black list. It was OK.

VP: You told me recently a rather moving story of going back to your hometown, and even going back to the block in which you lived, and the very building in which you lived, and what had happened to that building.

LS: Yes. We lived in the French Quarter. It was the French concession. Opposite us was the French police station, and they had gendarmes wearing funny shaped hats. We had a rather nice, large French colonial-style house and I used to walk to school, which was in the English concession. As you crossed the border there were English soldiers standing there, with the funny hats. It was kind of normal, we went to school and so on. Anyway, when we came to Tianjing, they had very nicely done some work beforehand, and they said, "Do you remember the Address?" and I said, "Yes. 38 Harbin Road — used to be 40 Rue Dillon." They found 38 Harbin, found the house. They'd chatted up the people inside, and we went in. I had tea with the people living there. It was very moving. There was in fact one resident from my boyhood, and I said to her, "I was there at your wedding." And she said, "Yes!" She was a grandmother by then. There was a very welcoming atmosphere, so we went in and wandered upstairs. My bedroom, I discovered, had been divided into two floors: there was a mezzanine floor because old-style French architecture has tall ceilings. There was a whole family living there; I actually felt a little strange saying, "This used to be my bedroom."

VP: Those of us at the Shanghai dinner on Saturday night will see some films that were made around this time by a gentleman who ended up in Australia in the late '40s by the name of C.F. Bliss. He was an Austrian Jew who escaped Europe during the war, and who was an amateur filmmaker, and made his way to Australia via London and Shanghai. The movies that he made in Shanghai in the early '40s — we've had a look at some — are very good home movies without sound. They give an indication of everything you talked about. In fact, do you remember what you said as you were watching them with me?

LS: Yes, I think there was a shot of an Indian directing traffic. I remember that this also was not unusual. Depending on which concession you were at, there was someone of a different hue — if you can put it that way — directing traffic. The

Indian was part of the British March, and he was doing his duty for the Empire, you know.

VP: I remember you said to me, "This could be the home movie film of my boyhood." So that's the film that you'll see as the backdrop. John: the visit of the Philadelphia Orchestra was the first major orchestra from the West post-Red Guard revolution. That was in '76.

JC: It was right after the Cultural Revolution had run its course.

VP: Yes, so the introduction occurred very quickly. One of the things on Kissinger's own agenda was to bring orchestras and musicians. Many of us have seen the film From Mao to Mozart with Isaac Stern; we could have made another film about you.

JC: Yes, you could have, no doubt about that. Would the fee have been good for me, do you think — as good as Mel Gibbs'?

VP: Well, maybe in 1979 it would have been as good as Mel Gibbs' fee.

JC: The thing about the early, early days is that there was nobody else there, there was just me. And the second visit was just Jan and me. There was nobody from the West coming in there yet. In fact, you really had to be very careful what you said and what you did. Every time I talked about something-or-other and they said "No, no, this is impossible," I'd get out my little red book, which I'd studied before I went, and I'd say,

FIGURE 2 — John Curro with young Chinese students. Photograph courtesy of John Curro.

"In here, the Chairman says we must not only develop ourselves now, but me must protect the old traditions. You're telling me you can't do so-and-so, but you can!" There would be confusion, and they'd rush around and look at the book wondering if I was right.

VP: This was the general protocol.

JC: Oh, yes. I had a lot of fun with that. The thing I really remember about that first visit is that we tried and tried to play some Western music with the Shanghai Philharmonic, which is a really good orchestra. I think I became certainly the first Australian expert on the Yellow River concerto, there's no question about that.

VP: Did you inflict it on us?

JC: I did, once. It was here at the Con.

VP: That's the end of diplomacy.

JC: It's a pretty hotch-potch piece, and then I discovered that the committee wrote it anyway. But there was something rather beautiful about the opening of the second movement, which used a traditional flute. It's really quite beautiful, and I said to them, "Let's try just a little bit of a — " "No, you can't do that!" "Why can't I do that?" "Because the official interpretation is that you can't do that." So I said "Oh, OK." So there you go, you see: even the way you interpreted a work in those days in China was forbidden unless it complied to the party line. The big people that suffered from all this I think were the composers, because the composers had to write according to the formula all the time. And the formula was: "long live Chairman Mao, and long live the People's War."

There were two wonderful violin pieces. This is hilarious. They can't just write pieces that don't resemble Wieniavski, Sarasati or Paganini if you want to write violin pieces, so we have these two fabulous little Chinese "violin pieces" written during this period when they couldn't play Western music. They were pure Sarasati, pure Wieniavski; but the titles were these: *We bring Chairman Mao a Piece of Tibetan Brickade*, and *The Sun Shines Brightly Over the Steel Smelter*. Even the titles had a political purpose. And the composers, if they'd had any talent, must have been incredibly frustrated.

LS: I can tell you a lovely story about one of the composers. We went out on a boat — a river trip — with a group of Shanghai composers. There were no officials with us, so it was fairly open. One of them told me a lovely story. He submitted a piece called *Symphonic Poem* to the committee for approval. It was not backed. The reason: it was formal music, and it had to mean something before they would approve the piece to be played. I said "Well, what did you do?" He said "Oh, I changed the title. It was called *Chairman Mao Contemplating the Swans on the Lake*." He sent the same piece in, and it was fine, they played it.

JC: Yes, it was like that, all right. It was really like that.

LS: This is what happens when you have fat commissars in charitable culture. The same thing happened in Russia, after all.

VP: At this point we move on; or back. Larry, from Brisbane you went to Canberra in 1966 as one of the foundation staff members of the new Canberra School of Music, which was founded by Ernest Lewellyn, the former concert master of the Sydney Symphony Orchestra. And you've been in Canberra for forty-five years, on and off. You're one of ALIA's most lustrous professors, and you were awarded its first higher doctorate in fine arts in 1997.

LS: And as far as I know there is only one of them.

VP: Your move to Canberra makes you then more accessible to the machines of government, and to the Department of Foreign Affairs. And, as more people **become** aware of your presence, largely as a pianist I suspect — and we all know that pianists are harmless …

LS: Mostly.

VP: You get offered invitations to go to Russia, first, as a diplomatic visitor. But in Russia you begin to find things.

LS: Well it was a similar experience. You see, I wasn't born in Russia but my background, through my parents, is Russian.

VP: When I knew your parents briefly in Bondi, they used to speak Russian to each other.

LS: Yes.

VP: So Russian was spoken in the home.

LS: Oh, yes, of course. So, when I went back to Russia it was again a kind of weird homecoming. And there I discovered that there was a hidden chapter — is this what you're leading to?

VP: Yes.

LS: In Russian history there's a gaping black hole, which, to this day, hasn't been explored, although it's beginning to be looked at. The hole was there because the fat commissars decided that there was a small group of composers that were officially *kosher* (can I use that?). The others were written out of the history books, or went of doing something else. I discovered the full truth when, in revenge for my visit, the Russians sent Khachaturian here to Australia. I took him to Bateman's Bay — we got fairly tipsy on fairly bad vodka, but the fate was familiar — and asked him about this period. He knew that the room wasn't bugged, you know; we were having oysters and vodka there by the sea. And he said yes, there was a whole movement of composers, and he named a few. But then he said they either left, or — I forget the word he used, but it meant "silenced" — they might have seen the error of their ways. In the official encyclopedias, when you looked up *Kildish* (which is the Russian *Grove*), if you look up a composer like Mosolov, who began forging an international career and so on, it says, cryptically, that *earlier in his career this composer made artistic mistakes.* So this was what interested me. I wrote a book, which might well be in your library here. It's called *Music of the repressed Russian avant-garde.* It covers that period from the beginning of the century, up to the revolution, until 1929, which is basically the year when Stalin assumed total control.

VP: John, when you first began to go to Shanghai and other places, was there a sense of Big Brother Russian musical process over the conservatory tradition?

JC: No. I think at the time I went they hated the Russians. That was the time they were more or less at war with the Russians.

VP: What I am asking is the Russian concerto tradition, and the competition tradition …

JC: You mean how they devised the official music? Yes, it was a combination of Rachmaninov, Liszt, Chopin a little bit. Yes, all that stuff which they reckon was revolutionary and/or sensual. And they used exactly those models to create these Yellow River concertos, the *Red Detachment of Women, Taking Tiger Mountain by Strategy*; these funny, revolutionary scores.

VP: Larry, I'll throw the ball to you. Were you aware of there being any sense of the Russian dominance in the pedagogy?

LS: There were still a few Russian teachers left here and there as we worked our way through the conservatoria: highly respected on the staff. So they hadn't gotten rid of everyone and I think, culturally, they felt OK with that; politically it was, as John points out, a totally different issue because the Russians thought that China would become part of the Russian Empire. But, culturally, there'd been a fair bit of traffic both ways, and yes, the modelling was Rachmaninov more than anyone else probably. It was the big Romantic gesture; all, naturally, contradictory because the composers that they admired were the products of the Imperialist system.

JS: They weren't allowed to be played at the time either.

LS: I love the *Yellow River concerto* because you get all the clichés over in the one piece. It's a piece built on a succession of clichés.

VP: John, can we talk about the sorts of students that you found in Shanghai in the early days and moving ahead?

JC: I've told you about the unfortunate viola situation in '75. Coming back to Brisbane I photocopied the whole of my viola library, put it into two or three boxes and sent it off to the viola teacher at Shanghai Con. When I returned in '79, only four years later, there were thirty viola students there and at least half of them were very good., so I patted myself on the back a couple of times for that. But in both visits I was confronted by students of twelve and thirteen years old, who could play the socks off anything at all that you would put in front of them. They were fantastic. And when it came to whose turn it was between Jan and I to take the class, we'd say "You take it." "No, you take it, what am I going to say?" And finally I landed a guy who'd just payed the *Carmen* fantasy, the Waxman version. He was fifteen, and played just like Heifetz. Jan said "You conduct opera, tell him about the story of the opera." Then I started getting involved in the story of the opera, and about how these were all prostitutes. And I thought "Oh no, they hate prostitutes in China, you can't talk about prostitutes!"

VP: You said he sounded like Heifetz. Was it because he was listening to Heifetz? Did they learn from recordings?

JC: Let me tell you what the situation was in China at the time. This is a lesson for us all to learn in Australia right now, where principal study lesson times are being progressively cut down. And if the principal study lesson times are cut at the conservatorium, what on Earth are they doing to make up for that? In any case, the statistics in Shanghai — and this is extreme of course — are: 268 students; about 289 teachers, which meant that each student got at least one lesson a day. That means that all they were doing really was supervised practice the whole time. Take that back to the beginnings of their program, which are in places called Children's Palaces, where littleys — three, four and five years old — are taken out and tested for their skills. Some of them go on to be acrobats, some sportsmen and some musicians. And those are progressively screened, tested, developed until entering the conservatorium. No wonder he can play like Heifetz. They're only incredibly gifted and incredibly motivated. The other aspect of it was that if you didn't do music or something like that, the alternatives were the army, or the farms, or the factories. So the kids that went through music, and got a job in music, were relatively better-off citizens.

VP: Those of us who have seen *Mao's Last Dancer* will relate to that. Larry, your trips to China were as a composer though, not as a pianist per se. There were remarkable trips by Ernie Lewellyn, Donald Westlake, all from Canberra, and others who brought people back from time to time. Ernie actually had them at his farm in the Southern Highlands and would have masterclasses for them over several weeks. So there was already a sense of bringing people out to the West.

LS: It had to be subsidised in those days, because the Chinese themselves could not afford to pay for the costs. Now it's different; well, everything's different. The exchange was wonderful because Ernie found, like John did and like Jan did, that the wealth of talent was huge. Because of the huge population, and the selection process, you were dealing with the top level of a very musical and highly gifted nation with a culture going back thousands of years. And so, when they would ask me about Australia, and the population, and our history, I could see they were barely suppressing giggles when I would explain that our population was somewhere around 20 million, which meant nothing really, and that our culture really only began around

1900, if you can pin a date on it. To someone from a country like that that's really small bikkies.

JC: There's a kind of a feeling that those kids were just technical machines and were not musical. That's been said a lot, but it's not true at all. I think the Chinese, if anything, have had this cosmopolitan influence for many more generations than Korea or Japan. So they had been exposed to the Western influence much earlier than the other Asian countries were.

LS: For some reason I just remembered that the Shanghai Conservatory when I was there the first time, was on the premises of the Jewish Cultural Centre. There were so many buildings put up by people who came from Europe and wherever else. They were solidly built, and many of them are still there.

VP: Often the Chinese students who have come to Australia have all the technical chops, but then there's the issue of interpretation. I've actually been in rooms at music camps where they say, "Teach me interpretation."

JC: Let me just go a bit further about that second visit to Shanghai, where we established a string orchestra. Orchestrally they were less secure than they were as soloists, interpretively speaking.

VP: Because you can't make an orchestra out of soloists.

JC: Exactly. I had this funny experience. We had set up this string orchestra, and the players were terrific. The harder the piece I put in front of them, the better it went. The stuff like Handel, or Bach, they'd stop and break down every couple of bars; there's not enough to do, they just didn't know where they were. They had nothing to hold on to. The most work went onto the easier pieces; when it came to Hindemith or something like that there was no problem at all. But orchestrally, I think, there was a bit of a problem because anybody in an orchestra in China had spent their whole lives playing the Chinese national propaganda music. They had no idea about Beethoven, or Vaughan-Williams. When I went back later on, in '79, my old orchestra, the Shanghai Philharmonic, gave a concert that I went to. On the program the main work was Vaughan-Williams' 2nd Symphony. And I said to them "Wow, you've come a long way in four years," and they said "Yes, but we worry that we don't know how to play it." It's interesting: players of this calibre who don't know how to play it.

VP: Larry, you've had Chinese students come to you in Canberra. "Teach me interpretation."

LS: What is different is the relationship between the master and the student. In Australia we're very laid-back with the relationship. First-year students come in, and it's "Larry" on the first day. I'm OK with that, that's perfectly alright; but a Chinese student would not do that. You'd have to expressly say to them "Please call me Larry." The point I'm making is that the tradition is more a relic of the passing-on of knowledge and information by aural means. So the teacher tells you what to do and you do it, usually without question. And of course in Australia, John alluded to our somewhat abbreviated teaching here. In Canberra it's like everywhere else. We teach students for twenty-six weeks of the year, so you get to train a musician for half a year. It can't be done. And of course any teacher worth their salt, and at their own expense, gives lessons during the breaks which, according university rules, is not legal because you might be favouring some students. So we've got all of that as well. I must say that that's one of the first things that strikes you when you start comparing the cultural backgrounds and the work ethics. We're very relaxed, generally. I'm actually delighted to have more and more students from Asia — from China — because the work ethic is incredibly high. I hope to God they don't learn too much from our lot.

VP: I want to change tack and talk about your personal relationship and how that has actually created an extraordinary body of work. In fact, in a couple of weeks' time, on the Saturday 29th of this month, John your orchestra is premiering Larry's third symphony. You've appeared as pianist with the orchestra: I recall a memorable performance of the Brahms' *Piano Concerto No. 2*. So it goes a long way back.

LS: Oh, yes. We gave any number of concerts in the early days in Brisbane. The Busoni Two.

JC: Yes, it was fondly called the "International Contemporary Music Society." And we played things like Block and Busoni! That must have been along time ago: seventy or eighty years or so!

LS: I can tell you a funny story. When I saw John, a while back, he said something about, "Your pieces are all too hard, too complicated, to cerebral." He turns to me and says — cheekily, I thought — "Have you discovered C Major yet?" And I said to him, "John, if you want C Major you can have it in spades." So the *Third Symphony* uses three notes: C, E and G. There are no other notes except for the last bar. In the last bar, one other note creeps in. It's a B flat. A second inversion C chord with a B flat stuck up top. So I guess it's a second inversion tonic 7th.

VP: Stravinsky said that he discovered C Major for himself.

LS: Well, this isn't strictly C Major. I played with different notes, but they happened to be the C Major triad because of what he said.

JC: It serves me right. Having delivered it, I thought, "Well, I have to play it, don't I? I can't wriggle out of it this time, so it's on."

LS: I'm going to find out on Saturday what's going on with it. It's easy. I'll say to the orchestra, "If you're playing something other than C, E or G, you're wrong."

VP: I at least it will test our ears for intonation issues.

LS: It sounds easy, but the tricky part is that once you write octaves — big ones, for the whole orchestra — then the truth comes out.

JC: This reminds me of the Chinese with all these directions in their scores: "*Surge forward! Fight to the end!*" are the conductor's directions for the orchestra. I don't know what they mean. Larry's got one for three piccolos in unison. And the little direction says: *"This is written on the assumption that, in the normal course of events, none of these three players will be able to play in tune with each other."*

LS: Well have you heard three piccolos trying to play the same note?

JC: You'll see.

VP: You've got a minute worth or retaliation, John.

JC: Oh, no. I accept my medicine, after having made the comment. He's delivered the repost, and I think it was well done, and I accept the challenge.

VP: This is a relationship of long-standing, and a very solid foundation, and it ain't over yet, folks.

Questions from the audience

Anonymous (for LS): *Were you exposed to traditional Chinese instruments as a child?*

LS: Oh, very much so. Not far away from us there were two places that I haunted. One was a place where Chinese opera was performed, and the other was a Buddhist temple. The temple was particularly fascinating because of the serenity and the beautiful chanting. I couldn't tear myself away from it. After a while the monks noticed that there was this strange, Russian kid there, and they would say, "Come in if you want to, come in and sit and listen," which I did. The opera was fantastically exciting because the massed percussion was something that has been with me all my life. My mother was worried about me going to the opera only because I had a habit of buying food from the street stores. She was quite right, because I managed to get typhoid as a result of buying a glazed apple; but that, as they say, is another story. As well as buskers on the streets, there were opportunities, if you wanted them, to hear a lot of Chinese music, uncontaminated by any European influence at that stage. We're talking about the late '30s, the '40s. The opera was fabulous.

JC: One of the things that Mao actually did decide was a good thing, and that was to retain the traditional forms of music and training. When I was there, even in the '70s, there was a very strong traditional instrument movement. They were playing traditional songs; there was some revolutionary music written for ancient instruments. What was that famous *pipa*[2] piece? *Ambush on All Sides*. It's a famous piece — one of the early historical pieces. They were all still permitted to play the early music.

Peter Roennfeldt (for LS): Larry, could you talk briefly about the *Violin Concerto*?

VP: The *3rd Violin Concerto* being played tomorrow night.

LS: As it happens, the concerto was written as a result of Jan Sedivka going to China a couple of times. He used to come and visit, and we'd sit around talking about the next possible piece. This idea of writing something new based on something very old came up in the conversation, and that's how the concerto happened. It's partly my response to Jan discovering Chinese music, and it's full of slides and so on that the players have to cope with; not just the soloist, but the cellos and basses have the Chinese slides. Partly, also, it's what I remember, acoustically, of China. So, it's a kind of internal travel log that's occurred; to you, of course, it will sound like something else, I don't know what. It's Chinese in the sense that they're fragments of remembered melodies. There are segments of a kind of pentatonic — but coloured and chromaticised — and there's a lot of percussion. It's the memory of the opera, you see. That's the genesis of the piece. It has nothing to do with being politically correct with China or any of that; it's just me remembering. What I remember most is the beautiful operatic gestures of singing, which is now in the violin part, and the percussion. There are no opera strings at all, so it's the solo voice with percussion, but I've added some brass because it's also part of the grandeur of China and the age and the civilisation. That's what prompted the piece.

Endnotes

1   *Yellow River Piano Concerto* was collaboratively arranged by a group of revolutionary Chinese musicians including pianist and composer Yin Chengzong and composer Chu Wanghua. The work was based on the Yellow River Cantata by composer Xian Xinghai.
2   Chinese four-stringed lute.

CHAPTER

15

Conversations with Ash Dargan

9 May 2010 — Research Fellows' Room, Queensland Conservatorium
Transcribed by Nicholas Ng on 10 December 2010, Brisbane

NN: Hello Ash.

AD: G'day Nick!

NN: It's great to have you here at Queensland Conservatorium. Maybe we can begin by asking some questions about your background: where you were born, and maybe you can tell us something about your heritage and your upbringing as well, and where you grew up.

AD: OK, well, I'd like to begin this story with where I was conceived. Where I was conceived was in Darwin, Northern Territory on Larrakia land. My background is from there, although I didn't grow up there and I wasn't birthed there, but I was certainly conceived there. I was actually born in Chincilla, just west of Brisbane and was adopted ... grew up on the Gold Coast. Had a wonderful life, just a very normal life.

But my heritage was a mystery to me, and in 1992, that all changed because the government changed the freedom of information act. That was a big year for Indigenous people and the stolen generation.

And so armed with that new amendment, I was able to find my mother and my Aboriginal heritage. I moved back to Darwin. I got in contact with my mother, she invited me back, and I moved up on a one-way ticket and started the next chapter of my life, which was all about Aboriginal culture, the Larrakia people and my grandmother (a traditional elder of the Larrakia tribe) who were the traditional land owners of Darwin in the Northern Territory. So I identify now as an Aboriginal man from the top end of Australia, the Larrakia nation.

NN: When did you discover music?

AD: Music, oh, in Grade 4. Growing up on the Gold Coast, I went to the Broadbeach

State School, and there were music opportunities there for students, and I put my hand up. I started the cornet in Grade 4 and I remember my teacher's name, Mr Hughes. He used to conduct the mighty big band at the time.

He was prolific on the Gold Coast as a musical teacher and conductor, and he inspired me. So that's when I started. I eventually graduated to trumpet a year later.

NN: And when was it that you discovered the didgeridoo and flutes?

AD: The didgeridoo didn't … I didn't discover that until I was 21, which was in 1992. So, that was parallel to my returning home to my culture. The didgeridoo came with that. I remember it was only a couple of days of me being in Darwin for the first time—21 years old, meeting all my family, going through some ceremonies, reconnecting with the greater family, the greater tribe. And my uncle, my great uncle, one of my grandmother's brothers, actually passed the *mamalima* to me (the didgeridoo, in our language is "mamalima"), and he looked at me and he told me: "this is part of who you are." And he held the didgeridoo up to me. "This is a part of who you are. Are you gonna take it up? Are you gonna continue?"

And I looked at him and look at this strange instrument, and you know growing up playing trumpet, I thought 'yeah, I'll give it a go' and I remember saying to my uncle, "Uncle, I'm not really sure. Why don't you leave it with me, and I'll get back to you in a couple of days."

And what happened is I just feel in love with it. It was like a duck to water. It made sense to me even though I didn't grow up playing it. And I wouldn't call it … it's actually more complex than the trumpet in many ways with the techniques of playing it. But for me it became something that I held on to in my personal journey of finding out about my Aboriginality, finding out the history, finding out the stories.

The didgeridoo for me, being able to have it in my life and constantly be playing and practising, somehow helped my journey of reconnection.

NN: Yes, and it was wonderful to have you here playing the didgeridoo at the opening [of the festival]. Certainly you're a very special person for us for ENCOUNTERS, not only because of your musicality but also because of your heritage. I know that you are partly of Chinese descent, which is why in many ways you're the embodiment of ENCOUNTERS for us: the Australia-China connection.

AD: That's right, I was so pleased to be invited and you're right, Chinese is part of my heritage as well. My grandfather was responsible for that. He was a second generation Australian Chinaman. He was from Canton and he worked on the Pine Creek goldmines and he married my grandmother. So … my mother and all my aunties and uncles are half-half. And so that's where I have this rich Chinese heritage from.

You know, by the time I got back to my people when I was 21, my grandfather had passed away early in his 50s, from cancer, and so I didn't actually get to meet this man that now plays a mythic role in my life because my family talks about him. These were very tough days in Darwin. He spoke both Cantonese and Mandarin. He was an epic gambler, all the Chinese were. He was a part of his culture — the Chinese community brought their culture with them, of course, and he was very involved in that, so he knew his culture. Unfortunately for me, I ... never met him, and I'm sure for me that piece of the puzzle is still unfolding. What is that part of myself? I need to have that dialogue in my life so that I can understand that incredible lineage within me.

I've been given the opportunity to follow the Aboriginal side, and boy, I can't wait to touch and dance, and live and breathe the Chinese heritage side. So when you invited me to *Encounters*, it was this opportunity for me to meet Chinese people, to be amongst that culture, and to breathe as much of that in, to get as much as I could from that, and it was really special for me, thank you.

NN: You're very welcome. It's very special for *us* to have you here. And maybe there are musical avenues that we can explore together between the didgeridoo and your other instruments.

AD: Yeah, you know, I remember asking my mother on the phone because we did the panel in *Encounters*. I really wanted to come in informed about any possible musical relationship that the Chinese and Aboriginal people had ... back in those days, and she ... gave me a lot of information on that.

And you know, we were all poor people back in those days, so people just couldn't afford pianos ... It was all just about real *hard* life, and ... things were very, very different back then. But what I like about any opportunities say if *we* were to play together, we could explore: well, if our ancestors had the opportunity to play, because they had their culture with them (that's a given-music was so much a part of their culture) had they been given that opportunity, if life hadn't been so hard. What might have come ... in this joint living together, these Aboriginal Chinese families living in the north of Australia? If they had instruments and the freedom to explore that, what would it have sounded like?

And that's where we get to explore now, and I think that's a very beautiful concept because we get to honour them in a way, to honour our ancestors to by giving them music that we can play together and offer it up to them, and for me that is a way that we would approach it. Because these people lived in hard times, they didn't get the opportunity to, but we do ... We're they offspring and so we can offer that up.

NN: That's wonderful, Ash. So I look forward to ... exploring this connection, even musically and in research too. A joint publication, who knows?

And so is there anything significant you might like to say about yourself? Your career highlights, your plans for the future? Working with intercultural music ...

AD: Having travelled the world, having so many opportunities being a mamalima player, and using my background of music to develop myself and explore myself musically as a serious artist, as a professional artist — I consider myself very fortunate. Through successive opportunities, I have been able to travel a lot and meet a lot of other cultures around the world. And I became fascinated just with meeting other cultures. I loved seeking out the old people, sitting around the fire and just dialoguing, and always in English ... seems to be the one language that all cultural people around the world can speak in, thankfully.

But there was also our musical instruments, and quite often I got the opportunity to dialogue over the fire in other places in other natural environments overseas. Other places that people called home, culturally, and I got to explore this wordless dialogue through these ancient musical instruments that actually share a great many things in common. And this is what I started to understand, and this understanding birthed in me, and I hold that very close to me.

It's personally what I honour most about sitting with other cultures that have ancient forms of music, and I enjoy speaking and dialoguing with those instruments with each other, because what I find and what a great deal of other cultural people that I've sat with dialoguing in this way, that we see and explore and share parts of ourselves that simply can't be spoken. It seems to me we're really sharing on a multi-dimensional level through the power of music, and you know, that's just a wonderful thing.

So, I hope top continue doing that, because I just seem to understand so much about myself and other people through the act of dialogue, of just sitting around the fire. Simple, simple, simple. But there's also the sharing of food; there's the sharing of time together. There's looking into each others' eyes and telling the story of your people, and all of these moments are synonymous with coming together with other cultural people, because these things are as important as music. Music is a part of that. It's one of the dimensions that we share in, and it's a beautiful one.

BIOGRAPHIES

傳記

Kim Cunio

Dr Kim Cunio has studied with a number of Australia's finest musicians including Australian composer Nigel Butterly, conductor and producer Eric Clapham, and Jazz guitar legend Ike Isaacs. His work with the ABC has seen him compose and produce music projects for CD, radio and television over the last decade. He is one of Australia's most accomplished researching composers and was awarded an ABC Golden Manuscript Award in 2004 in recognition of his work with traditional and Islamic music. Kim works in new art music, music research, traditional music, acousmatics and screen. He plays a large number of traditional instruments and has appeared at a number of local and international festivals including the Festival of Universal Sacred Music (New York). Kim's music is expansive, beautiful and multi layered. He has a state of the art studio and lectures at Queensland Conservatorium Griffith University.

Shan Deng

Winner of the Sydney International Piano Competition's Best Australian Pianist Prize, Shan Deng is a well known Australian-Chinese pianist now working in Hobart, Tasmania. Her successes include winning the keyboard final of the ABC Young Performer of the year award, and representing the Arts as a national finalist in the Young Australian of the Year competition. Shan has also received Churchill and Fulbright fellowships to travel and study in the USA and South Africa.

Shan's early music studies were undertaken in the gifted children's program at the Central Conservatory of Music in Beijing. Studying with Leah Horwitz, she obtained her Bachelor of Music at Queensland Conservatorium Griffith University with first class honours and a university medal. Shan then completed a Master of Music, with a scholarship at Manhattan School of Music, where she studied under Professor Phillip Kawin.

Concert demands have taken Shan around the world, and she has performed in Australia, Asia, the USA, South Africa and Europe. She has toured overseas as a soloist with the Queensland Philharmonic Orchestra, and has appeared with all the Australian Symphony Orchestras. Shan has been featured in numerous Australian, Chinese and South African radio and television programs.

In 2001 Shan accepted an appointment at Conservatorium of Music, University of Tasmania, where she is currently Lecturer in piano and co-ordinator of the keyboard department. Shan is in demand around the world as a concert artist, teacher and adjudicator.

> *A stunning repertoire, played with distinction* — The Mercury
>
> *Shan Deng is a pianist of precision and flair* — Cape Times
>
> *Mozart's sonata in C major... was poetically charged and played with style, intelligence and amazing energy* — Courier Mail
>
> *An ecstatic audience returned this wonderful performer back to the piano for many encores with enormous enthusiasm* — Kapati News
>
> *Here was a pianist of great charm and elegance* — The Advocate

Erik Griswold

Eclectic composer-pianist Erik Griswold fuses experimental, jazz and world music traditions to create works of striking originality. Specializing in prepared piano, percussion and toy instruments, he has created a musical universe all his own that is "sincere" (neural.it), "playful" (igloo magazine), "colourful and refreshingly unpretentious" (Paris Transatlantic).

Since the late 1980s he has composed solo and chamber works for many adventurous performers in the U.S. and Australia, such as Margaret Leng Tan, Steven Schick, Either/Or Ensemble, Southern Cross Soloists, red fish blue fish, Speak Percussion, and many others. In 2012, new works include "Drifting cowboys in a mist" for Kurilpa String Quartet, "Bury the sound" for Decibel, and "Time Crystals" for Clocked Out Duo.

Griswold has received grants, commissions, and/or fellowships from the Australia Council for the Arts, Arts Queensland, Brisbane City Council, Melbourne City Council, Asialink Foundation, Queensland Music Festival, Melbourne Jazz Fringe Festival, Civitella Ranieri Foundation, and the InterArts Consortium of the University of California. His work can be heard on Mode Records, Room:40, Listen/Hear Collective, Einstein Records, Accretions/Circumvention, Move, Clocked Out, and Innova.

His music has been performed at major festivals and venues throughout Australia, the U.S., Asia, and Europe, including: Carnegie Hall, Asia Pacific Festival (Wellington), Bang on a Can Festival (New York), Big Sur Experimental Music Festival, Chengdu Arts Centre, El Cruce (Madrid), Los Angeles Philharmonic Green Umbrella Series (Los Angeles), London Jazz Festival, Queensland Music Festival (Brisbane), Shanghai International Festival, Sydney Opera House, Roulette and Tonic (New York).

Together with Vanessa Tomlinson, Griswold directs Clocked Out, which produces innovative concert series, events and tours. Clocked Out recently received the APRA-AMCOS "Award for Excellence by an Organisation" for their 2009-10 programs.

Griswold has lived in San Diego, Los Angeles, New York, Melbourne, Adelaide, and now calls Brisbane home. He is currently adjunct professor at Queensland Conservatorium, Griffith University, and holds a PhD from University of California, San Diego.

Catherine Ingram

Dr Catherine Ingram commenced a postdoctoral fellowship in the Department of Music, School of Oriental and African Studies, University of London, in January 2013. She is also an Honorary fellow at the University of Melbourne, Australia, where she completed her PhD in Ethnomusicology and Chinese Studies in 2010. Her doctoral dissertation was an ethnographic study of Kam villagers singing Kam "big song," the Kam minority musical tradition of southwestern China inscribed on UNESCO's Representative List of the Intangible Cultural Heritage of Humanity in 2009. She is a former recipient of an Endeavour Australia Cheung Kong Research Fellowship and of a Postdoctoral Fellowship from the International Institute of Asian Studies (Universities of Amsterdam and Leiden, The Netherlands). Since 2004 she has conducted extensive participant-observation research into Kam singing traditions, and has published in the areas of ethnomusicology, anthropology, research methodology and ethics, culture and ecology, gender and cultural development, intangible cultural heritage, and digital musical archiving.

Her articles—several of which have been co-authored with Kam village song experts and singers—have appeared in edited volumes such as Women, Gender and Rural Development in China (edited by T. Jacka and S. Sargeson), Music as Intangible Cultural Heritage: Policy, Ideology and Practice in the Preservation of East Asian Traditions (edited by K. Howard) and Sustainable Data from Digital Research: Humanities Perspectives on Digital Scholarship (edited by N. Thieberger et al.), in journals such as Context and Asian Studies Review, and in various other print and online sources. In 2011, Catherine received the inaugural Nadel Essay Award for a paper submitted to The Asia Pacific Journal of Anthropology. Since 2006 she has also lectured courses in Ethnomusicology and Asian Studies at The University of Melbourne, and has given twenty guest lectures at various institutes in Australia, China, Hong Kong, Taiwan and The Netherlands.

Tony Mitchell

Dr Tony Mitchell is a senior lecturer in cultural studies and popular music at the University of Technology, Sydney. He is the author of Dario Fo: People's Court Jester (1999), Popular Music and Local Identity: Pop, Rock and Rap in Europe and Oceania (1996) and the editor of Global Noise: Rap and Hip hop outside the USA (2001). He co-edited Sounds of Then, Sounds of Now: Popular Music in Australia (2008), North meets South: Popular Music in Aotearoa/New Zealand, (1994), and Home, Land and Sea: Situating Popular Music in Aotearoa New Zealand (2011).

Aline Scott-Maxwell

Dr Aline Scott-Maxwell is an ethnomusicologist and Lecturer in Music in the School of Music-Conservatorium, Monash University. Previous positions have included Lecturer in Music at the Department of Music, University of Sydney, and head of the Asian Studies Research Collection, Monash University Library. She was awarded her PhD from Monash University, titled 'The Dynamics of the Yogyakarta Gamelan Music Tradition', building on a long residence in Indonesia where she studied Javanese gamelan music. She continues to maintain her gamelan performing and teaching interests. She was co-General Editor of the Currency Companion to Music and Dance in Australia (Currency House, 2003) and is a long-term member of the International Association for the Study of Popular Music. Her current research areas include Australia's musical engagement with Asia and music and migration with reference to Australia. Recent publications have focused on issues of community and identity in Indonesian and Italian popular music in Australia and development of a framework for understanding the history of Australian musical interactions with Asia.

Nicholas Ng

Dr Nicholas Ng is a composer/performer and Research Fellow at Queensland Conservatorium. His music may be heard on the radio (ABC), in dance and theatre productions (Australian Choreographic Centre), and as art exhibition installations (Art Gallery of NSW, Queensland Art Gallery | Gallery of Modern Art). Nicholas has performed at venues such as Merkin Concert Hall (New York City), 'The Studio', Sydney Opera House, and at festivals including the Chinese Gardens Chamber Music Festival (Sydney), KunstenFESTIVALdesarts (Brussels), Melbourne International Arts Festival, the OzAsia Festival (Adelaide), the Push Festival (Vancouver) and Woodford Folk Festival. Published by Orpheus Music, he has been commissioned by the Melbourne Symphony Orchestra and The Australian Voices, and collaborates regularly with William Yang (photography), Anna Yen (circus, movement) and Julian Wong (movement, dance, music).

Nicholas is a PhD graduate from the Australian National University and researches Chinese music in Australia and the greater Chinese diaspora. He curated the festival 'ENCOUNTERS: Musical meetings between Australia and China' (May 2010) and awaits the publication of his first book based on this event. He is currently co-directing ENCOUNTERS: India (9-19 May 2013) while developing two cross-art productions: tunCLOUD (National Film and Sound Archive), and Annette Shun Wah's The Serpent's Table (Performance 4a and Griffin Theatre).

Vanessa Tomlinson

Australian percussionist Vanessa Tomlinson is active in the fields of solo percussion, contemporary chamber music, improvisation, installation and composition. She has performed at festivals around the world such as Wien Modern, London Jazz Festival,

Green Umbrella Series LA, Bang-on-a-Can Marathon NY, The Adelaide Festival of Arts, Shanghai Festival. She is the recipient of 2 Green Room Awards, the 2011 APRA/AMC Award for Excellence by an organization or individual, and has been awarded artist residencies through Asialink (University of Melbourne), Civitella Ranieri (Italy), Banff (Canada) and Bundanon (NSW). She has recorded on numerous labels including Mode Records, Tzadik, ABC Classics, Etcetera, Clocked Out and Innova.

Vanessa performs regularly as the percussionist with The Australian Art Orchestra, The Golden Orb, Clocked Out Duo and The Lunaire Collective. She was a founding member of percussion group red fish blue fish, and is co-founder and artistic director of Clocked Out, one of Australia's most important and eclectic musical organisations. Vanessa is also founder and director of Ba Da Boom, the in-residence percussion ensemble at Queensland Conservatorium, and the training ground for a wide cross-section of the percussion community.

She is wellknown for her interpretations of the music of Pateras, Griswold and Globokar, her improvisational language that incorporates sonic investigations of found objects, nature, and toy instruments, and her tireless advocacy for awareness of the plethora of high quality music-making happening in Australia.

Vanessa studied at the University of Adelaide, Hochschule fur Musik in Freiburg and received her Masters and Doctorate from the University of California, San Diego where she worked closely with Steven Schick and George Lewis. In addition Vanessa has studied Sichuan Opera with Master Zhong Kaichi in Chengdu, China. Vanessa was recently appointed Associate Professor in Music at Queensland Conservatorium, Griffith University.

Wang Zheng-Ting

Dr Wang Zheng-Ting, honorary research fellow at Monash University and lecturer on Chinese music at the University of Melbourne, graduated from Shanghai Music Conservatory and completed a MA in Ethnomusicology at Monash University and a PhD in Ethnomusicology at the University of Melbourne Australia. He is the founder and director of the Australian Chinese Music Ensemble. In 2007 and 2001 he was invited by the City University of New York as a visiting scholar. In 2007 he invited as adjudicator for the Arts Grants Program City of Melbourne. As an educator, in 2001-1998 he lectured on Chinese instrumental music at the University of Melbourne, in 1995 he lectured on Chinese instrumental music at Monash University. As a lecture and solo performer on the Sheng (Chinese mouth organ), he has performed many recitals: Center for study of free reed instrument the City University of New York (2003, 2001, 1999); the Victoria University Wellington in New Zealand (2002); Hoch Schule Fur Music Koln, in Wuppertal, Germany (2001); Mahasarakham University, Thailand (2001); St. Paul's School London, England (1999); New York's Lincoln Center (1997). He performed at China Festival, in Amsterdam, Holland (2005); performed with Christine Sullivan's jazz band, Mara Jazz Band, Zydeco Jump and

Women in Docs at the Shanghai International Spring Festival (2004 and 2001); performed at the International Double Reed Society World Conference in Melbourne (2004). performed with the Venice Chamber Orchestra, in Venice (2001); performed at the University of Michigan, USA (2003). His performance lecture includes: Musikwissenschaftliches Institut der Universitat Basel, Switzerland (2006); Schweizerische Musikforschende Gesellschaft, Ortsgruppe, Zurich, Switzerland (2006); Universitat Mozarteum Salzburg, in Innsbruck and at Universitat Wien, in Vienna, Austria (2006); Tokai University, Japan (2000); Performance and Lecture at Tokyo University, Japan (2000); University of California Los Angeles (1999). He got many awards: City of Melbourne Arts Grant (2006); Australia Council Grant (2006, 2004, 2002, 2001); Australia-China Council Grant (2006, 2001); Arts Victoria Grant (2005, 2003, 2002, 2001); the University of Melbourne PhD scholarship (2001-1998); Asialink Residency Grant (2008, 1999); American Composers Forum's composition grant (1996). He also acted as organizer for the cultural event: one of the company coordinators for Melbourne International Festival (2002, 1999); Music and cultural coordinator for Asian Food Festival, Melbourne (1996); Music coordinator for Chinese New Year Festival, Melbourne (1996). His book Chinese Music in Australia: Victoria,1850s to mid -1990s was published in 1997. Many of his articles were published by international press which included Cambridge Scholars Press.

Tony Wheeler

Performer on clarinet, saxophone, guqin (Ancient 7-stringed Chinese zither), ruan (Chinese 4-stringed guitar), composer, and teacher Tony Wheeler was born in New Zealand in 1958, and has spent most of his life in Australia, as well as a considerable number of years in Asia. He studied clarinet and composition at the Queensland Conservatorium of Music, where he also had his first contact with Chinese traditional music. After graduating in 1982 with a B.Mus. with Distinction, he worked as a freelance player and teacher, before being awarded a scholarship to spend two years (1985-87) at the Shanghai Conservatory, studying Chinese composition, ruan and guqin. After leaving Shanghai, Tony then spent four years studying and teaching at the University of Hong Kong, before receiving a Master's Degree in composition for Chinese instruments.

As well as maintaining a busy teaching schedule, Tony is active in a wide variety of musical genres and styles. He frequently performs on Chinese and Western instruments in a contemporary and or improvisatory context, but has also played clarinet and saxophone in major orchestras including the Queensland Symphony and Sydney Symphony. He is currently employed by four educational institutions as a clarinet and saxophone teacher. He also teaches the guqin and ruan.

In 2000, Tony recorded a CD for the Celestial Harmonies label, entitled Moon Road To Dawn, in collaboration with the shakuhachi Master James Franklin. He also appears on the CD East, released by the Australian Institute of Eastern Music. Another CD Nine Elemental Songs, which he recorded in collaboration with James

Franklin and Michael Atherton, was released by Wirripang in 2008. Many of his compositions have been published in printed form by Wirripang, and his reconstruction of "Gu Jiao Xing - Walking With the Ancients" was published in China in 2011. In 2011 Tony was also elected as a council member of the China Kun Opera and Gu Qin Research Institute.

Yang Mu

Dr YANG Mu is currently a senior lecturer in the School of International Studies at the University of New South Wales, Australia. His earlier career and undergraduate education were in China while his PhD research and subsequent academic career have been in Australia. The main area of his research has been traditional musical cultures of China, and over the past forty years he has conducted intensive fieldwork in that country. In recent years his research interests have resided mainly in contemporary change in Chinese society and musical traditions, including the performance of music, dance, and theater associated with local customs. He publishes widely in both English and Chinese in the fields of ethnomusicology, cultural anthropology, linguistics, and current affairs.

William Yang

William Yang is one of Australia's greatest storytellers. The fact that his stories are image based makes them all the more powerful and unique. He is a fine and prolific photographer as well as a renowned theatre performer. His very personal stories describe the experience of being Chinese in an Australia that was not always hospitable to people of different appearances or of a different sexual persuasion. He says his mother wanted desperately to fit in, wanting her children to be more Australian than Australians. As a result Yang claimed his Chinese heritage and celebrated Sydney's gay culture of which he was part.

William Yang has presented over twenty individual exhibitions across Asia, Australia, Europe and North America. These have included Claiming China (2008) reflecting on his experiences as an openly gay person with Chinese Heritage, shown at the Australian Centre for Photography, Sydney and Monash Gallery of Art, Victoria. In 2008 Yang also exhibited William Yang Portraits at Global Art Projects and Sofitel Melbourne and was included in the group survey show Yin-Yang: China in Australia, S.H.Ervin Gallery, Sydney. A retrospective exhibition of Yang's photographic work, Diaries was held in 1998 at the New South Wales State Library. His works are in the collections of Art Gallery of New South Wales, Museum of Contemporary Art, National Gallery of Australia, National Portrait Gallery, Queensland Art Gallery, State Library of New South Wales and National Library of Australia, Canberra.

The Song Company (Roland Peelman, director) and The Golden Orb (Vanessa Tomlinson, director) with William Yang and Nicholas Ng in the premiere of *The Harvest of Endurance*, the Encounters festival finale item composed by 18 Australian composers and based on the historical scroll of the same name. Photo courtesy of William Yang.

www.ingramcontent.com/pod-product-compliance
Lightning Source LLC
Chambersburg PA
CBHW051523230426
43668CB00012B/1723